What Readers Are Saying About *Seven Languages in Seven Weeks*

Knowing multiple paradigms greatly influences our design abilities, so I'm always on the lookout for good books that'll help me learn them. This book nicely brings prominent paradigms together. Bruce has experience learning and using multiple languages. Now you can gain from his experience through this book. I highly recommend it.

► **Dr. Venkat Subramaniam**
Award-winning author and founder, Agile Developer, Inc.

As a programmer, the importance of being exposed to new programming languages, paradigms, and techniques cannot be overstated. This book does a marvelous job of introducing seven important and diverse languages in a concise—but nontrivial—manner, revealing their strengths and reasons for being. This book is akin to a dim-sum buffet for any programmer who is interested in exploring new horizons or evaluating emerging languages before committing to studying one in particular.

► **Antonio Cangiano**
Software engineer and technical evangelist, IBM

Fasten your seat belts, because you are in for a fast-paced journey. This book is packed with programming-language-learning action. Bruce puts it all on the line, and the result is an engaging, rewarding book that passionate programmers will thoroughly enjoy. If you love learning new languages, if you want to challenge your mind, if you want to take your programming skills to the next level—this book is for you. You will not be disappointed.

► **Frederic Daoud**
Author, *Stripes ...and Java Web Development Is Fun Again* and *Getting Started with Apache Click*

Do you want seven kick starts into learning your "language of the year"? Do you want your thinking challenged about programming in general? Look no further than this book. I personally was taken back in time to my undergraduate computer science days, coasting through my programming languages survey course. The difference is that Bruce won't let you coast through this course! This isn't a leisurely read—you'll have to work this book. I believe you'll find it both mind-blowing and intensely practical at the same time.

► **Matt Stine**
Group leader, Research Application Development at St. Jude Children's Research Hospital

I spent most of my time as a computer sciences student saying I didn't want to be a software developer and then became one anyway. *Seven Languages in Seven Weeks* expanded my way of thinking about problems and reminded me what I love about programming.

► **Travis Kaspar**
Software engineer, Northrop Grumman

I have been programming for 25 years in a variety of hardware and software languages. After reading *Seven Languages in Seven Weeks*, I am starting to understand how to evaluate languages for their objective strengths and weaknesses. More importantly, I feel as if I could pick one of them to actually get some work done.

► **Chris Kappler**
Senior scientist, Raytheon BBN Technologies

Seven Languages in Seven Weeks

A Pragmatic Guide to Learning Programming Languages

Seven Languages in Seven Weeks

A Pragmatic Guide to Learning Programming Languages

Bruce A. Tate

The Pragmatic Bookshelf
Raleigh, North Carolina Dallas, Texas

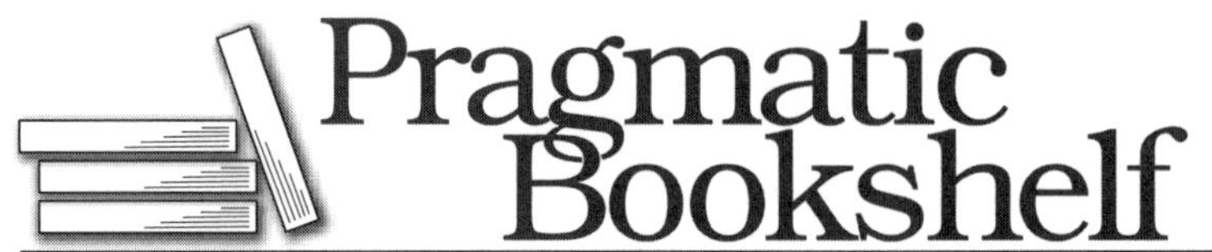

Our Pragmatic courses, workshops, and other products can help you and your team create better software and have more fun. For more information, as well as the latest Pragmatic titles, please visit us at http://www.pragprog.com.

The team that produced this book includes:

Editor:	Jackie Carter
Indexing:	Potomac Indexing, LLC
Copy edit:	Kim Wimpsett
Layout:	Steve Peter
Production:	Janet Furlow
Customer support:	Ellie Callahan
International:	Juliet Benda

Printed in the United States of America.

ISBN-10: 1-934356-59-X

ISBN-13: 978-1-934356-59-3

Printed on acid-free paper.

P1.0 printing, October 2010

Version: 2010-10-13

Contents

Dedication

The five months from December 2009 through April 2010 were among the most difficult of my life. My brother, not yet 47 years old, had emergency bypass surgery. No one had any clue that anything was wrong at all. (He came through the surgery without further incident and is doing well.) In late March, my sister was diagnosed with breast cancer. The biggest shock of all came in early March. My mother was diagnosed with terminal cancer. A few short weeks later, she was gone.

As you would expect, I am left to struggle with the grief of a jarring and unexpected loss because of a brutally efficient disease. I would not be human otherwise. But strangely, this experience has not been an entirely negative one. You see, my mother was at peace with the remarkable life she lived, her relationships with her family were strong and fulfilling, and she was exactly where she wanted to be with her faith.

Lynda Lyle Tate put her creative energy into painting with watercolors. She shared her art primarily through her Madison Avenue Art Gallery and her classes. Before I left home, I had the opportunity to take a few lessons from her. For someone from a technical profession, the experience was always a little disorienting. I would visualize the masterpiece on my blank canvas. As the actual image took shape, it drifted further and further from my original vision. When I despaired that things were beyond my ability to fix, Mom looked over my shoulder and told me what she saw. After a few flicks of her talented wrist added darks to accentuate depth and highlights to add clarity and detail, I would realize that I had not been too far astray at all. It just took a gifted touch to bring back my creation from the brink of disaster. Then, I would throw my excited arms up in victory and tell everyone in the class about this thing I had created, not yet realizing that each member of the class was going through their own private burst of joy.

After a little while, I learned that Mom was working on another canvas as well. Through her church and through her profession, she'd find broken people. Encountering a lost spouse here or a troubled marriage there, my mother would bring them into class where she would use the paint and paper to slightly open a door that had been slammed shut. As we spent our last week together, person after person would come through her room devastated at the thought of losing their teacher, but Mom would tell the perfect joke or offer the right word of kindness, comforting those who came to comfort her. I got to meet the human canvases who had been put right by the master and gone on to do great things. It was a humbling experience.

When I told my mother that I would dedicate this book to her, she said that she would like that, but she had nothing to do with computers. That is true enough. The very thought of Windows would leave her helpless. But Mom, you have had everything to do with *me*. Your well-timed words of encouragement inspired me, your love of creativity shaped me, and your enthusiasm and love of life guide me even now. As I think about these experiences, I can't help but feel a little better and a little stronger because I, too, am a canvas shaped by the master.

This book is dedicated with love to Lynda Lyle Tate, 1936–2010.

Acknowledgments

This is the most demanding book I have ever written. It's also the most rewarding. The people who have offered to help in various ways have made it so. Thanks first and foremost to my family. Kayla and Julia, your writing amazes me. You can't yet imagine what you can accomplish. Maggie, you are my joy and inspiration.

In the Ruby community, thanks to Dave Thomas for turning me on to the language that turned my career upside down and helped me have fun again. Thanks also to Matz for your friendship and your offer to share your thoughts with my readers. You invited me to Japan to visit the place where Ruby was born, and that experience inspired me much more than you will ever know. To Charles Nutter, Evan Phoenix, and Tim Bray, thanks for the conversations about topics in this book that must have seemed tiresome but helped me refine and shape the message.

In the Io community, thanks to Jeremy Tregunna for helping me get plugged in and sharing some cool examples for the book. Your reviews were among the best. They were timely and helped build a much stronger chapter. Steve Dekorte, you've created something special, whether or not the marketplace ever recognizes it as so. The concurrency features rock, and the language has intrinsic beauty. I can definitely appreciate how much of this language feels right. Thanks for helping this neophyte debug his installation. Thanks also for your thoughtful reviews and your interview that helped me capture the essence of Io. You captured the imagination of the beta readers and created the favorite language of many of them.

In the Prolog community, thanks to Brian Tarbox for sharing your remarkable experience with my readers. The dolphin projects, featured on Nova, certainly add a dramatic flair to the Prolog chapter. Special thanks go to Joe Armstrong. You can see how much your feedback shaped the chapter and the overall book. Thanks also for contributing your map-coloring example and your ideas for Append. They were the right examples delivered at the right time.

In the Scala community, thanks to my good friend Venkat Subramaniam. Your Scala book is both rich and understandable. I leaned on it heavily. I greatly appreciate your review and the little bits of help that you offered along the way. Those little bits of your time saved me tremendous anguish and let me focus on the task of teaching. Thanks also to Martin Odersky for helping this stranger by sharing your thoughts with my readers. Scala takes a unique and brave approach to integrating functional programming paradigms with object-oriented paradigms. Your efforts are greatly appreciated.

In the Erlang community, I again thank Joe Armstrong. Your kindness and energy have helped me form the ideas in this book. Your tireless promotion of the way distributed, fault-tolerant systems should be built is working. More than any other idea in any other language in this book, Erlang's "Let it crash" philosophy makes sense to me. I hope to see those ideas more broadly adopted.

In the Clojure community, thanks to Stuart Halloway for your reviews and ideas that forced me to work harder to bring a better book to my readers. Your insights into Clojure and your instincts helped me understand what was important. Your book was also hugely influential in the Clojure chapter and actually changed the way I attacked some problems in other chapters as well. Your approach in your consulting practice is greatly appreciated. You're bringing much-needed simplicity and productivity to this industry. Thanks also to Rich Hickey for your thoughtful ideas on the creation of the language and what it means to be a Lisp dialect. Some ideas in Clojure are intensely radical and yet so practical. Congratulations. You've found a way to make Lisp revolutionary. Again.

In the Haskell community, thanks to Phillip Wadler for the opportunity to look inside the process that created Haskell. We share a passion for teaching, and you're very good at it. Thanks also to Simon Peyton-Jones. I enjoyed working through your interview, the insights you added, and the unique perspective you brought to these readers.

The reviewers did an outstanding job with this book. Thanks to Vladimir G. Ivanovic, Craig Riecke, Paul Butcher, Fred Daoud, Aaron Bedra, David Eisinger, Antonio Cangiano, and Brian Tarbox. You formed the most effective review team I've ever worked with. The book is much stronger for it. I know that reviewing a book at this level of detail is thankless, demanding work. Those of us who still like technical books thank you. The publishing business could not exist without you.

I also want to thank those of you who shared your ideas about language choice and programming philosophy. At various times, Neal Ford, John Heintz, Mike Perham, and Ian Warshak made significant contributions. These kinds of conversations made me look smarter than I really am.

Beta readers, thank you for reading the book and keeping me working. Your comments have shown me that a good number of you are working through the languages rather than casually skimming. I've changed the book based on hundreds of comments so far and expect to do even more throughout the life of the book.

Finally, to the team at the Pragmatic Bookshelf, I offer my sincerest gratitude. Dave Thomas and Andy Hunt, you have had an incalculable impact on my career as a programmer and again as an author. This publishing platform has made writing viable again for me. We can take a book like this one that might not be as attractive to the mass market and make it financially worthwhile. Thanks to all the members of the publishing team. Jackie Carter, your gentle hand and guidance were what this book needed, and I hope you enjoyed our conversations as much as I did. Thanks to those who labored in my shadow to make this book the best it could be. Specifically, I want to thank the team that labored so hard to make this book look good and correct all of my bad habits, including Kim Wimpsett, the copy editor; Seth Maislin, the indexer; Steve Peter, the typesetter; and Janet Furlow, the producer. This book would not be what it is without you.

As always, mistakes that slipped through this fine team are all mine. For those of you I missed, I offer my sincerest apologies. Any oversight was not intentional.

Finally, thanks to all of my readers. I think that real hard-copy books have value, and I can follow my passion and write because you do, too.

Bruce Tate

Foreword

From the yet to be written "How Proust Can Make You a Better Programmer"
by Joe Armstrong, Creator of Erlang

"The Gmail editor cannot get typographic quotes right."

"Disgraceful," said Margery, "the sign of an illiterate programmer and a decadent culture."

"What should we do about it?"

"We must insist that the next programmer we hire has read all of 'A la recherche du temps perdu."'

"All seven volumes?"

"All seven volumes."

"Will it make them better at punctuation and make them get their quotes right?"

"Not necessarily, but it will make them a better programmer. It's a Zen thing...."

Learning to program is like learning to swim. No amount of theory is a substitute for diving into the pool and flailing around in the water gasping for air. The first time you sink under the water, you panic, but when you bob to the surface and gulp in some air, you feel elated. You think to yourself, "I can swim." At least that's how I felt when I learned to swim.

It's the same with programming. The first steps are the most difficult, and you need a good teacher to encourage you to jump into the water.

Bruce Tate is such a teacher. This book gives you the opportunity to start with what is the most difficult part of learning to program, namely, getting started.

Let's assume that you've actually managed the difficult task of downloading and installing the interpreter or compiler for the language you are interested in. What should you do next? What will be your first program?

Bruce neatly answers this question. Just type in the programs and program fragments in this book to see whether you can reproduce his results. Don't think about writing your own programs yet—just try to reproduce the examples in the book. As you grow in confidence, you will be able to tackle your own programming projects.

The first step in acquiring any new skill is not being able to do your own thing but being able to reproduce what other people have done before you. This is the quickest way to mastering a skill.

Getting started with programming in a new language is not so much a deep exercise in understanding the underlying principles that a language embodies; it is rather a matter of getting the semicolons and commas in the right places and understanding the weird error messages that the system spits out when you make an error. It is not until you get beyond the messy business of entering a program and getting it through the compiler that you can even start to think about the meaning of the different language constructs.

Once you've gotten through the mechanics of entering and running programs, you can sit back and relax. Your subconscious does the rest. While your conscious brain is figuring out where to put the semicolons, your subconscious is figuring out the deep meaning that lies underneath the surface structures. Then you'll wake up one day suddenly understanding the deeper meaning of a logic program or why a particular language had a particular construct.

Knowing a small amount about many languages is a useful skill. I often find that I need to understand a bit of Python or Ruby to solve a particular problem. The programs I download from the Internet are often written in a variety of languages and need a little tweaking before I can use them.

Each language has its own set of idioms, its strengths, and its weaknesses. By learning several different programming languages, you will be able to see which language is best suited to the kinds of problems that interest you most.

I'm pleased to see that Bruce's taste in programming languages is eclectic. He covers not only the well-established languages such as Ruby but also less-well-appreciated languages like Io. Ultimately, programming is about understanding, and understanding is about ideas. So, exposure to new ideas is essential to a deeper understanding of what programming is all about.

A Zen master might tell you that to be better at mathematics you'd better study Latin. Thus it is with programming. To better understand the essence of OO programming, you should study logic or functional programming (FP). To be better at FP, you should study Assembler.

Books on comparative programming languages were popular when I grew up as a programmer, but most of these were academic tomes that gave little practical guidance to how to actually go about using a language. This reflected the technology of the age. You could read about the ideas in a language, but actually trying it out was virtually impossible.

Today, not only can we read about the ideas, but we can try them in practice. This makes the difference between standing on the poolside wondering whether it would be nice to swim and diving in and enjoying the water.

I warmly recommend this book and hope that you enjoy reading it as much as I have.

Joe Armstrong, creator of Erlang
2 March 2010
Stockholm

Chapter 1

Introduction

People learn spoken languages for different reasons. You learned your first language to live. It gave you the tools to get through your everyday life. If you learned a second language, the reasons could be very different. Sometimes, you might have to learn a second language to further your career or adapt to a changing environment. But sometimes you decide to conquer a new language not because you have to but because you want to learn. A second language can help you encounter new worlds. You may even seek enlightenment, knowing every new language can shape the way you think.

So it is with programming languages. In this book, I will introduce you to seven different languages. My goal is not to make a motherly demand like your morning spoonful of cod liver oil. I want to guide you through a journey that will enlighten you and change the way you look at programming. I won't make you an expert, but I'll teach you more than "Hello, World."

1.1 Method to the Madness

Most of the time, when I'm learning a new programming language or framework, I'll look for a quick interactive tutorial. My goal is to experience the language in a controlled environment. If I want, I can go off script and explore, but I'm basically looking for a quick jolt of caffeine, a snapshot of syntactic sugar, and core concepts.

But usually, the experience is not fulfilling. If I want to get the true flavor of a language that is more than a subtle extension of one I already know, a short tutorial is *never* going to work. I need a deep, fast dive.

This book will give you such an experience not once but seven times. You'll find answers to the following questions:

- *What is the typing model?* Typing is strong (Java) or weak (C), static (Java) or dynamic (Ruby). The languages in this book lean on the strong typing end of the spectrum, but you'll encounter a broad mix of static and dynamic. You will find how the trade-offs impact a developer. The typing model will shape the way you attack a problem and control the way the language works. Every language in this book has its own typing idiosyncrasies.

- *What is the programming model?* Is it object-oriented (OO), functional, procedural, or some type of hybrid? This book has languages spanning four different programming models and, sometimes, combinations of more than one. You will find a logic-based programming language (Prolog), two languages with full support for object-oriented concepts (Ruby, Scala), four languages that are functional in nature (Scala, Erlang, Clojure, Haskell), and one prototype language (Io). Several of the languages are multiparadigm languages, like Scala. Clojure's multimethods will even let you implement your own paradigm. Learning new programming paradigms is one of the most important concepts in this book.

- *How will you interact with it?* Languages are compiled or interpreted, and some have virtual machines while others don't. In this book, I'll begin to explore with an interactive shell, if there is one. I will move on to files when it's time to attack bigger projects. We won't attack large enough projects to fully dive into packaging models.

- *What are the decision constructs and core data structures?* You'd be surprised how many languages can make decisions with things other than variations of ifs and whiles. You'll see pattern matching in Erlang and unification in Prolog. Collections play a vital role in just about any language. In languages such as Smalltalk and Lisp, the collections are defining characteristics of the language. In others, like C++ and Java, collections are all over the place, defining the user's experience by their absence and lack of cohesion. Either way, you'll need a sound understanding of the collections.

- *What are the core features that make the language unique?* Some of the languages will support advanced features for concurrent programming. Others provide unique high-level constructs such as Clojure's macros or Io's message interpretation. Others will give you a supercharged virtual machine, like Erlang's BEAM. Because of it, Erlang will let you build fault-tolerant distributed systems much more quickly than you can in other languages. Some languages support programming models that are laser-focused on a particular problem, such as using logic to solve constraints.

When you're through, you will not be an expert in any of these languages, but you *will* know what each uniquely has to offer. Let's get to the languages.

1.2 The Languages

Choosing the languages in this book was much easier than you might imagine. I simply asked potential readers. When we rolled up all the data, we had eight potential candidates. I struck JavaScript because it was *too* popular and replaced it with the next most popular prototype language, Io. I also struck Python because I wanted no more than one object-oriented language, and Ruby was higher on the list. That made room for a surprising candidate, Prolog, which was a top-ten language on the list. These are the languages that did make the cut and the reasons I picked them:

- *Ruby.* This object-oriented language gets high marks for ease of use and readability. I briefly considered not including any object-oriented language at all, but I found myself wanting to compare the different programming paradigms to object-oriented programming (OOP), so including at least one OOP language was important. I also wanted to push Ruby a little harder than most programmers do and give readers a flavor for the core decisions that shaped the design of Ruby. I decided to take a dive into Ruby metaprogramming, allowing me to extend the syntax of the language. I'm quite happy with the result.

- *Io.* Along with Prolog, Io is the most controversial language I included. It is not commercially successful, but the concurrency constructs with the simplicity and uniformity of syntax are important concepts. The minimal syntax is powerful, and the similarities to Lisp are sometimes striking. Io has a small footprint, is a prototype language like JavaScript, and has a unique message dispatch mechanism that I think you'll find interesting.

- *Prolog.* Yes, I know it's old, but it is also extremely powerful. Solving a Sudoku in Prolog was an eye-opening experience for me. I've worked hard to solve some difficult problems in Java or C that would have been effortless in Prolog. Joe Armstrong, creator of Erlang, helped me gain a deeper appreciation of this language that strongly influenced Erlang. If you've never had an occasion to use it, I think you will be pleasantly surprised.

- *Scala.* One of a new generation of languages on the Java virtual machine, Scala has brought strong functional concepts to the Java ecosystem. It also embraces OOP. Looking back, I see a striking similarity to C++, which was instrumental to bridging procedural programming and OOP. As you dive into the Scala community, you'll see why Scala represents pure heresy to pure functional programmers and pure bliss to Java developers.

- *Erlang.* One of the oldest languages on this list, Erlang is gathering steam as a functional language that gets concurrency, distribution, and fault tolerance right. The creators of CouchDB, one of the emerging cloud-based databases, chose Erlang and have never looked back. After spending a little time with this distributed language, you'll see why. Erlang makes designing concurrent, distributed, fault-tolerant applications much easier than you could have ever thought possible.

- *Clojure.* Another JVM language, this Lisp-dialect makes some radical changes in the way we think about concurrency on the JVM. It is the only language in this book that uses the same strategy in versioned databases to manage concurrency. As a Lisp dialect, Clojure packs plenty of punch, supporting perhaps the most flexible programming model in the book. But unlike other Lisp dialects, the parentheses are greatly reduced, and you have a huge ecosystem to lean on, including a huge Java library and widely available deployment platforms.

- *Haskell.* This language is the only pure functional language in the book. That means you won't find mutable state anywhere. The same function with the same input parameters will give you the same output, every time. Of all the strongly typed languages, Haskell supports the most widely respected typing model. Like Prolog, it will take a little while to understand, but the results will be worth it.

I'm sorry if your favorite language didn't make the list. Believe me, I've already gotten hate mail from more than a few language enthusiasts. We included several dozen languages in the survey mentioned earlier.

Those languages that I picked are not necessarily the best, but each one is unique, with something important to teach you.

1.3 Buy This Book

...if you are a competent programmer who wants to grow. That claim might seem a little nebulous, but indulge me.

Learning to Learn

Dave Thomas is one of the founders of this publishing company. He has challenged thousands of students to learn a new language every year. At worst, by learning languages, you'll learn to fold new concepts back into the code that you write in your chosen language.

Writing this book has had a profound impact on the Ruby code that I write. It is more functional and is easier to read with less repetition. I reach for mutable variables less and do a better job with code blocks and higher-order functions. I also use some techniques that are unconventional in the Ruby community, but they make my code more concise and readable.

At best, you could launch a new career. Every ten years or so, programming paradigms change. As the Java language became more limiting for me, I experimented with Ruby to better understand its approach to web development. After a couple of successful side projects, I pushed my career hard in that direction and have never looked back. My Ruby career started with basic experimentation and grew into more.

Help for Dangerous Times

Many of the readers of this book won't be old enough to remember the last time our industry switched programming paradigms. Our shift to object-oriented programming had a couple of false starts, but the old structural programming paradigm was simply unable to handle the complexity required for modern web applications. The successful Java programming language gave us a hard shove in that direction, and the new paradigm stuck. Many developers got caught with old skills and had to completely retool the way they thought, the tools they used, and the way they designed applications.

We may be in the midst of another transformation. This time, new computer designs will be the driver. Five of the seven languages in this book have compelling concurrency models. (Ruby and Prolog are the exceptions.) Whether or not your programming language changes right away, I'm going to go out on a limb and say that the languages in this book have some compelling answers to offer. Check out Io's implementation of futures, Scala's actors, or Erlang's "Let it crash" philosophy. Understand how Haskell programmers leave mutable state behind or how Clojure uses versioning to solve some of the most difficult concurrency problems.

You can also find insight in surprising places. Erlang, the language behind the scenes for several of the cloud-style databases, is a great example. Dr. Joe Armstrong started that language from a Prolog foundation.

1.4 Don't Buy This Book

...until you've read this section and agree. I am going to make a deal with you. You agree to let me focus on the programming language rather than installation details. My part of the deal is to teach you more in a shorter time. You'll have to Google a little more, and you can't rely on me to support your installation, but when you're through the book, you'll know much more because I'll be able to dive deeper.

Please recognize that seven languages is an ambitious undertaking for both of us. As a reader, you're going to have to stretch your brain around seven different syntax styles, four programming paradigms, four decades worth of language development, and more. As an author, I have to cover an enormously broad set of topics for you. I learned several of these languages to support this book. To successfully cover the most important details of each language, I need to make some simplifying assumptions.

I Will Take You Beyond Syntax

To really get into the head of a language designer, you're going to have to be willing to go beyond the basic syntax. That means you'll have to code something more than the typical "Hello, World" or even a Fibonacci series. In Ruby, you will get to do some metaprogramming. In Prolog, you'll solve a full Sudoku. And in Erlang, you'll write a monitor that can detect the death of another process and launch another one or inform the user.

The second that I decided to go deeper than the basics, I made a commitment to you and a compromise. The commitment: I won't settle for a superficial treatment. And the compromise: I won't be able to cover some basics that you'd expect to find in dedicated language books. I will rarely go through exception processing, except where it's a fundamental feature of the language. I will not go into packaging models in detail because we'll be dealing with small projects that do not require them. I will not go over primitives that we don't need to solve the basic problems I lay out for you.

I Won't Be Your Installation Guide

One of my biggest challenges is the platform. I have had direct contact from readers of various books using three different Windows platforms, OS X, and at least five different Unix versions. I've seen comments on various message boards of many more. Seven languages on seven platforms is an insurmountable topic for a single author and probably for a multiauthor book. I can't support installation for seven languages, so I'm not going to try.

I suspect that you're not remotely interested in reading another outdated installation guide. Languages and platforms change. I'll tell you where to go to install the language, and I'll tell you what version I'm using. That way, you'll be working from up-to-date instructions from the same list as everyone else. I cannot support your installations.

I Won't Be Your Programming Reference

We've tried hard to get you strong programming reviews for this book. In some cases, we are lucky enough to get a review from the person who designed the language. I'm confident that this material will capture the spirit of each programming language pretty well by the time it has gone through the entire review process. That said, please understand that I cannot possibly fully support your endeavors in each language. I would like to make a comparison to spoken languages.

Knowing a language as a tourist passing through is far different from being a native speaker. I speak English fluently and Spanish haltingly. I know a few phrases in three other languages. I ordered fish in Japan. I asked to find a restroom in Italy. But I know my limitations. From the programming side, I speak Basic, C, C++, Java, C#, JavaScript, Ruby, and a few others fluently. I speak dozens of others haltingly, including the languages in this book. I'm not qualified to support six of the languages on this list. I write Ruby full-time and have for five years now. But I couldn't tell you how to write a web server in Io or a database in Erlang.

I would fail badly if I tried to provide an exhaustive reference for each of these languages. I could make a programming guide that's at least as long as this book on any of the separate languages in here. I will give you enough information to get started. I will walk you through examples in each languages, and you'll see examples of those programs. I will do my best to compile everything and make sure it all runs. But I couldn't support your programming efforts even if I wanted.

The languages on this list all have exceptional support communities. That's part of the reason I picked them. In each of the exercises, I try to have a section that asks you to find resources. This idea is intentional. It will make you self-reliant.

I Am Going to Push You Hard

This book is going to take you one step beyond your twenty-minute tutorial. You know Google as well as I do, and you'll be able to find one of those simple primers for every language on this list. I will give you a quick interactive tour. You'll also get some small programming challenges and one programming project every week. It's not going to be easy, but it will be informative and fun.

If you simply read this book, you'll experience the flavor of the syntax and no more. If you look online for the answers before trying to code the exercises yourself, you'll fail. You will want to try the exercises first, fully recognizing that you'll fail at a few of them. Learning syntax is always easier than learning to reason.

If you find yourself nervous after reading this description, I suggest that you put down this book and pick up another. You won't be happy with me. You would probably be better served by seven different programming books. But if you find yourself excited about the prospect of coding better quickly, let's push on.

1.5 A Final Charge

At this point, I expected to have some sweeping, motivational words to say, but it all seemed to boil down to two words.

Have fun.

A spoonful of sugar makes the medicine go down.
► Mary Poppins

Chapter 2

Ruby

If you are sampling this book, chances are we have something in common: learning programming languages intrigues us. To me, learning a language is like learning a character. Throughout my career, I've experienced scores of languages firsthand. Like any person, each language took on a distinct personality. Java was like having a rich lawyer as a brother. He was fun when he was younger, but now he's a black hole that sucks away all the joy in a 100-mile radius. Visual Basic was like that bleached-blond cosmetologist. She's not going to solve global warming, but she's always good for a haircut and tremendously fun to talk to. Throughout the book, I will compare the languages you will encounter to popular characters. I hope the comparisons will help you unlock a little bit about the character that makes each language special.

Meet Ruby, one of my favorites. She's sometimes quirky, always beautiful, a little mysterious, and absolutely magical. Think Mary Poppins,[1] the British nanny. At the time, most nannies were like most of the C family of languages—draconian beasts who were mercilessly efficient but about as fun as taking that shot of cod liver oil every night. With a spoonful of sugar, everything changed. Mary Poppins made the household more efficient by making it fun and coaxing every last bit of passion from her charges. Ruby does the same thing and with more syntactic sugar[2] than a spoonful. Matz, Ruby's creator, doesn't worry

---

1. *Mary Poppins*. DVD. Directed by Robert Stevenson. 1964; Los Angeles, CA: Walt Disney Video, 2004.
2. Syntactic sugar describes a language feature that makes code easier to read and write, though there are alternative ways to express the same code.

about the efficiency of the language. He optimizes the efficiency of the *programmers*.

2.1 Quick History

Yukihiro Matsumoto created Ruby in about 1993. Most people just call him Matz. As a language, Ruby is an interpreted, object-oriented, dynamically typed language from a family of so-called scripting languages. Interpreted means that Ruby code is executed by an interpreter rather than a compiler. Dynamically typed means that types are bound at execution time rather than compile time. In general, the trade-off for such a strategy is flexibility versus execution safety, but we'll get into that a little more later. Object-oriented means the language supports encapsulation (data and behavior are packaged together), inheritance through classes (object types are organized in a class tree), and polymorphism (objects can take many forms). Ruby patiently waited for the right moment and then burst onto the scene around 2006 with the emergence of the Rails framework. After wandering for ten years in the enterprise jungles, programming was fun again. Ruby is not hugely efficient in terms of execution speed, but it makes programmers very productive.

Interview with Yukihiro (Matz) Matsumoto

I had the pleasure to travel to Matsumotosan's hometown of Matsue, Japan. We had the chance to have some conversations about the foundations of Ruby, and he agreed to answer some questions for this book.

Bruce: *Why did you write Ruby?*

Matz: *Right after I started playing with computers, I got interested in programming languages. They are the means of programming but also enhancers for your mind that shape the way you think about programming. So for a long time, for a hobby, I studied a lot of programming languages. I even implemented several toy languages but no real ones.*

In 1993, when I saw Perl, I was somehow inspired that an object-oriented language that combines characteristics from Lisp, Smalltalk, and Perl would be a great language to enhance our productivity. So, I started developing such a language and named it Ruby. The primary motivation was to amuse myself. It was mere hobby at the beginning, trying to create a language that fit my taste. Somehow, other programmers all over the world have felt sympathy for that language and the policy behind it. And it became very popular, far beyond my expectation.

Bruce: *What is the thing you like about it the most?*

Matz: *I like the way it makes my programming enjoyable. As a particular technical issue, I like blocks most. They are tamed higher-order functions but open up great possibilities in DSL and other features as well.*

Bruce: *What is a feature that you would like to change, if you could go back in time?*

Matz: *I would remove the thread and add actors or some other more advanced concurrency features.*

As you read through this chapter, whether or not you already know Ruby, try to keep an eye out for trade-offs that Matz made along the way. Look for syntactic sugar, those little features that break the basic rules of the language to give programmers a little friendlier experience and make the code a little easier to understand. Find places where Matz used code blocks for marvelous effect in collections and elsewhere. And try to understand the trade-offs that he made along the way between simplicity and safety and between productivity and performance.

Let's get started. Take a peek at some Ruby code:

```
>> properties = ['object oriented', 'duck typed', 'productive', 'fun']
=> ["object oriented", "duck typed", "productive", "fun"]
>> properties.each {|property| puts "Ruby is #{property}."}
Ruby is object oriented.
Ruby is duck typed.
Ruby is productive.
Ruby is fun.
=> ["object oriented", "duck typed", "productive", "fun"]
```

Ruby is the language that taught me to smile again. Dynamic to the core, Ruby has a marvelous support community. The implementations are all open source. Most commercial support comes from smaller companies, and that has insulated Ruby from some of the over-reaching frameworks that plague some other kingdoms. Ruby has been slow to catch on in the enterprise, but it's taking hold now on the strength of its productivity, especially in the area of web development.

2.2 Day 1: Finding a Nanny

All magic aside, Mary Poppins is first and foremost a great nanny. When you first learn a language, your job is to learn how to use it to do the jobs you already know how to do. Treat this first conversation with Ruby as a dialogue. Does the conversation flow freely, or is it unnecessarily awkward? What's the core programming model? How does it treat types? Let's start digging for some answers.

Lightning Tour

As promised, I'm not going to take you through an exhaustive outdated installation process, but installing Ruby is a snap. Just go to http://www.ruby-lang.org/en/downloads/, find your platform, and install Ruby 1.8.6 or newer. I am running Ruby version 1.8.7 for this chapter, and version 1.9 will have some slight differences. If you're on Windows, there's a one-click installer that will work, and if you're on OS X Leopard or greater, Ruby comes with the Xcode disks.

To test your installation, just type irb. If you don't see any errors, you're ready to handle the rest of this chapter. If you do, don't be shy. Very few installation problems are unique. Google will show the way.

Using Ruby with the Console

If you haven't done so, type irb. You should see Ruby's interactive console. You'll type a command and get a response. Give these a try:

```
>> puts 'hello, world'
hello, world
=> nil
>> language = 'Ruby'
=> "Ruby"
>> puts "hello, #{language}"
hello, Ruby
=> nil
>> language = 'my Ruby'
=> "my Ruby"
>> puts "hello, #{language}"
hello, my Ruby
=> nil
```

If you don't already know Ruby, this brief example gives you many clues about the language. You know that Ruby can be interpreted. In fact, Ruby is almost always interpreted, though some developers are working on virtual machines that compile Ruby to byte code as it gets executed. I didn't declare any variables. Everything I did returned a value, even when I didn't ask Ruby to return anything. In fact, every piece of code in Ruby returns something.

You also saw at least two types of strings. One quote around a string means the string should be interpreted literally, and two quotes leads to string evaluation. One of the things that the Ruby interpreter evaluates is string substitution. In this example, Ruby substituted the value returned by the code language into the string. Let's keep going.

The Programming Model

One of the first questions about a language you should answer is, "What is the programming model?" It's not always a simple answer. You've probably been exposed to procedural languages such as C, Fortran, or Pascal. Most of us are using object-oriented languages right now, but many of those languages have procedural elements too. For example, 4 in Java is not an object. You may have picked up this book to explore functional programming languages. Some of those languages such as Scala mix programming models by throwing in object-oriented concepts. There are dozens of other programming models as well. Stack-based languages such as PostScript or Forth use one or more stacks as a central feature of the language. Logic-based languages such as Prolog build around rules. Prototype languages like Io, Lua, and Self use the object, not the class, as the basis for object definition and even inheritance.

Ruby is a pure object-oriented language. In this chapter, you'll see just how far Ruby takes this concept. Let's look at some basic objects:

```
>> 4
=> 4
>> 4.class
=> Fixnum
>> 4 + 4
=> 8
>> 4.methods
=> ["inspect", "%", "<<", "singleton_method_added", "numerator", ...
 "*", "+", "to_i", "methods", ...
 ]
```

I've omitted some of the methods from this list, but you get the picture. Just about everything in Ruby is an object, down to each individual number. A number is an object that has a class called Fixnum, and the method called methods returns an array of methods (Ruby represents arrays in square brackets). In fact, you can call any method on an object with the dot operator.

Decisions

Programs exist to make decisions, so it stands to reason that the way a language makes decisions is a central concept that shapes the way you code, and think, in a given language. Ruby is like most object-oriented and procedural languages in many ways. Check out these expressions:

```
>> x = 4
=> 4
>> x < 5
=> true
>> x <= 4
=> true
>> x > 4
=> false
>> false.class
=> FalseClass
>> true.class
=> TrueClass
```

So, Ruby has expressions that evaluate to true or false. True to form, true and false are also first-class objects. You can conditionally execute code with them:

```
>> x = 4
=> 4
>> puts 'This appears to be false.' unless x == 4
=> nil
>> puts 'This appears to be true.' if x == 4
This appears to be true.
=> nil
>> if x == 4
>>   puts 'This appears to be true.'
>> end
This appears to be true.
=> nil
>> unless x == 4
>>   puts 'This appears to be false.'
>> else
?>   puts 'This appears to be true.'
>> end
This appears to be true.
=> nil
>> puts 'This appears to be true.' if not true
=> nil
>> puts 'This appears to be true.' if !true
=> nil
```

I really like Ruby's design choice for simple conditionals. You can use both block forms (if *condition*, *statements*, end) or one-line forms (*statement* if *condition*) when you're working with if or unless. To some, the one-line version of the if is off-putting. To me, it allows you to express a single thought in a line of code:

```
order.calculate_tax unless order.nil?
```

Sure, you can express the previous in a block, but you would add additional noise to what should be a single, coherent thought. When you can distill a simple idea into one line, you make reading your code less of a burden. I also like the idea of unless. You could express the same idea with not or !, but unless expresses the idea much better.

while and until are similar:

```
>> x = x + 1 while x < 10
=> nil
>> x
=> 10
>> x = x - 1 until x == 1
=> nil
>> x
=> 1
>> while x < 10
>>   x = x + 1
>>   puts x
>> end
2
3
4
5
6
7
8
9
10
=> nil
```

Notice that = is for assignment and == tests for equality. In Ruby, each object will have its notion of equality. Numbers are equal if their values are equal.

You can use values other than true and false as expressions too:

```
>> puts 'This appears to be true.' if 1
This appears to be true.
=> nil
>> puts 'This appears to be true.' if 'random string'
(irb):31: warning: string literal in condition
This appears to be true.
=> nil
>> puts 'This appears to be true.' if 0
This appears to be true.
=> nil
```

```
>> puts 'This appears to be true.' if true
This appears to be true.
=> nil
>> puts 'This appears to be true.' if false
=> nil
>> puts 'This appears to be true.' if nil
=> nil
```

So, everything but nil and false evaluate to true. C and C++ programmers, take note. 0 is true!

Logical operators work like they do in C, C++, C#, and Java, with a few minor exceptions. and (alternatively &&) is a logical and. or (alternatively ||) is a logical or. With these tests, the interpreter will execute code only until the value of the test is clear. Use & or | to compare while executing the whole expression. Here are these concepts in action:

```
>> true and false
=> false
>> true or false
=> true
>> false && false
=> false

>> true && this_will_cause_an_error
NameError: undefined local variable or method `this_will_cause_an_error'
    for main:Object
        from (irb):59
>> false && this_will_not_cause_an_error
=> false
>> true or this_will_not_cause_an_error
=> true
>> true || this_will_not_cause_an_error
=> true
>> true | this_will_cause_an_error
NameError: undefined local variable or method `this_will_cause_an_error'
    for main:Object
        from (irb):2
        from :0
>> true | false
=> true
```

There's no magic here. You'll normally use the short-circuit version of these commands.

Duck Typing

Let's get into Ruby's typing model a little. The first thing you need to know is how much protection Ruby will give you when you make a mistake with types. We're talking about type safety. Strongly typed languages check types for certain operations and check the types before you can do any damage. This check can happen when you present the code to an interpreter or a compiler or when you execute it. Check out this code:

```
>> 4 + 'four'
TypeError: String can't be coerced into Fixnum
        from (irb):51:in `+'
        from (irb):51

>> 4.class
=> Fixnum
>> (4.0).class
=> Float

>> 4 + 4.0
=> 8.0
```

So, Ruby is strongly typed,[3] meaning you'll get an error when types collide. Ruby makes these type checks at run time, not compile time. I'm going to show you how to define a function a little before I normally would to prove the point. The keyword def defines a function but doesn't execute it. Enter this code:

```
>> def add_them_up
>>   4 + 'four'
>> end
=> nil
>> add_them_up
TypeError: String can't be coerced into Fixnum
        from (irb):56:in `+'
        from (irb):56:in `add_them_up'
        from (irb):58
```

So, Ruby does not do type checking until you actually try to execute code. This concept is called *dynamic typing*. There are disadvantages: you can't catch as many errors as you can with static typing because compilers and tools can catch more errors with a statically typed system. But Ruby's type system also has several potential advantages. Your classes don't have to inherit from the same parent to be used in the same way:

```
>> i = 0
=> 0
```

3. I'm lying to you a little, but only a little. Two examples from here, you'll see me change an existing class at run time. Theoretically, a user can change a class beyond all recognition and defeat type safety, so in the strictest sense, Ruby is not strongly typed. But for the most part, Ruby behaves like a strongly typed language most of the time.

```
>> a = ['100', 100.0]
=> ['100', 100.0]
>> while i < 2
>>   puts a[i].to_i
>>   i = i + 1
>> end
100
100
```

You just saw duck typing in action. The first element of the array is a String, and the second is a Float. The same code converts each to an integer via to_i. Duck typing doesn't care what the underlying type might be. If it walks like a duck and quacks like a duck, it's a duck. In this case, the quack method is to_i.

Duck typing is extremely important when it comes to clean object-oriented design. An important tenet of design philosophy is to code to interfaces rather than implementations. If you're using duck typing, this philosophy is easy to support with very little added ceremony. If an object has push and pop methods, you can treat it like a stack. If it doesn't, you can't.

What We Learned in Day 1

So far, you've just waded through the basics. It's an interpreted object-oriented language. Just about everything is an object, and it's easy to get at any object's parts, like the methods and the class. Ruby is duck typed, and Ruby behaves mostly like a strongly typed language, though some academics would argue with that distinction. It's a free-spirited language that will let you do just about anything, including changing core classes like NilClass and String. Now let me turn you loose for a little self-study.

Day 1 Self-Study

So, you've had your first date with Ruby. Now, it's time to write a little code. In this session, you're not going to write whole programs. Instead, you'll use irb to execute a few Ruby snippets. As always, you can find the answers in the back of the book.

Find:

- The Ruby API
- The free online version of *Programming Ruby: The Pragmatic Programmer's Guide* [TFH08]

- A method that substitutes part of a string
- Information about Ruby's regular expressions
- Information about Ruby's ranges

Do:

- Print the string "Hello, world."
- For the string "Hello, Ruby," find the index of the word "Ruby."
- Print your name ten times.
- Print the string "This is sentence number 1," where the number 1 changes from 1 to 10.
- Run a Ruby program from a file.
- Bonus problem: If you're feeling the need for a little more, write a program that picks a random number. Let a player guess the number, telling the player whether the guess is too low or too high.

  (Hint: `rand(10)` will generate a random number from 0 to 9, and `gets` will read a string from the keyboard that you can translate to an integer.)

2.3 Day 2: Floating Down from the Sky

At the time, one of the most striking scenes in *Mary Poppins* was her entrance. She floated into town on her umbrella. My kids will never understand why that entrance was groundbreaking stuff. Today, you're going to experience a little bit of the magic that makes Ruby click. You'll learn to use the basic building blocks of objects, collections, and classes. You'll also learn the basics of the code block. Open up your mind to a little magic.

Defining Functions

Unlike Java and C#, you don't have to build a whole class to define a function. You can define a function right in the console:

```
>> def tell_the_truth
>>   true
>> end
```

Every function returns something. If you do not specify an explicit return, the function will return the value of the last expression that's processed before exiting. Like everything else, this function is an object.

Later, we'll work on strategies to pass functions as parameters to other functions.

Arrays

Arrays are Ruby's workhorse ordered collection. Ruby 1.9 introduces ordered hashes too, but in general, arrays are Ruby's primary ordered collection. Take a look:

```
>> animals = ['lions', 'tigers', 'bears']
=> ["lions", "tigers", "bears"]
>> puts animals
lions
tigers
bears
=> nil
>> animals[0]
=> "lions"
>> animals[2]
=> "bears"
>> animals[10]
=> nil
>> animals[-1]
=> "bears"
>> animals[-2]
=> "tigers"
>> animals[0..1]
=> ['lions', 'tigers']
>> (0..1).class
=> Range
```

You can see that Ruby collections will give you some freedom. If you access any undefined array element, Ruby will simply return nil. You will also find some features that don't make arrays more powerful but just make them easier to use. animals[-1] returned the first element from the end, animals[-2] returned the second, and so on. These features are called *syntactic sugar*, an added feature for convenience. The animals[0..1] expression might look like syntactic sugar, but it's not. 0..1 is actually a Range, meaning all numbers from 0 to 1, inclusive.

Arrays can hold other types as well:

```
>> a[0] = 0
NameError: undefined local variable or method `a' for main:Object
from (irb):23
>> a = []
=> []
```

Oops. I tried to use an array before it was an array. That error gives you a clue to the way Ruby arrays and hashes work. [] is actually a method on Array:

```
>> [1].class
=> Array
>> [1].methods.include?('[]')
=> true
>> # use [1].methods.include?(:[]) on ruby 1.9
```

So, [] and []= are just syntactic sugar to allow access to an array. To do this right, I need to put an empty array into it first, and then I can play around with it some:

```
>> a[0] = 'zero'
=> "zero"
>> a[1] = 1
=> 1
>> a[2] = ['two', 'things']
=> ["two", "things"]
>> a
=> ["zero", 1, ["two", "things"]]
```

Arrays don't need to be homogeneous.

```
>> a = [[1, 2, 3], [10, 20, 30], [40, 50, 60]]
=> [[1, 2, 3], [10, 20, 30], [40, 50, 60]]
>> a[0][0]
=> 1
>> a[1][2]
=> 30
```

And multidimensional arrays are just arrays of arrays.

```
>> a = [1]
=> [1]
>> a.push(1)
=> [1, 1]
>> a = [1]
=> [1]
>> a.push(2)
=> [1, 2]
>> a.pop
=> 2
>> a.pop
=> 1
```

Arrays have an incredibly rich API. You can use an array as a queue, a linked list, a stack, or a set. Now, let's take a look at the other major collection in Ruby, the hash.

Hashes

Remember that collections are buckets for objects. In the hash bucket, every object has a label. The label is the key, and the object is the value. A hash is a bunch of key-value pairs:

```
>> numbers = {1 => 'one', 2 => 'two'}
=> {1=>"one", 2=>"two"}
>> numbers[1]
=> "one"
>> numbers[2]
=> "two"
>> stuff = {:array => [1, 2, 3], :string => 'Hi, mom!'}
=> {:array=>[1, 2, 3], :string=>"Hi, mom!"}
>> stuff[:string]
=> "Hi, mom!"
```

This is not too complicated. A hash works a lot like an array, but instead of an integer index, the hash can have any arbitrary key. The last hash is interesting because I'm introducing a symbol for the first time. A symbol is an identifier preceded with a colon, like :symbol. Symbols are great for naming things or ideas. Although two strings with the same value can be different physical strings, identical symbols are the same physical object. You can tell by getting the unique object identifier of the symbol several times, like so:

```
>> 'string'.object_id
=> 3092010
>> 'string'.object_id
=> 3089690
>> :string.object_id
=> 69618
>> :string.object_id
=> 69618
```

Hashes sometimes show up in unusual circumstances. For example, Ruby does not support named parameters, but you can simulate them with a hash. Throw in a little syntactic sugar, and you can get some interesting behavior:

```
>> def tell_the_truth(options={})
>>   if options[:profession] == :lawyer
>>     'it could be believed that this is almost certainly not false.'
>>   else
>>     true
>>   end
>> end
=> nil
>> tell_the_truth
=> true
```

```
>> tell_the_truth :profession => :lawyer
=> "it could be believed that this is almost certainly not false."
```

This method takes a single optional parameter. If you pass nothing in, options will be set to an empty hash. If you pass in a :profession of :lawyer, you will get something different. The result is not fully true, but it is almost just as good, because the system will evaluate it as true. Notice that you didn't have to type in the braces. These braces are optional for the last parameter of a function. Since array elements, hash keys, and hash values can be almost anything, you can build some incredibly sophisticated data structures in Ruby, but the real power comes when you start to get into code blocks.

Code Blocks and Yield

A code block is a function without a name. You can pass it as a parameter to a function or a method. For example:

```
>> 3.times {puts 'hiya there, kiddo'}
hiya there, kiddo
hiya there, kiddo
hiya there, kiddo
```

The code between braces is called a *code block*. times is a method on Fixnum that simply does something some number of times, where something is a code block and number is the value of the Fixnum. You can specify code blocks with {/} or do/end. The typical Ruby convention is to use braces when your code block is on one line and use the do/end form when the code blocks span more than one line. Code blocks can take one or more parameters:

```
>> animals = ['lions and ', 'tigers and', 'bears', 'oh my']
=> ["lions and ", "tigers and", "bears", "oh my"]
>> animals.each {|a| puts a}
lions and
tigers and
bears
oh my
```

This code begins to display the power of the code block. That code told Ruby what to do for every item in the collection. With a fraction of the syntax, Ruby iterated over each of the elements, printing each one. To really get a feel for what's going on, here's a custom implementation of the times method:

```
>> class Fixnum
>>   def my_times
>>     i = self
```

```
>>     while i > 0
>>       i = i - 1
>>       yield
>>     end
>>   end
>> end
=> nil
>> 3.my_times {puts 'mangy moose'}
mangy moose
mangy moose
mangy moose
```

This code opens up an existing class and adds a method. In this case, the method called my_times loops a set number of times, invoking the code block with yield. Blocks can also be first-class parameters. Check out this example:

```
>> def call_block(&block)
>>   block.call
>> end
=> nil
>> def pass_block(&block)
>>   call_block(&block)
>> end
=> nil
>> pass_block {puts 'Hello, block'}
Hello, block
```

This technique will let you pass around executable code. Blocks aren't just for iteration. In Ruby, you'll use blocks to delay execution...

```
execute_at_noon { puts 'Beep beep... time to get up'}
```

conditionally execute something...

```
...some code...
in_case_of_emergency do
  use_credit_card
  panic
end

def in_case_of_emergency
  yield if emergency?
end
...more code...
```

enforce policy...

```
within_a_transaction do
  things_that
  must_happen_together
end
```

```
def within_a_transaction
  begin_transaction
  yield
  end_transaction
end
```

and many other places. You'll see Ruby libraries that use blocks to process each line of a file, do work within an HTTP transaction, and do complex operations over collections. Ruby is a block party.

Running Ruby from a File

The code examples are getting a little more complicated, so working from the interactive console isn't all that convenient anymore. You'll use the console to explore short bits of code, but you'll primarily put your code into files. Create a file called hello.rb. You can include any Ruby code that you'd like:

```
puts 'hello, world'
```

Save it to your current directory, and then execute it from the command line:

```
batate$ ruby hello.rb
hello, world
```

A few people are using Ruby from full integrated development environments, but many are happy to use a simple editor with files. My favorite is TextMate, but vi, emacs, and many other popular editors have Ruby plug-ins. With this understanding in our back pocket, we can move on to the reusable building blocks of Ruby programs.

Defining Classes

Like Java, C#, and C++, Ruby has classes and objects. Think cookie cutter and cookie—classes are templates for objects. Of course, Ruby supports inheritance. Unlike C++, a Ruby class can inherit from only one parent, called a *superclass*. To see it all in action, from the console, type the following:

```
>> 4.class
=> Fixnum
>> 4.class.superclass
=> Integer
>> 4.class.superclass.superclass
=> Numeric
>> 4.class.superclass.superclass.superclass
=> Object
>> 4.class.superclass.superclass.superclass.superclass
=> nil
```

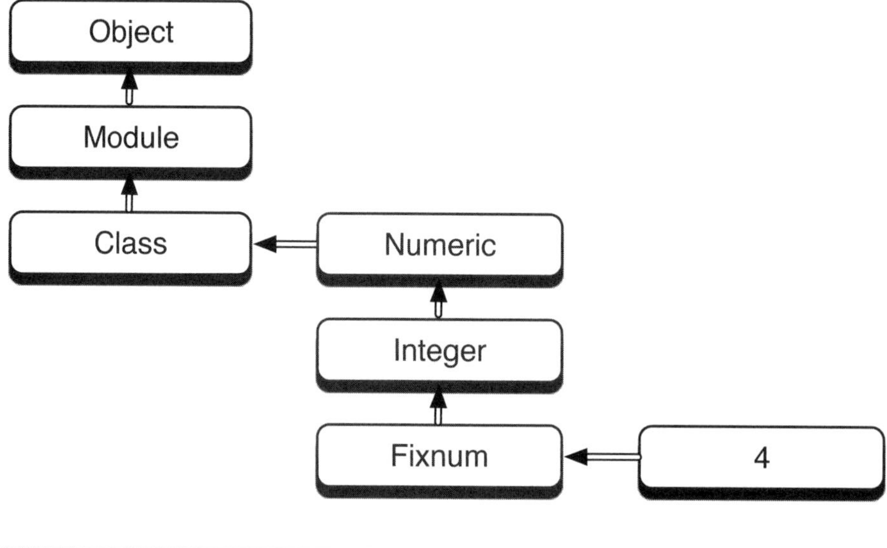

Figure 2.1: RUBY METAMODEL

So far, so good. Objects are derived from a class. The 4's class is Fixnum, which inherits from Integer, Numeric, and ultimately Object.

Check out Figure 2.1 to see how things fit together. Everything eventually inherits from Object. A Class is also a Module. Instances of Class serve as templates for objects. In our case, Fixnum is an instance of a class, and 4 is an instance of Fixnum. Each of these classes is also an object:

```
>> 4.class.class
=> Class
>> 4.class.class.superclass
=> Module
>> 4.class.class.superclass.superclass
=> Object
```

So, Fixnum is derived from the class Class. From there, it really gets confusing. Class inherits from Module, and Module inherits from Object. When all is said and done, everything in Ruby has a common ancestor, Object.

ruby/tree.rb

```
class Tree
  attr_accessor :children, :node_name

  def initialize(name, children=[])
    @children = children
    @node_name = name
  end

  def visit_all(&block)
    visit &block
    children.each {|c| c.visit_all &block}
  end

  def visit(&block)
    block.call self
  end
end

ruby_tree = Tree.new( "Ruby",
  [Tree.new("Reia"),
   Tree.new("MacRuby")] )

puts "Visiting a node"
ruby_tree.visit {|node| puts node.node_name}
puts

puts "visiting entire tree"
ruby_tree.visit_all {|node| puts node.node_name}
```

This power-packed class implements a very simple tree. It has three methods, initialize, visit, and visit_all, and two instance variables, children and node_name. initialize has special meaning. Ruby will call it when the class instantiates a new object.

I should point out a few conventions and rules for Ruby. Classes start with capital letters and typically use CamelCase to denote capitalization. You must prepend instance variables (one value per object) with @ and class variables (one value per class) with @@. Instance variables and method names begin with lowercase letters in the underscore_style. Constants are in ALL_CAPS. This code defines a tree class. Each tree has two instance variables: @children and @node_name. Functions and methods that test typically use a question mark (if test?).

The attr keyword defines an instance variable. Several versions exist. The most common are attr (defining an instance variable and a method of the same name to access it) and attr_accessor, defining an instance variable, an accessor, and a setter.

Our dense program packs a punch. It uses blocks and recursion to allow any user to visit all nodes in a tree. Each instance of Tree has one node of a tree. The initialize method provides the starting values for children and node_name. The visit method calls the inbound code block. The visit_all method calls visit for the node and then recursively calls visit_all for each of the children.

The remaining code uses the API. It defines a tree, visits one node, and then visits all nodes. Running it produces this output:

```
Visiting a node
Ruby

visiting entire tree
Ruby
Reia
MacRuby
```

Classes are only part of the equation. You've briefly seen modules in the code on page 26. Let's go back and take a closer look.

Writing a Mixin

Object-oriented languages use inheritance to propagate behavior to similar objects. When the behaviors are not similar, either you can allow inheritance from more than one class (multiple inheritance) or you can look to another solution. Experience has shown that multiple inheritance is complicated and problematic. Java uses interfaces to solve this problem. Ruby uses modules. A module is a collection of functions and constants. When you include a module as part of a class, those behaviors and constants become part of the class.

Take this class, which adds a to_f method to an arbitrary class:

ruby/to_file.rb

```
module ToFile
  def filename
    "object_#{self.object_id}.txt"
  end

  def to_f
    File.open(filename, 'w') {|f| f.write(to_s)}
  end
end
```

```
class Person
  include ToFile
  attr_accessor :name

  def initialize(name)
    @name = name
  end

  def to_s
    name
  end
end

Person.new('matz').to_f
```

Start with the module definition. This module has two methods. The to_f method writes the output of the to_s method to a file with a filename supplied by the filename method. What's interesting here is that to_s is used in the module but implemented in the class! The class has not even been defined yet. The module interacts with the including class at an intimate level. The module will often depend on several class methods. With Java, this contract is explicit: the class will implement a formal interface. With Ruby, this contract is implicit, through duck typing.

The details of Person are not at all interesting, and that's the point. The Person includes the module, and we're done. The ability to write to a file has nothing to do with whether a class is actually a Person. We add the capability to add the contents to a file by mixing in the capability. We can add new mixins and subclasses to Person, and each subclass will have the capabilities of all the mixins without having to know about the mixin's implementation. When all is said and done, you can use a simplified single inheritance to define the essence of a class and then attach additional capabilities with modules. This style of programming, introduced in Flavors and used in many languages from Smalltalk to Python, is called a *mixin*. The vehicle that carries the mixin is not always called a module, but the premise is clear. Single inheritance plus mixins allow for a nice packaging of behavior.

Modules, Enumerable, and Sets

A couple of the most critical mixins in Ruby are the enumerable and comparable mixins. A class wanting to be enumerable must implement each, and a class wanting to be comparable must implement <=>. Called the *spaceship* operator, <=> is a simple comparison that returns -1 if b is greater, 1 if a is greater, and 0 otherwise. In exchange for implementing these methods, enumerable and comparable provide many convenience methods for collections. Crack open the console:

```
>>  'begin' <=> 'end'
=> -1
>> 'same' <=> 'same'
=> 0
>> a = [5, 3, 4, 1]
=> [5, 3, 4, 1]
>> a.sort
=> [1, 3, 4, 5]
>> a.any? {|i| i > 6}
=> false
>> a.any? {|i| i > 4}
=> true
>> a.all? {|i| i > 4}
=> false
>> a.all? {|i| i > 0}
=> true
>> a.collect {|i| i * 2}
=> [10, 6, 8, 2]
>> a.select {|i| i % 2 == 0 } # even
=> [4]
>> a.select {|i| i % 2 == 1 } # odd
=> [5, 3, 1]
>> a.max
=> 5
>> a.member?(2)
=> false
```

any? returns true if the condition is true for any of the elements; all? returns true if the condition is true for all elements. Since the spaceship is implemented on these integers through Fixnum, you can sort and compute the min or max.

You can also do set-based operations. collect and map apply a function to each of the elements and return an array of the results. find finds one element matching the condition, and both select and find_all return all elements matching a condition. You can also compute the total of a list or the product with inject:

```
>> a
=> [5, 3, 4, 1]
>> a.inject(0) {|sum, i| sum + i}
=> 13
>> a.inject {|sum, i| sum + i}
=> 13
>> a.inject {|product, i| product * i}
=> 60
```

inject seems tricky, but it's not too complicated. It takes a code block with two arguments and an expression. The code block will be executed for each item in the list, with inject passing each list element to the code block as the second argument. The first argument is the result of the previous execution of the code block. Since the result won't have a value the first time the code block is executed, you just pass the initial value as the argument to inject. (If you don't specify a value, inject will use the first value in the collection.) Take a second look, with a little help:

```
>> a.inject(0) do |sum, i|
?>  puts "sum: #{sum}  i: #{i}   sum + i: #{sum + i}"
?>  sum + i
?>end
sum: 0  i: 5   sum + i: 5
sum: 5  i: 3   sum + i: 8
sum: 8  i: 4   sum + i: 12
sum: 12  i: 1   sum + i: 13
```

As expected, the result of the previous line is always the first value passed to the next line. Using inject, you can compute the word count of many sentences, find the largest word in a paragraph of lines, and do much more.

What We Learned in Day 2

This is your first chance to see some of Ruby's sugar and also a little of the magic. You're starting to see how flexible Ruby can be. The collections are dead simple: two collections with multiple APIs layered on top. Application performance is secondary. Ruby is about the performance of the programmer. The enumerable module gives you a flavor of just how well-designed Ruby can be. The single-inheritance object-oriented structure certainly isn't novel, but the implementation is packed with intuitive design and useful features. This level of abstraction gives you a marginally better programming language, but serious mojo is on the way.

Day 2 Self-Study

These problems will be a little more demanding. You've used Ruby a little longer, so the gloves are off. These examples will force you to do a little more analytical thinking.

Find:

- Find out how to access files with and without code blocks. What is the benefit of the code block?

- How would you translate a hash to an array? Can you translate arrays to hashes?
- Can you iterate through a hash?
- You can use Ruby arrays as stacks. What other common data structures do arrays support?

Do:

- Print the contents of an array of sixteen numbers, four numbers at a time, using just each. Now, do the same with each_slice in Enumerable.
- The Tree class was interesting, but it did not allow you to specify a new tree with a clean user interface. Let the initializer accept a nested structure with hashes and arrays. You should be able to specify a tree like this: {'grandpa' => { 'dad' => {'child 1' => {}, 'child 2' => {} }, 'uncle' => {'child 3' => {}, 'child 4' => {} } } }.
- Write a simple grep that will print the lines of a file having any occurrences of a phrase anywhere in that line. You will need to do a simple regular expression match and read lines from a file. (This is surprisingly simple in Ruby.) If you want, include line numbers.

2.4 Day 3: Serious Change

The whole point of Mary Poppins is that she made the household better as a whole by making it fun and changing the hearts of the people in it with passion and imagination. You could back off a little and play it safe, using Ruby to do the same things you already know how to do in other languages. But when you change the way a language looks and works, you can capture magic that makes programming fun. In this book, each chapter will show you some nontrivial problem that the language solves well. In Ruby, that means metaprogramming.

Metaprogramming means writing programs that write programs. The ActiveRecord framework that's the centerpiece of Rails uses metaprogramming to implement a friendly language for building classes that link to database tables. An ActiveRecord class for a Department might look like this:

```
class Department < ActiveRecord::Base
  has_many :employees
  has_one :manager
end
```

has_many and has_one are Ruby methods that add all the instance variables and methods needed to establish a has_many relationship. This class specification reads like English, eliminating all the noise and baggage that you usually find with other database frameworks. Let's look at some different tools you can use for metaprogramming.

Open Classes

You've already had a brief introduction to open classes. You can change the definition of any class at any time, usually to add behavior. Here's a great example from the Rails framework that adds a method to NilClass:

ruby/blank.rb

```
class NilClass
  def blank?
    true
  end
end

class String
  def blank?
    self.size == 0
  end
end

["", "person", nil].each do |element|
  puts element unless element.blank?
end
```

The first invocation of class defines a class; once a class is already defined, subsequent invocations modify that class. This code adds a method called blank? to two existing classes: NilClass and String. When I check the status of a given string, I often want to see whether it is blank. Most strings can have a value, be empty, and be possibly nil. This little idiom lets me quickly check for the two empty cases at once, because blank? will return true. It doesn't matter which class String points to. If it supports the blank? method, it will work. If it walks like a duck and quacks like a duck, it is a duck. I don't need to draw blood to check the type.

Watch what's going on here. You're asking for a very sharp scalpel, and Ruby will gladly give it to you. Your open classes have redefined both String and Nil. It's possible to completely disable Ruby by redefining, say, Class.new. The trade-off is freedom. With the kind of freedom that lets you redefine any class or object at any time, you can build some amazingly readable code. With freedom and power come responsibility.

Open classes are useful when you're building languages to encode your own domain. It's often useful to express units in a language that works for your business domain. For example, consider an API that expresses all distance as inches:

ruby/units.rb

```
class Numeric
  def inches
    self
  end

  def feet
    self * 12.inches
  end

  def yards
    self * 3.feet
  end

  def miles
    self * 5280.feet
  end

  def back
    self * -1
  end

  def forward
    self
  end
end

puts 10.miles.back
puts 2.feet.forward
```

The open classes make this kind of support possible with minimal syntax. But other techniques can stretch Ruby even further.

Via method_missing

Ruby calls a special debugging method each time a method is missing in order to print some diagnostic information. This behavior makes the language easier to debug. But sometimes, you can take advantage of this language feature to build some unexpectedly rich behavior. All you need to do is override method_missing. Consider an API to represent Roman numerals. You could do it easily enough with a method call, with an API something like Roman.number_for "ii". In truth, that's not too bad. There are no mandatory parentheses or semicolons to get in the way. With Ruby, we can do better:

ruby/roman.rb

```
class Roman
  def self.method_missing name, *args
    roman = name.to_s
    roman.gsub!("IV", "IIII")
    roman.gsub!("IX", "VIIII")
    roman.gsub!("XL", "XXXX")
    roman.gsub!("XC", "LXXXX")

    (roman.count("I") +
     roman.count("V") * 5 +
     roman.count("X") * 10 +
     roman.count("L") * 50 +
     roman.count("C") * 100)
  end
end

puts Roman.X
puts Roman.XC
puts Roman.XII
puts Roman.X
```

This code is a beautiful example of method_missing in action. The code is clear and simple. We first override method_missing. We'll get the name of the method and its parameters as input parameters. We're interested only in the name. First, we convert that to String. Then, we replace the special cases, like iv and ix, with strings that are easier to count. Then, we just count Roman digits and multiply by the value of that number. The API is so much easier: Roman.i versus Roman.number_for "i".

Consider the cost, though. We do have a class that will be much more difficult to debug, because Ruby can no longer tell you when a method is missing! We would definitely want strong error checking to make sure it was accepting valid Roman numerals. If you don't know what you're looking for, you could have a tough time finding that implementation of that ii method on Roman. Still, it's another scalpel for the tool bag. Use it wisely.

Modules

The most popular metaprogramming style in Ruby is the module. You can literally implement def or attr_accessor with a few lines of code in a module. You can also extend class definitions in surprising ways. A common technique lets you design your own domain-specific language

(DSL) to define your class.[4] The DSL defines methods in a module that adds all the methods and constants needed to manage a class.

I'm going to break an example down using a common superclass first. Here's the type of class that we want to build through metaprogramming. It's a simple program to open a CSV file based on the name of the class.

ruby/acts_as_csv_class.rb

```
class ActsAsCsv
  def read
    file = File.new(self.class.to_s.downcase + '.txt')
    @headers = file.gets.chomp.split(', ')

    file.each do |row|
      @result << row.chomp.split(', ')
    end
  end

  def headers
    @headers
  end

  def csv_contents
    @result
  end

  def initialize
    @result = []
    read
  end
end

class RubyCsv < ActsAsCsv
end

m = RubyCsv.new
puts m.headers.inspect
puts m.csv_contents.inspect
```

This basic class defines four methods. headers and csv_contents are simple accessors that return the value of instance variables. initialize initializes the results of the read. Most of the work happens in read. The read method opens a file, reads headings, and chops them into individual fields. Next, it loops over lines, placing the contents of each line in an

4. DSLs let you tailor a language for a specific domain. For perhaps the best-known example in Ruby, the ActiveRecord persistence framework uses domain-specific languages to map a class to a database table.

array. This implementation of a CSV file is not complete because it does not handle edge cases like quotes, but you get the idea.

The next step is to take the file and attach that behavior to a class with a module method often called a *macro*. Macros change the behavior of classes, often based on changes in the environment. In this case, our macro opens up the class and dumps in all the behavior related to a CSV file:

ruby/acts_as_csv.rb

```
class ActsAsCsv
  def self.acts_as_csv

    define_method 'read' do
      file = File.new(self.class.to_s.downcase + '.txt')
      @headers = file.gets.chomp.split(', ')

      file.each do |row|
        @result << row.chomp.split(', ')
      end
    end

    define_method "headers" do
      @headers
    end

    define_method "csv_contents" do
      @result
    end

    define_method 'initialize' do
      @result = []
      read
    end
  end
end

class RubyCsv < ActsAsCsv
  acts_as_csv
end

m = RubyCsv.new
puts m.headers.inspect
puts m.csv_contents.inspect
```

The metaprogramming happens in the acts_as_csv macro. That code calls define_method for all the methods we want to add to the target class. Now, when the target class calls acts_as_csv, that code will define all four methods on the target class.

So, the acts_as macro code does nothing but add a few methods we could have easily added through inheritance. That design does not seem like much of an improvement, but it's about to get more interesting. Let's see how the same behavior would work in a module:

ruby/acts_as_csv_module.rb

```
module ActsAsCsv

  def self.included(base)
    base.extend ClassMethods
  end

  module ClassMethods
    def acts_as_csv
      include InstanceMethods
    end
  end

  module InstanceMethods

    def read
      @csv_contents = []
      filename = self.class.to_s.downcase + '.txt'
      file = File.new(filename)
      @headers = file.gets.chomp.split(', ')

      file.each do |row|
        @csv_contents << row.chomp.split(', ')
      end
    end

    attr_accessor :headers, :csv_contents

    def initialize
      read
    end

  end

end

class RubyCsv  # no inheritance! You can mix it in
  include ActsAsCsv
  acts_as_csv
end

m = RubyCsv.new
puts m.headers.inspect
puts m.csv_contents.inspect
```

Ruby will invoke the included method whenever this module gets included into another. Remember, a class is a module. In our included method, we extend the target class called base (which is the RubyCsv class), and that module adds class methods to RubyCsv. The only class method is acts_as_csv. That method in turn opens up the class and includes all the instance methods. And we're writing a program that writes a program.

The interesting thing about all these metaprogramming techniques is that your programs can change based on the state of your application. ActiveRecord uses metaprogramming to dynamically add accessors that are the same name as the columns of the database. Some XML frameworks like builder let users define custom tags with method_missing to provide a beautiful syntax. When your syntax is more beautiful, you can let the reader of your code get past the syntax and closer to the intentions. That's the power of Ruby.

What We Learned in Day 3

In this section, you learned to use Ruby to define your own syntax and change classes on the fly. These programming techniques fall in the category of metaprogramming. Every line of code that you write has two kinds of audiences: computers and people. Sometimes, it's hard to strike a balance between building code that can pass through the interpreter or compiler and is also easy to understand. With metaprogramming, you can close the gap between valid Ruby syntax and sentences.

Some of the best Ruby frameworks, such as Builder and ActiveRecord, heavily depend on metaprogramming techniques for readability. You used open classes to build a duck-typed interface supporting the blank? method for String objects and nil, dramatically reducing the amount of clutter for a common scenario. You saw some code that used many of the same techniques. You used method_missing to build beautiful Roman numerals. And finally, you used modules to define a domain-specific language that you used to specify CSV files.

Day 3 Self-Study

Do:

Modify the CSV application to support an each method to return a CsvRow object. Use method_missing on that CsvRow to return the value for the column for a given heading.

For example, for the file:

```
one, two
lions, tigers
```

allow an API that works like this:

```
csv = RubyCsv.new
csv.each {|row| puts row.one}
```

This should print "lions".

2.5 Wrapping Up Ruby

We have covered a lot of ground in this chapter. I hope you can see the comparison to Mary Poppins. After speaking at dozens of Ruby conferences, I have heard scores of people profess their love for Ruby because it is fun. To an industry that grew up embracing the C family of languages including C++, C#, Java, and others, Ruby is a breath of fresh air.

Core Strengths

Ruby's pure object orientation allows you to treat objects in a uniform and consistent way. The duck typing allows truer polymorphic designs based on what an object can support rather than that object's inheritance hierarchy. And Ruby's modules and open classes let a programmer attach behavior to syntax that goes beyond the typical method or instance variable definitions in a class.

Ruby is ideal as a scripting language, or as a web development language if the scaling requirements are reasonable. The language is intensely productive. Some of the features that enable that productivity make Ruby hard to compile and make the performance suffer.

Scripting

Ruby is a fantastic scripting language. Writing glue code to munge two applications together, writing a spider to scrape web pages for a stock quote or book price, or running local build environments or automated tests are excellent uses for Ruby.

As a language with a presence on most major operating systems, Ruby is a good choice for scripting environments. The language has a wide variety of libraries included with the base, as well as thousands of gems, or prepackaged plug-ins, that can be used for loading CSV files, processing XML, or working with low-level Internet APIs.

Web Development

Rails is already one of the most successful web development frameworks of all time. The design is based on well-understood model-view-controller paradigms. The many naming conventions for database and application elements allow a typical application to be built with few lines of configuration at all. And the framework has plug-ins that handle some difficult production issues:

- The structure of Rails applications is always consistent and well understood.
- Migrations handle changes in the database schema.
- Several well-documented conventions reduce the total amount of configuration code.
- Many different plug-ins are available.

Time to Market

I would consider the productivity of Ruby and Rails to be an important component in its success. In the mid-2000s, you could not throw a rock in San Francisco without hitting someone who worked at a start-up powered by Rails. Even today, Ruby is prolific in these kinds of companies, including mine. The combination of the beautiful syntax and the community of programmers, tools, and plug-ins is extremely powerful. You can find Ruby gems to find the ZIP code of a surfer and another to calculate all address codes in a fifty-mile radius. You can process images and credit cards, work with web services, and communicate across many programming languages.

Many large, commercial websites use Ruby and Ruby on Rails. The original Twitter implementation was in Ruby, and the extraordinary productivity of the language allowed the website to grow to huge proportions. Eventually, the core of Twitter was rewritten in Scala. There are two lessons here. First, Ruby is a great language for getting a viable product to market quickly. Second, the scalability of Ruby is limited in some ways.

In formal big enterprises with distributed transactions, fail-safe messaging, and internationalization, the role of Ruby is often seen as a little more limited, but Ruby can do all of these things. Sometimes, concerns about the right application frameworks and scalability are well-founded, but too many people focus on enough scalability to build the next eBay when they can't deliver any software on time. Often, Ruby would be more than adequate considering the time-to-market pressures many enterprises face.

Weaknesses

No language is perfect for all applications. Ruby has its share of limitations too. Let's walk through some of the major ones.

Performance

Ruby's primary weakness is performance. Sure, Ruby is getting faster. Version 1.9 is up to ten times faster for some use cases. A new Ruby virtual machine written by Evan Phoenix called Rubinius has the potential to compile Ruby using a just-in-time compiler. This approach looks at an interpreter's usage patterns for a block of code to anticipate which code is likely to be needed again. This approach works well for Ruby, a language where syntax clues are usually not enough to allow compilation. Remember, the definition of a class can change at any time.

Still, Matz is very clear. He works to optimize the programmer's experience, not the performance of the language. Many of the language's features such as open classes, duck typing, and method_missing defeat the very tools that enable compilation and the associated performance gains.

Concurrency and OOP

Object-oriented programming has a critical limitation. The whole premise of the model depends on wrapping behavior around state, and usually the state can be changed. This programming strategy leads to serious problems with concurrency. At best, significant resource contentions are built into the language. At worst, object-oriented systems are next to impossible to debug and cannot be reliably tested for concurrent environments. As of this writing, the Rails team is only now starting to address the problem of managing concurrency effectively.

Type Safety

I'm a firm believer in duck typing. With this typing strategy, you can generally have cleaner abstractions with concise, readable code. But duck typing comes at a price, too. Static typing allows a whole range of tools that make it easier to do syntax trees and thus provide integrated development environments. IDEs for Ruby are more difficult to build, and so far, most Ruby developers do not use them. Many times, I've lamented the loss of an IDE-style debugger. I know I'm not alone.

Final Thoughts

So, Ruby's core strengths are its syntax and flexibility. The core weaknesses are around performance, though the performance is reasonable for many purposes. All in all, Ruby is an excellent language for object-oriented development. For the right applications, Ruby can excel. As with any tool, use it to solve the right set of problems, and you're not likely to be disappointed. And keep your eyes open for a little magic along the way.

The question isn't, "What are we going to do?" The question is, "What aren't we going to do?"

► Ferris Bueller

Chapter 3

Io

Meet Io. Like Ruby, Io is a rule bender. He's young, wicked smart, and easy to understand but hard to predict. Think Ferris Bueller.[1] If you like a good party, you'll have to let Io show you around the town. He'll try anything once. He might give you the ride of your life, wreck your dad's car, or both. Either way, you will not be bored. As the quote above says, you won't have many rules to hold you back.

3.1 Introducing Io

Steve Dekorte invented the Io language in 2002. It's always written with an uppercase *I* followed by a lowercase *o*. Io is a prototype language like Lua or JavaScript, meaning every object is a clone of another.

Written as an exercise to help Steve understand how interpreters work, Io started as a hobbyist language and remains pretty small today. You can learn the syntax in about fifteen minutes and the basic mechanics of the language in thirty. There are no surprises. But the libraries will take you a little longer. The complexity and the richness comes from the library design.

Today, most of Io's community is focused on Io as an embeddable language with a tiny virtual machine and rich concurrency. The core strengths are richly customizable syntax and function, as well as a strong concurrency model. Try to focus on the simplicity of the syntax and the prototype programming model. I found that after Io, I had a much stronger understanding of how JavaScript worked.

---

1. *Ferris Bueller's Day Off*. DVD. Directed by John Hughes. 1986; Hollywood, CA: Paramount, 1999.

3.2 Day 1: Skipping School, Hanging Out

Meeting Io is like meeting any language. You'll have to put in a little keyboard time to get properly acquainted. It will be much easier if we can interact outside of stifled conversations in the hallway before history class. Let's cut school and skip straight to the good stuff.

Names are sometimes deceiving, but you can tell a lot from Io. It's simultaneously reckless (ever try Googling for *Io*?)[2] and brilliant. You get only two letters, both vowels. The language's syntax is simple and low-level, like the name. Io syntax simply chains messages together, with each message returning an object and each message taking optional parameters in parentheses. In Io, everything is a message that returns another receiver. There are no keywords and only a handful of characters that behave like keywords.

With Io, you won't worry about both classes and objects. You'll deal exclusively in objects, cloning them as needed. These clones are called *prototypes*, and Io is the first and only prototype-based language we'll look at. In a *prototype* language, every object is a clone of an existing object rather than a class. Io gets you about as close to object-oriented Lisp as you're likely to get. It's too early to tell whether Io will have lasting impact, but the simplicity of the syntax means it has a fighting chance. The concurrency libraries that you'll see in day 3 are well conceived, and the message semantics are elegant and powerful. Reflection is everywhere.

Breaking the Ice

Let's crack open the interpreter and start the party. You can find it at http://iolanguage.com. Download it and install it. Open the interpreter by typing io, and enter the traditional "Hello, World" program:

```
Io> "Hi ho, Io" print
Hi ho, Io==> Hi ho, Io
```

You can tell exactly what's going on here. You're sending the print message to the string "Hi ho, Io". Receivers go on the left, and messages go on the right. You won't find much syntactic sugar at all. You'll just send messages to objects.

In Ruby, you created a new object by calling new on some class. You created a new kind of object by defining a class. Io makes no distinction

2. Try Googling for *Io language* instead.

between these two things. You'll create new objects by cloning existing ones. The existing object is a prototype:

```
batate$ io
Io 20090105
Io> Vehicle := Object clone
==>  Vehicle_0x1003b61f8:
  type             = "Vehicle"
```

Object is the root-level object. We send the clone message, which returns a new object. We assign that object to Vehicle. Here, Vehicle is not a class. It's not a template used to create objects. It *is* an object, based on the Object prototype. Let's interact with it:

```
Io> Vehicle description := "Something to take you places"
==> Something to take you places
```

Objects have slots. Think of the collection of slots as a hash. You'll refer to each slot with a key. You can use := to assign something to a slot. If the slot doesn't exist, Io will create it. You can also use = for assignment. If the slot doesn't exist, Io throws an exception. We just created a slot called description.

```
Io> Vehicle description = "Something to take you far away"
==> Something to take you far away
Io> Vehicle nonexistingSlot = "This won't work."

  Exception: Slot nonexistingSlot not found.
    Must define slot using := operator before updating.
  ---------
  message 'updateSlot' in 'Command Line' on line 1
```

You can get the value from a slot by sending the slot's name to the object:

```
Io> Vehicle description
==> Something to take you far away
```

In fact, an object is little more than a collection of slots. We can look at the names of all the slots on Vehicle like this:

```
Io> Vehicle slotNames
==> list("type", "description")
```

We sent the slotNames method to Vehicle and got a list of slot names back. There are two slots. You've seen the description slot, but we also have a type slot. Every object supports type:

```
Io> Vehicle type
==> Vehicle
Io> Object type
==> Object
```

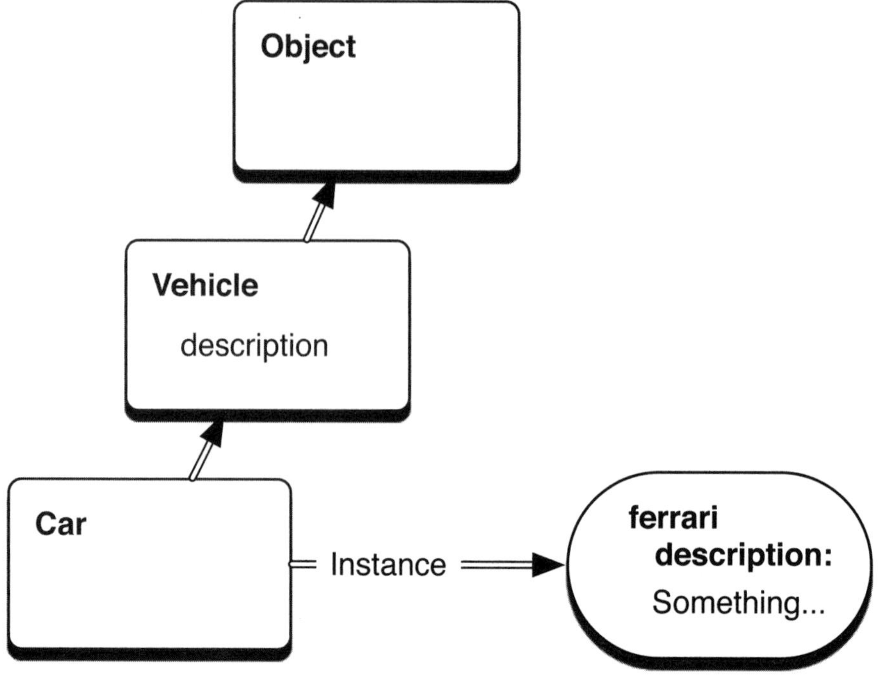

Figure 3.1: AN OBJECT-ORIENTED DESIGN

We'll get to types in a few paragraphs. For now, know that type represents the kind of object you're dealing with. Keep in mind that a type is an object, not a class. Here's what we know so far:

- You make objects by cloning other objects.
- Objects are collections of slots.
- You get a slot's value by sending the message.

You can already see that Io is simple and fun. But sit back. We're only scratching the surface. Let's move on to inheritance.

Objects, Prototypes, and Inheritance

In this section, we're going to deal with inheritance. Given a car that's also a vehicle, think of how you would model a ferrari object that is an instance of a car. In an object-oriented language, you'd do something like Figure 3.1.

Let's see how you'd solve the same problem in a prototype language. We're going to need a few extra objects. Let's create another:

```
Io> Car := Vehicle clone
==>  Car_0x100473938:
  type             = "Car"

Io> Car slotNames
==> list("type")
Io> Car type
==> Car
```

In Io-speak, we created a new object called Car by sending the clone message to the Vehicle prototype. Let's send description to Car:

```
Io> Car description
==> Something to take you far away
```

There's no description slot on Car. Io just forwards the description message to the prototype and finds the slot in Vehicle. It's dead simple but plenty powerful. Let's create another car, but this time, we'll assign it to ferrari:

```
Io> ferrari := Car clone
==>  Car_0x1004f43d0:

Io> ferrari slotNames
==> list()
```

A-ha! There's no type slot. By convention, types in Io begin with uppercase letters. Now, when you invoke the type slot, you'll get the type of your prototype:

```
Io> ferrari type
==> Car
```

This is how Io's object model works. Objects are just containers of slots. Get a slot by sending its name to an object. If the slot isn't there, Io calls the parent. That's all you have to understand. There are no classes or metaclasses. You don't have interfaces or modules. You just have objects, like you see in Figure 3.2, on the next page.

Types in Io are just conveniences. Idiomatically, an object that begins with an uppercase name is a type, so Io sets the type slot. Any clones of that type starting with lowercase letters will simply invoke their parents' type slot. Types are just tools that help Io programmers better organize code.

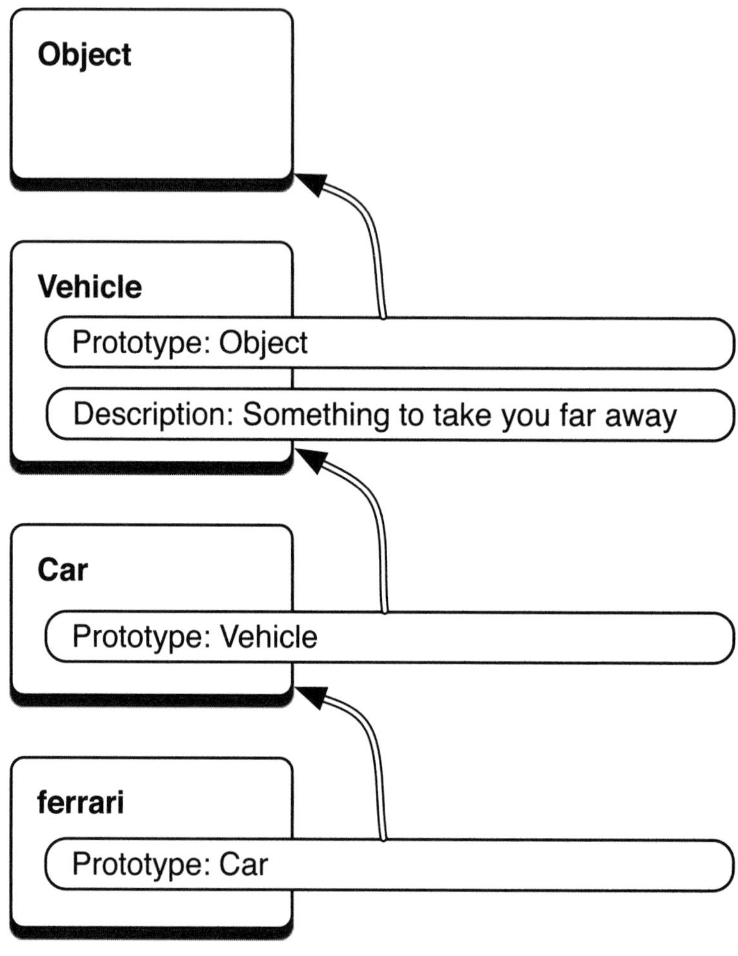

Figure 3.2: INHERITANCE IN IO

If you wanted ferrari to be a type, you would have it begin with an uppercase letter, like this:

```
Io> Ferrari := Car clone
==> Ferrari_0x9d085c8:
type = "Ferrari"

Io> Ferrari type
==> Ferrari

Io> Ferrari slotNames
==> list("type")
Io> ferrari slotNames
==> list()
Io>
```

Notice that ferrari has no type slot, but Ferrari does. We're using a simple coding convention rather than a full language feature to distinguish between types and instances. In other cases, they behave the same way.

In Ruby and Java, classes are templates used to create objects. bruce = Person.new creates a new person object from the Person class. They are different entities entirely, a class and an object. Not so in Io. bruce := Person clone creates a clone called bruce from the prototype called Person. Both bruce and Person are objects. Person is a type because it has a type slot. In most other respects, Person is identical to bruce. Let's move on to behavior.

Methods

In Io, you can create a method easily, like this:

```
Io> method("So, you've come for an argument." println)
==> method(
    "So, you've come for an argument." println
)
```

A method is an object, just like any other type of object. You can get its type:

```
Io> method() type
==> Block
```

Since a method is an object, we can assign it to a slot:

```
Io> Car drive := method("Vroom" println)
==> method(
    "Vroom" println
)
```

If a slot has a method, invoking the slot invokes the method:

```
Io> ferrari drive
Vroom
==> Vroom
```

Believe it or not, you now know the core organizational principles of Io. Think about it. You know the basic syntax. You can define types and objects. You can add data and behavior to an object by assigning contents to its slots. Everything else involves learning the libraries.

Let's dig a little deeper. You can get the contents of slots, whether they are variables or methods, like this:

```
Io> ferrari getSlot("drive")
==> method(
    "Vroom" println
)
```

getSlot will give you your parent's slot if the slot doesn't exist:

```
Io> ferrari getSlot("type")
==> Car
```

You can get the prototype of a given object:

```
Io> ferrari proto
==>  Car_0x100473938:
  drive            = method(...)
  type             = "Car"

Io> Car proto
==>  Vehicle_0x1003b61f8:
  description      = "Something to take you far away"
  type             = "Vehicle"
```

These were the prototypes that you used to clone ferrari and Car. You also see their custom slots for convenience.

There's a master namespace called Lobby that contains all the named objects. All of the assignments you've done in the console, plus a few more, are on Lobby. You can see it like this:

```
Io> Lobby
==>  Object_0x1002184e0:
  Car              = Car_0x100473938
  Lobby            = Object_0x1002184e0
  Protos           = Object_0x1002184e0
  Vehicle          = Vehicle_0x1003b61f8
  exit             = method(...)
  ferrari          = Car_0x1004f43d0
  forward          = method(...)
```

You see the exit implementation, forward, Protos, and the stuff we defined.

The prototype programming paradigm seems clear enough. These are the basic ground rules:

- Every *thing* is an object.
- Every *interaction* with an object is a message.
- You don't instantiate classes; you clone other objects called *prototypes*.
- Objects remember their prototypes.
- Objects have slots.
- Slots contain objects, including method objects.
- A message returns the value in a slot or invokes the method in a slot.
- If an object can't respond to a message, it sends that message to its prototype.

And that's most of it. Since you can see or change any slot or any object, you can do some pretty sophisticated metaprogramming. But first, you need to see the next layer of building blocks: collections.

Lists and Maps

Io has a few types of collections. A list is an ordered collection of objects of any type. List is the prototype for all lists, and Map is the prototype for key-value pairs, like the Ruby hash. Create a list like this:

```
Io> toDos := list("find my car", "find Continuum Transfunctioner")
==> list("find my car", "find Continuum Transfunctioner")

Io> toDos size
==> 2

Io> toDos append("Find a present")
==> list("find my car", "find Continuum Transfunctioner", "Find a present")
```

There's a shortcut way of representing a list. Object supports the list method, which wraps the arguments up into a list. Using list, you can conveniently create a list, like this:

```
Io> list(1, 2, 3, 4)
==> list(1, 2, 3, 4)
```

List also has convenience methods for math and to deal with the list as other data types, such as stacks:

```
Io> list(1, 2, 3, 4) average
==> 2.5

Io> list(1, 2, 3, 4) sum
==> 10

Io> list(1, 2, 3) at(1)
==> 2

Io> list(1, 2, 3) append(4)
==> list(1, 2, 3, 4)

Io> list(1, 2, 3) pop
==> 3

Io> list(1, 2, 3) prepend(0)
==> list(0, 1, 2, 3)

Io> list() isEmpty
==> true
```

The other major collection class in Io is the Map. Io maps are like Ruby hashes. Since there's no syntactic sugar, you'll work with them with an API that looks like this:

```
Io> elvis := Map clone
==>  Map_0x115f580:

Io> elvis atPut("home", "Graceland")
==>  Map_0x115f580:

Io> elvis at("home")
==> Graceland

Io> elvis atPut("style", "rock and roll")
==>  Map_0x115f580:

Io> elvis asObject
==>  Object_0x11c1d90:
  home                 = "Graceland"
  style                = "rock and roll"

Io> elvis asList
==> list(list("style", "rock and roll"), list("home", "Graceland"))

Io> elvis keys
==> list("style", "home")
```

```
Io> elvis size
==> 2
```

When you think about it, a hash is a lot like an Io object in structure where the keys are slots that are tied to values. The combination of slots that can be rapidly translated to objects is an interesting one.

Now that you've seen the basic collections, you'll want to use them. We'll need to introduce control structures, and those will depend on boolean values.

true, false, nil, and singletons

Io's conditions are pretty similar to those of other object-oriented languages. Here are a few:

```
Io> 4 < 5
==> true
Io> 4 <= 3
==> false
Io> true and false
==> false
Io> true and true
==> true
Io> true or true
==> true
Io> true or false
==> true
Io> 4 < 5 and 6 > 7
==> false
Io> true and 6
==> true
Io> true and 0
==> true
```

That's simple enough. Make a note: 0 is true as in Ruby, not false as in C. So, what is true?

```
Io> true proto
==>  Object_0x200490:
                        = Object_()
  !=                    = Object_!=()
...

Io> true clone
==> true
Io> false clone
==> false
Io> nil clone
==> nil
```

Now, that's interesting! true, false, and nil are singletons. Cloning them just returns the singleton value. You can do the same pretty easily. Create your own singleton like this:

```
Io> Highlander := Object clone
==>  Highlander_0x378920:
  type              = "Highlander"

Io> Highlander clone := Highlander
==>  Highlander_0x378920:
  clone             = Highlander_0x378920
  type              = "Highlander"
```

We've simply redefined the clone method to return Highlander, rather than letting Io forward requests up the tree, eventually getting to Object. Now, when you use Highlander, you'll get this behavior:

```
Io> Highlander clone
==>  Highlander_0x378920:
  clone             = Highlander_0x378920
  type              = "Highlander"
Io> fred := Highlander clone
==>  Highlander_0x378920:
  clone             = Highlander_0x378920
  type              = "Highlander"

Io> mike := Highlander clone
==>  Highlander_0x378920:
  clone             = Highlander_0x378920
  type              = "Highlander"

Io> fred == mike
==> true
```

Two clones are equal. That's not generally true:

```
Io> one := Object clone
==>  Object_0x356d00:

Io> two := Object clone
==>  Object_0x31eb60:

Io> one == two
==> false
```

Now, there can be only one Highlander. Sometimes, Io can trip you up. This solution is simple and elegant, if a little unexpected. We've blasted through a lot of information, but you know enough to do some pretty radical things, such as changing an object's clone method to make a singleton.

Be careful, though. Love him or hate him, you can't deny that Io is interesting. As with Ruby, Io can be a love-hate relationship. You can change just about any slot on any object, even the ones that define the language. Here's one that you may not want to try:

```
Object clone := "hosed"
```

Since you overrode the clone method on object, nothing can create objects anymore. You can't fix it. You just have to kill the process. But you can also get some pretty amazing behaviors in a short time. Since you have complete access to operators and the slots that make up any object, you can build domain-specific languages with a few short fascinating lines of code. Before we wrap up the day, let's hear what the inventor of the language has to say.

An Interview with Steve Dekorte

Steve Dekorte is an independent consultant in the San Francisco area. He invented Io in 2002. I had the pleasure of interviewing him about his experiences with creating Io.

Bruce Tate: *Why did you write Io?*

Steve Dekorte: *In 2002, my friend Dru Nelson wrote a language called Cel (inspired by Self) and was asking for feedback on its implementation. I didn't feel I understood how programming languages work well enough to have anything useful to say, so I started writing a small language to understand them better. It grew into Io.*

Bruce Tate: *What is the thing that you like about it the most?*

Steve Dekorte: *I like the simple and consistent syntax and semantics. They help with understanding what's going on. You can quickly learn the basics. I have a terrible memory. I constantly forget the syntax and weird semantic rules for C and have to look them up. (ed. Steve implemented Io in C.) That's one of the things I don't want to do when I use Io.*

For example, you can see the code, such as people select(age > 20) map(address) println*, and get a pretty good idea of what is going on. You're filtering a list of people based on age, getting their addresses, and printing them out.*

If you simplify the semantics enough, things become more flexible. You can start to compose things that you did not understand when you implemented the language. Here's an example. There are video games that are puzzle games that assume a solution, and there are more games that are open-ended. The open-ended ones are fun because you can do things that the designers of the game never imagined. Io is like that.

Sometimes other languages make syntactic shortcuts. That leads to extra parsing rules. When you program in a language, you need to have the parser in your head. The more complicated a language, the more of the parser you need to have in your head. The more work a parser has to do, the more work you have to do.

Bruce Tate: *What are some limitations of Io?*

Steve Dekorte: *The cost of Io's flexibility is that it can be slower for many common uses. That said, it also has certain advantages (such as coroutines, async sockets, and SIMD support), which can also make it much faster than even C apps written with traditional thread per socket concurrency or non-SIMD vector ops.*

I've also had some complaints that the lack of syntax can make quick visual inspection trickier. I've had similar problems with Lisp, so I understand. Extra syntax makes for quick reading. New users sometimes say Io has too little syntax, but they usually warm up to it.

Bruce Tate: *Where is the strangest place you've seen Io in production?*

Steve Dekorte: *Over the years, I've heard rumors of Io from place to place like on a satellite, in a router configuration language, and as a scripting language for video games. Pixar uses it too. They wrote a blog entry about it.*

It was a busy first day, so it's time to break for a little bit. You can now pause and put some of what you've learned into practice.

What We Learned in Day 1

You're now through a good chunk of Io. So far, you know a good deal about the basic character of Io. The prototype language has very simple syntax that you can use to build new basic elements of the language itself. Even core elements lack even the simplest syntactic sugar. In some ways, this minimal approach will make you work a little harder to read the syntax.

A minimal syntax has some benefits as well. Since there is not much going on syntactically, you don't have to learn any special rules or exceptions to them. Once you know how to read one sentence, you can read them all. Your learning time can go toward establishing your vocabulary.

Your job as a new student is greatly simplified:

- Understand a few basic syntactical rules.
- Understand messages.
- Understand prototypes.
- Understand the libraries.

Day 1 Self-Study

When you're looking for Io background, searching for answers is going to be a little tougher because Io has so many different meanings. I recommend Googling for *Io language*.

Find:

- Some Io example problems
- An Io community that will answer questions
- A style guide with Io idioms

Answer:

- Evaluate `1 + 1` and then `1 + "one"`. Is Io strongly typed or weakly typed? Support your answer with code.
- Is 0 true or false? What about the empty string? Is `nil` true or false? Support your answer with code.
- How can you tell what slots a prototype supports?
- What is the difference between `=` (equals), `:=` (colon equals), and `::=` (colon colon equals)? When would you use each one?

Do:

- Run an Io program from a file.
- Execute the code in a slot given its name.

Spend a little time playing with slots and prototypes. Make sure you understand how prototypes work.

3.3 Day 2: The Sausage King

Think back to Ferris Bueller for a moment. In the movie, the middle-class high-school student represented himself as the sausage king of Chicago in a classic bluff. He got a great table in a great restaurant because he was willing to bend the rules. If you're coming from a Java background and you liked it, you're thinking about what could have happened—too much freedom is not always a good thing. Bueller probably deserved to be thrown out. In Io, you're going to need to relax a little and take advantage of the power. If you're coming from a Perl scripting background, you probably liked Bueller's bluff because of the result of the bluff. If you've traditionally played things a little fast and loose, you're going to have to pull back a little and inject some discipline. In day 2, you'll start to see how you might use Io's slots and messages to shape core behaviors.

Conditionals and Loops

All of Io's conditional statements are implemented without syntactical sugar. You'll find they are easy to understand and remember, but they're a little harder to read because of fewer syntactic clues. Setting up a simple infinite loop is easy. Type Control+C to break out:

```
Io> loop("getting dizzy..." println)
getting dizzy...
getting dizzy...
...
getting dizzy.^C
IoVM:
        Received signal. Setting interrupt flag.
...
```

Loops will often be useful with the various concurrency constructs, but you'll normally want to choose one of the conditional looping constructs, such as a while loop. A while loop takes a condition and a message to evaluate. Keep in mind that a semicolon concatenates two distinct messages:

```
Io> i := 1
==> 1
Io> while(i <= 11, i println; i = i + 1); "This one goes up to 11" println
1
2
...
10
11
This one goes up to 11
```

You could do the same with a for loop. The for loop takes the name of the counter, the first value, the last value, an optional increment, and a message with sender.

```
Io> for(i, 1, 11, i println); "This one goes up to 11" println
1
2
...
10
11
This one goes up to 11
==> This one goes up to 11
```

And with the optional increment:

```
Io> for(i, 1, 11, 2, i println); "This one goes up to 11" println
1
3
5
7
9
11
This one goes up to 11
==> This one goes up to 11
```

In fact, you can often have an arbitrary number of parameters. Did you catch that the optional parameter is the third one? Io will allow you to attach extra parameters. That may seem to be convenient, but you need to watch carefully because there is no compiler to babysit you:

```
Io> for(i, 1, 2, 1, i println, "extra argument")
1
2
==> 2
Io> for(i, 1, 2, i println, "extra argument")
2
==> extra argument
```

In the first form, "extra argument" is really extra. In the second form, you've omitted the optional increment argument, and that effectively shifted everything to the left. Your "extra argument" is now the message, and you're working in steps of i println, which returns i. If that line of code is buried deeply into a complex package, Io just puked in your car. Sometimes, you have to take the bad with the good. Io gives you freedom. Sometimes, freedom hurts.

The if control structure is implemented as a function with the form if(condition, true code, false code). The function will execute true code if condition is true; otherwise, it will execute false code:

```
Io> if(true, "It is true.", "It is false.")
==> It is true.
```

```
Io> if(false) then("It is true") else("It is false")
==> nil
Io> if(false) then("It is true." println) else("It is false." println)
It is false.
==> nil
```

You've spent some time on control structures. Now, we can use them to develop our own operators.

Operators

Like with object-oriented languages, many prototype languages allow for syntactic sugar to allow *operators*. These are special methods like + and / that take a special form. In Io, you can see the operator table directly, like this:

```
Io> OperatorTable
==> OperatorTable_0x100296098:
Operators
  0   ? @ @@
  1   **
  2   % * /
  3   + -
  4   << >>
  5   < <= > >=
  6   != ==
  7   &
  8   ^
  9   |
  10  && and
  11  or ||
  12  ..
  13  %= &= *= += -= /= <<= >>= ^= |=
  14  return

Assign Operators
  ::= newSlot
  :=  setSlot
  =   updateSlot

To add a new operator: OperatorTable addOperator("+", 4)
    and implement the + message.
To add a new assign operator: OperatorTable addAssignOperator(
    "=", "updateSlot") and implement the updateSlot message.
```

You can see that an assignment is a different kind of operator. The number to the left shows the level of precedence. Arguments closer to 0 bind first. You can see that + evaluates before ==, and * before +, just as you would expect. You can override the precedence with (). Let's define an exclusive or operator. Our xor returns true if exactly one of the arguments is true, and false otherwise. First, we add the operator to the table:

```
Io> OperatorTable addOperator("xor", 11)
==> OperatorTable_0x100296098:
Operators
  ...
  10  && and
  11  or xor ||
  12  ..
  ...
```

You can see the new operator in the right place. Next, we need to implement the xor method on true and false:

```
Io> true xor := method(bool, if(bool, false, true))
==> method(bool,
    if(bool, false, true)
)
Io> false xor := method(bool, if(bool, true, false))
==> method(bool,
    if(bool, true, false)
)
```

We're using brute force here to keep the concepts simple. Our operator behaves exactly like you would expect:

```
Io> true xor true
==> false
Io> true xor false
==> true
Io> false xor true
==> true
Io> false xor false
==> false
```

When all is said and done, true xor true gets parsed as true xor(true). The method in the operator table determines the order of precedence and the simplified syntax.

Assignment operators are in a different table, and they work a little bit differently. Assignment operators work as messages. You'll see an example of them in action in Section 3.4, *Domain-Specific Languages*, on page 68. For now, that's all we'll say about operators. Let's move on to messages, where you will learn to implement your own control structures.

Messages

As I was working through this chapter, one of the Io committers was helping me through a moment of frustration. He said, "Bruce, there's something you have to understand about Io. Almost everything is a message." If you look at Io code, everything but comment markers and the comma (,) between arguments are messages. Everything. Learning Io well means learning to manipulate them beyond just basic invocation. One of the most crucial capabilities of the language is message reflection. You can query any characteristic of any message and act appropriately.

A message has three components: the sender, the target, and the arguments. In Io, the sender sends a message to a target. The target executes the message.

The call method gives you access to the meta information about any message. Let's create a couple of objects: the postOffice that gets messages and the mailer that delivers them:

```
Io> postOffice := Object clone
==>  Object_0x100444b38:

Io> postOffice packageSender := method(call sender)
==> method(
    call sender
)
```

Next, I'll create the mailer to deliver a message:

```
Io> mailer := Object clone
==>  Object_0x1005bfda0:

Io> mailer deliver := method(postOffice packageSender)
==> method(
    postOffice packageSender
)
```

There's one slot, the deliver slot, that sends a packageSender message to postOffice. Now, I can have the mailer deliver a message:

```
Io> mailer deliver
==>  Object_0x1005bfda0:
  deliver          = method(...)
```

So, the deliver method is the object that sent the message. We can also get the target, like this:

```
Io> postOffice messageTarget := method(call target)
==> method(
    call target
)
```

```
Io> postOffice messageTarget
==>  Object_0x1004ce658:
  messageTarget    = method(...)
  packageSender    = method(...)
```

Simple enough. The target is the post office, as you can see from the slot names. Get the original message name and arguments, like this:

```
Io> postOffice messageArgs := method(call message arguments)
==> method(
    call message arguments
)
Io> postOffice messageName := method(call message name)
==> method(
    call message name
)
Io> postOffice messageArgs("one", 2, :three)
==> list("one", 2, : three)
Io> postOffice messageName
==> messageName
```

So, Io has a number of methods available to let you do message reflection. The next question is, "When does Io compute a message?"

Most languages pass arguments as values on stacks. For example, Java computes each value of a parameter first and then places those values on the stack. Io doesn't. It passes the message itself and the context. Then, the receivers evaluate the message. You can actually implement control structures with messages. Recall the Io if. The form is if(booleanExpression, trueBlock, falseBlock). Let's say you wanted to implement an unless. Here's how you'd do it:

io/unless.io

```
unless := method(
    (call sender doMessage(call message argAt(0))) ifFalse(
    call sender doMessage(call message argAt(1))) ifTrue(
    call sender doMessage(call message argAt(2)))
)

unless(1 == 2, write("One is not two\n"), write("one is two\n"))
```

This little example is beautiful, so read it carefully. Think of doMessage as somewhat like Ruby's eval but at a lower level. Where Ruby's eval evaluates a string as code, doMessage executes an arbitrary message. Io is interpreting the message parameters but delaying binding and execution. In a typical object-oriented language, the interpreter or compiler would compute all the arguments, including both code blocks, and place their return values on the stack. In Io, that's not what happens at all.

Say the object westley sends the message princessButtercup unless(trueLove, ("It is false" println), ("It is true" println)). The result is this flow:

1. The object westley sends the previous message.
2. Io takes the interpreted message and the context (the call sender, target, and message) and puts it on the stack.
3. Now, princessButtercup evaluates the message. There is no unless slot, so Io walks up the prototype chain until it finds unless.
4. Io begins executing the unless message. First, Io executes call sender doMessage(call message argAt(0)). That code simplifies to westley trueLove. If you've ever seen the movie *The Princess Bride*, you know that westley has a slot called trueLove, and the value is true.
5. The message is not false, so we'll execute the third code block, which simplifies to westley ("It is true" println).

We're taking advantage of the fact that Io does not execute the arguments to compute a return value to implement the unless control structure. That concept is extremely powerful. So far, you've seen one side of reflection: behavior with message reflection. The other side of the equation is state. We'll look at state with an object's slots.

Reflection

Io gives you a simple set of methods to understand what's going on in the slots. Here are a few of them in action. This code creates a couple of objects and then works its way up the prototype chain with a method called ancestors:

io/animals.io

```
Object ancestors := method(
        prototype := self proto
        if(prototype != Object,
        writeln("Slots of ", prototype type, "\n---------------")
        prototype slotNames foreach(slotName, writeln(slotName))
        writeln
        prototype ancestors))

Animal := Object clone
Animal speak := method(
            "ambiguous animal noise" println)
```

```
Duck := Animal clone
Duck speak := method(
            "quack" println)

Duck walk := method(
            "waddle" println)

disco := Duck clone
disco ancestors
```

The code is not too complicated. First, we create an Animal prototype and use that to create a Duck instance, with a speak method. disco's prototype is Duck. The ancestors method prints the slots of an object's prototype and then calls ancestors on the prototype. Keep in mind that an object can have more than one prototype, but we don't handle this case. To save paper, we halt the recursion before printing all of the slots in the Object prototype. Run it with io animals.io:

Here's the output:

```
Slots of Duck
---------------
speak
walk
type

Slots of Animal
---------------
speak
type
```

No surprises there. Every object has a prototype, and those prototypes are objects that have slots. In Io, dealing with reflection has two parts. In the post office example, you saw message reflection. Object reflection means dealing with objects and the slots on those objects. No classes are involved, anywhere.

What We Learned in Day 2

If you're still following, day 2 should have been a breakthrough day of sorts. You should know enough Io to do basic tasks with a little support from the documentation. You know how to make decisions, define methods, use data structures, and use the basic control structures. In these exercises, we'll put Io through its paces. Get thoroughly familiar with Io. You will really want to have the basics down when we move into problems that stretch Io into the metaprogramming and concurrency spaces.

Day 2 Self-Study

Do:

1. A Fibonacci sequence starts with two 1s. Each subsequent number is the sum of the two numbers that came before: 1, 1, 2, 3, 5, 8, 13, 21, and so on. Write a program to find the nth Fibonacci number. fib(1) is 1, and fib(4) is 3. As a bonus, solve the problem with recursion and with loops.

2. How would you change / to return 0 if the denominator is zero?

3. Write a program to add up all of the numbers in a two-dimensional array.

4. Add a slot called myAverage to a list that computes the average of all the numbers in a list. What happens if there are no numbers in a list? (Bonus: Raise an Io exception if any item in the list is not a number.)

5. Write a prototype for a two-dimensional list. The dim(x, y) method should allocate a list of y lists that are x elements long. set(x, y, value) should set a value, and get(x, y) should return that value.

6. Bonus: Write a transpose method so that (new_matrix get(y, x)) == matrix get(x, y) on the original list.

7. Write the matrix to a file, and read a matrix from a file.

8. Write a program that gives you ten tries to guess a random number from 1–100. If you would like, give a hint of "hotter" or "colder" after the first guess.

3.4 Day 3: The Parade and Other Strange Places

My first few days with Io were frustrating, but after a couple of weeks, I found myself giggling like a school girl at the unexpected places the language would take me. It's like Ferris showing up on the news, at the ball park, in the parade—everywhere you don't expect him. In the end, I got out of Io exactly what I wanted, which was a language that changed the way I think.

Domain-Specific Languages

Just about everyone who is deeply involved with Io appreciates the power that Io gives you in the area of DSLs. Jeremy Tregunna, one of the core committers for Io, told me about an implementation of a subset of C in Io that took around 40 lines of code! Since that example is just a little too deep for us to consider, here's another one of Jeremy's gems. This one implements an API that provides an interesting syntax for phone numbers.

Say you want to represent phone numbers in this form:

```
{
    "Bob Smith": "5195551212",
    "Mary Walsh": "4162223434"
}
```

There are many approaches to the problem of managing such a list. Two that come to mind are parsing the list or interpreting it. Parsing it means that you would write a program to recognize the various elements of the syntax, and then you could place the code in a structure that Io understands. That's another problem for another day. It would be much more fun to interpret that code as an Io hash. To do this, you will have to alter Io. When you're done, Io will accept this list as a valid syntax for building hashes!

Here's how Jeremy attacked the problem, with an assist from Chris Kappler, who brought this example up to the current version of Io:

io/phonebook.io

```
OperatorTable addAssignOperator(":", "atPutNumber")
curlyBrackets := method(
  r := Map clone
  call message arguments foreach(arg,
       r doMessage(arg)
       )
  r
)
Map atPutNumber := method(
  self atPut(
       call evalArgAt(0) asMutable removePrefix("\"") removeSuffix("\""),
       call evalArgAt(1))
)
s := File with("phonebook.txt") openForReading contents
phoneNumbers := doString(s)
phoneNumbers keys   println
phoneNumbers values println
```

That code is slightly more complex than anything you've seen so far, but you know the basic building blocks. Let's deconstruct it:

```
OperatorTable addAssignOperator(":", "atPutNumber")
```

The first line adds an operator to Io's assignment operator table. Whenever : is encountered, Io will parse that as atPutNumber, understanding that the first argument is a name (and thus a string), and the second is a value. So, key : value will be parsed as atPutNumber("key", value). Moving on:

```
curlyBrackets := method(
  r := Map clone
  call message arguments foreach(arg,
       r doMessage(arg)
       )
  r
)
```

The parser calls the curlyBrackets method whenever it encounters curly brackets ({}). Within this method, we create an empty map. Then, we execute call message arguments foreach(arg, r doMessage(arg)) for each argument. That's a seriously dense line of code! Let's take it apart.

From left to right, we take the call message, which is the part of the code between the curly brackets. Then, we iterate through each of the phone numbers in the list with forEach. For each phone name and phone number, we execute r doMessage(arg). For example, the first phone number will execute as r "Bob Smith": "5195551212". Since : is in our operator table as atPutNumber, we'll execute r atPutNumber("Bob Smith", "5195551212"). That brings us to the following:

```
Map atPutNumber := method(
  self atPut(
       call evalArgAt(0) asMutable removePrefix("\"") removeSuffix("\""),
       call evalArgAt(1))
)
```

Remember, key : value will parse as atPutNumber("key", value). In our case, the key is already a string, so we strip the leading and trailing quotes. You can see that atPutNumber simply calls atPut on the target range, which is self, stripping the quotes off the first argument. Since messages are immutable, to strip the quotes, we have to translate the message to a mutable value for it to work.

You can use the code like this:

```
s := File with("phonebook.txt") openForReading contents
phoneNumbers := doString(s)
phoneNumbers keys   println
phoneNumbers values println
```

Understanding Io's syntax is trivial. You just have to know what's going on in the libraries. In this case, you see a few new libraries. The doString message evaluates our phone book as code, File is a prototype for working with files, with specifies a filename and returns a file object, openForReading opens that file and returns the file object, and contents returns the contents of that file. Taken together, this code will read the phone book and evaluate it as code.

Then, the braces define a map. Each line in the map "string1" : "string2" does a map atPut("string1", "string2"), and we're left with a hash of phone numbers. So, in Io, since you can redefine anything from operators to the symbols that make up the language, you can build DSLs to your heart's content.

So, now you can begin to see how you would change Io's syntax. How would you go about dynamically changing the language's behavior? That's the topic of the next section.

Io's method_missing

Let's review the flow of control. The behavior for what happens in a given message is all baked into Object. When you send an object a message, it will do the following:

1. Compute the arguments, inside out. These are just messages.
2. Get the name, target, and sender of the message.
3. Try to read the slot with the name of the message on the target.
4. If the slot exists, return the data or invoke the method inside.
5. If the slot doesn't exist, forward the message to the prototype.

These are the basic mechanics of inheritance within Io. You normally wouldn't mess with them.

But you can. You can use the forward message in the same way that you would use Ruby's method_missing, but the stakes are a little higher. Io doesn't have classes, so changing forward also changes the way you get any of the basic behaviors from object. It's a bit like juggling hatchets on the high wire. It's a cool trick if you can get away with it, so let's get started!

XML is a pretty way to structure data with an ugly syntax. You may want to build something that lets you represent XML data as Io code.

For example, you might want to express this:

```
<body>
<p>
This is a simple paragraph.
</p>
</body>
```

like this:

```
body(
    p("This is a simple paragraph.")
)
```

Let's call the new language LispML. We're going to use Io's forward like a missing method. Here's the code:

io/builder.io

```
Builder := Object clone

Builder forward := method(
  writeln("<", call message name, ">")
  call message arguments foreach(
        arg,
        content := self doMessage(arg);
        if(content type == "Sequence", writeln(content)))
  writeln("</", call message name, ">"))

Builder  ul(
        li("Io"),
        li("Lua"),
        li("JavaScript"))
```

Let's carve it up. The Builder prototype is the workhorse. It overrides forward to pick up any arbitrary method. First, it prints an open tag. Next, we use a little message reflection. If the message is a string, Io will recognize it as a sequence, and Builder prints the string without quotes. Finally, Builder prints a closing tag.

The output is exactly what you'd expect:

```
<ul>
<li>
Io
</li>
<li>
Lua
</li>
<li>
JavaScript
</li>
</ul>
```

I have to say, I'm not sure whether LispML is that much of an improvement over traditional XML, but the example is instructive. You've just completely changed the way inheritance works in one of Io's prototypes. Any instance of Builder will have the same behavior. Doing this, you can create a new language with Io's syntax but none of the same behaviors by defining your own Object and basing all of your prototypes on that new object. You can even override Object to clone your new object.

Concurrency

Io has outstanding concurrency libraries. The main components are coroutines, actors, and futures.

Coroutines

The foundation for concurrency is the coroutine. A coroutine provides a way to voluntarily suspend and resume execution of a process. Think of a coroutine as a function with multiple entry and exit points. Each yield will voluntarily suspend the process and transfer to another process. You can fire a message asynchronously by using @ or @@ before a message. The former returns a future (more later), and the second returns nil and starts the message in its own thread. For example, consider this program:

io/coroutine.io

```
vizzini := Object clone
vizzini talk := method(
            "Fezzik, are there rocks ahead?" println
            yield
            "No more rhymes now, I mean it." println
             yield)

fezzik := Object clone

fezzik rhyme := method(
                        yield
            "If there are, we'll all be dead." println
            yield
            "Anybody want a peanut?" println)

vizzini @@talk; fezzik @@rhyme

Coroutine currentCoroutine pause
```

fezzik and vizzini are independent instances of Object with coroutines. We fire asynchronous talk and rhyme methods. These run concurrently, voluntarily yielding control to the other at specified intervals with the yield message. The last pause waits until all async messages complete and then exits. Coroutines are great for solutions requiring cooperative multitasking. With this example, two processes that need to coordinate can easily do so, to read poetry, for example:

```
batate$ io code/io/coroutine.io
Fezzik, are there rocks ahead?
If there are, we'll all be dead.
No more rhymes now, I mean it.
Anybody want a peanut?
Scheduler: nothing left to resume so we are exiting
```

Java and C-based languages use a concurrency philosophy called *preemptive multitasking*. When you combine this concurrency strategy with objects that have changeable state, you wind up with programs that are hard to predict and nearly impossible to debug with the current testing strategies that most teams use. Coroutines are different. With coroutines, applications can voluntarily give up control at reasonable times. A distributed client could relinquish control when waiting for the server. Worker processes could pause after processing queue items.

Coroutines are the basic building blocks for higher levels of abstractions like actors. Think of actors as universal concurrent primitives that can send messages, process messages, and create other actors. The messages an actor receives are concurrent. In Io, an actor places an incoming message on a queue and processes the contents of the queue with coroutines.

Next, we'll look into actors. You won't believe how easy they are to code.

Actors

Actors have a huge theoretical advantage over threads. An actor changes its own state and accesses other actors only through closely controlled queues. Threads can change each other's state without restriction. Threads are subject to a concurrency problem called *race conditions*, where two threads access resources at the same time, leading to unpredictable results.

Here's the beauty of Io. Sending an asynchronous message to any object makes it an actor. End of story. Let's take a simple example. First, we'll create two objects called faster and slower:

```
Io> slower := Object clone
==>  Object_0x1004ebb18:

Io> faster := Object clone
==>  Object_0x100340b10:
```

Now, we'll add a method called start to each:

```
Io> slower start := method(wait(2); writeln("slowly"))
==> method(
    wait(2); writeln("slowly")
)
Io> faster start := method(wait(1); writeln("quickly"))
==> method(
    wait(1); writeln("quickly")
)
```

We can call both methods sequentially on one line of code with simple messages, like this:

```
Io> slower start; faster start
slowly
quickly
==> nil
```

They start in order, because the first message must finish before the second can begin. But we can easily make each object run in its own thread by preceding each message with @@, which will return immediately and return nil:

```
Io> slower @@start; faster @@start; wait(3)
quickly
slowly
```

We add an extra wait to the end so that all threads finish before the program terminates, but that's a great result. We are running in two threads. We made both of these objects actors, *just by sending an asynchronous message to them!*

Futures

I will finish up the concurrency discussion with the concept of futures. A future is a result object that is immediately returned from an asynchronous message call. Since the message may take a while to process, the future becomes the result once the result is available. If you ask for the value of a future before the result is available, the process blocks until the value is available. Say we have a method that takes a long time to execute:

```
futureResult := URL with("http://google.com/") @fetch
```

I can execute the method and do something else immediately until the result is available:

```
writeln("Do something immediately while fetch goes on in background...")
// ...
```

Then, I can use the future value:

```
writeln("This will block until the result is available.")
// this line will execute immediately

writeln("fetched ", futureResult size, " bytes")
// this will block until the computation is complete

// and Io prints the value
==> 1955
```

The futureResult code fragment will return a future object, immediately. In Io, a future is not a proxy implementation! The future will block until the result object is available. The value is a Future object until the result arrives, and then all instances of the value point to the result object. The console is going to print the string value of the last statement returned.

Futures in Io also provide automatic deadlock detection. It's a nice touch, and they are easy to understand and use.

Now that you've had a flavor of Io's concurrency, you have a sound foundation for evaluating the language. Let's wrap up day 3 so you can put what you know into practice.

What We Learned in Day 3

In this section, you learned to do something nontrivial in Io. First, we bent the rules of syntax and built a new hash syntax with braces. We added an operator to the operator table and wired that into operations on a hash table. Next, we built an XML generator that used method_missing to print XML elements.

Next, we wrote some code that used coroutines to manage concurrency. The coroutines differed from concurrency in languages like Ruby, C, and Java because threads could only change their own state, leading to a more predictable and understandable concurrency model and less of a need for blocking states that become bottlenecks.

We sent some asynchronous messages that made our prototypes actors. We didn't have to do anything beyond changing the syntax of our messages. Finally, we looked briefly at futures and how they worked in Io.

Day 3 Self-Study

Do:

- Enhance the XML program to add spaces to show the indentation structure.

- Create a list syntax that uses brackets.
- Enhance the XML program to handle attributes: if the first argument is a map (use the curly brackets syntax), add attributes to the XML program. For example:

  `book({"author": "Tate"}...)` would print `<book author="Tate">`:

3.5 Wrapping Up Io

Io is an excellent language for learning how to use prototype-based languages. Like Lisp, the syntax is stunningly simple, but the semantics of the language lend plenty of power. The prototype languages encapsulate data and behavior like object-oriented programming languages. Inheritance is simpler. There are no classes or modules in Io. One object inherits behavior directly from its prototype.

Strengths

Prototype languages are generally quite malleable. You can change any slot on any object. Io takes this flexibility to the max, allowing you to quickly create the syntax you want. Like Ruby, some of the trade-offs that make Io so dynamic tend to cap the performance, at least in a single thread. The strong, modern concurrency libraries often make Io a good language for parallel processing. Let's look at where Io is excelling today.

Footprint

Io's footprint is small. Most of the production Io applications are embedded systems. This application makes sense, since the language is small, powerful, and quite flexible. The virtual machine is easy to port to different operating environments.

Simplicity

Io's syntax is remarkably compact. You can learn Io very quickly. Once you understand the core syntax, everything else is learning the library structures. I found that I could work my way into metaprogramming quite quickly, within my first month of using the language. In Ruby, getting to the same point took a little longer. In Java, it took many months to get to the point where I could make any sense of metaprogramming at all.

Flexibility

Io's duck typing and freedom allow you to change any slot in any object at any time. This free-wheeling nature means you can change the basic rules of the language to suit your application. It's quite easy to add proxies at any place through changing the forward slot. You can also override key language constructs by changing their slots directly. You can even create your own syntax quickly.

Concurrency

Unlike Java and Ruby, the concurrency constructs are up-to-date and fresh. Actors, futures, and coroutines make it much easier to build multithreaded applications that are easier to test and have better performance. Io also gives considerable thought to mutable data and how to avoid it. Having these features baked into the core libraries made it easy to learn a robust concurrency model. Later, in other languages, we will build on these concepts. You'll see actors in Scala, Erlang, and Haskell.

Weaknesses

There's much to like about Io and some suboptimal aspects as well. Freedom and flexibility come at a price. Also, since Io has the smallest community of any of the languages in this book, it's a riskier choice for some projects. Let's take a look at the problems associated with Io.

Syntax

Io has very little syntax sugar. Simple syntax is a double-edged sword. On one side, the clean syntax makes Io, the language, easy to understand. But there's a cost. Simple syntax often makes it hard to communicate difficult concepts concisely. Said another way, you may find it easy to understand how a given program uses the Io language and, at the same time, have a difficult time understanding what your program is doing.

For a point of contrast, consider Ruby. At first, you may find the Ruby code `array[-1]` baffling because you don't understand the syntactic sugar: `-1` is shorthand for the last element in the array. You would also need to learn that `[]` is a method to get the value at a specified index of an array. Once you understood those concepts, you'd be able to process more code at a glance. With Io, the trade-off is the opposite. You don't have to learn very much to get started, but you do have to work a little harder to absorb concepts that might be otherwise communicated with sugar.

The balance of syntactic sugar is a difficult one. Add too much sugar, and it's too difficult to learn a language and remember how to use it. Add too little, and you need to spend more time to express code and potentially more energy to debug it. In the end, syntax is a matter of preference. Matz prefers plenty of sugar. Steve doesn't.

Community

Right now, the Io community is very small. You cannot always find libraries in Io like you can with other languages. It's also harder to find programmers. These issues are somewhat mitigated by having a good C interface (which talks to a variety of languages) and a syntax that is so easy to remember. Good JavaScript programmers could pick up Io quickly. But having a smaller community is a definite weakness and is the main thing that holds powerful, new languages back. Either Io will get a killer application that drives acceptance or it will remain a niche player.

Performance

Discussing performance in a vacuum of other issues such as concurrency and application design is not usually wise, but I should point out that Io has a number of features that will slow raw, single-threaded execution speed. This problem is somewhat mitigated by Io's concurrency constructs, but you should still keep this limitation in mind.

Final Thoughts

In general, I liked learning Io. The simple syntax and small footprint intrigued me. I also think that, like Lisp, Io has a strong overriding philosophy of simplicity and flexibility. By staying with this philosophy uniformly in the language creation, Steve Dekorte has created something like the Lisp of the prototype languages. I think the language has a shot to grow. Like Ferris Bueller, it has a bright, but perilous, future.

Sally Dibbs, Dibbs Sally. 461-0192.
► Raymond

Chapter 4
Prolog

Ah, Prolog. Sometimes spectacularly smart, other times just as frustrating. You'll get astounding answers only if you know how to ask the question. Think *Rain Man.*[1] I remember watching Raymond, the lead character, rattle off Sally Dibbs' phone number after reading a phone book the night before, without thinking about whether he should. With both Raymond and Prolog, I often find myself asking, in equal parts, "How did he know that?" and "How didn't he know that?" He's a fountain of knowledge, if you can only frame your questions in the right way.

Prolog represents a serious departure from the other languages we've encountered so far. Both Io and Ruby are called *imperative languages*. Imperative languages are recipes. You tell the computer exactly how to do a job. Higher-level imperative languages might give you a little more leverage, combining many longer steps into one, but you're basically putting together a shopping list of ingredients and describing a step-by-step process for baking a cake.

It took me a couple of weeks of playing with Prolog before I could make an attempt at this chapter. I used several tutorials as I ramped up, including a tutorial by J. R. Fisher[2] for some examples to wade through and another primer by A. Aaby[3] to help the structure and terminology gel for me, and lots of experimentation.

Prolog is a declarative language. You'll throw some facts and inferences at Prolog and let it do the reasoning for you. It's more like going to a

1. *Rain Man.* DVD. Directed by Barry Levinson. 1988; Los Angeles, CA: MGM, 2000.
2. http://www.csupomona.edu/~jrfisher/www/prolog_tutorial/contents.html
3. http://www.lix.polytechnique.fr/~liberti/public/computing/prog/prolog/prolog-tutorial.html

good baker. You describe the characteristics of cakes that you like and let the baker pick the ingredients and bake the cake for you, based on the rules you provided. With Prolog, you don't have to know *how*. The computer does the reasoning for you.

With a casual flip through the Internet, you can find examples to solve a Sudoku with fewer than twenty lines of code, crack Rubik's Cube, and solve famous puzzles such as the Tower of Hanoi (around a dozen lines of code). Prolog was one of the first successful logic programming languages. You make assertions with pure logic, and Prolog determines whether they are true. You can leave gaps in your assertions, and Prolog will try to fill in the holes that would make your incomplete facts true.

4.1 About Prolog

Developed in 1972 by Alain Colmerauer and Phillipe Roussel, Prolog is a logic programming language that gained popularity in natural-language processing. Now, the venerable language provides the programming foundation for a wide variety of problems, from scheduling to expert systems. You can use this rules-based language for expressing logic and asking questions. Like SQL, Prolog works on databases, but the data will consist of logical rules and relationships. Like SQL, Prolog has two parts: one to express the data and one to query the data. In Prolog, the data is in the form of logical rules. These are the building blocks:

- *Facts.* A fact is a basic assertion about some world. (Babe is a pig; pigs like mud.)
- *Rules.* A rule is an inference about the facts in that world. (An animal likes mud if it is a pig.)
- *Query.* A query is a question about that world. (Does Babe like mud?)

Facts and rules will go into a *knowledge base*. A Prolog compiler compiles the knowledge base into a form that's efficient for queries. As we walk through these examples, you'll use Prolog to express your knowledge base. Then, you'll do direct retrieval of data and also use Prolog to link rules together to tell you something you might not have known.

Enough background. Let's get started.

4.2 Day 1: An Excellent Driver

In *Rain Man*, Raymond told his brother he was an excellent driver, meaning he could do a fine job of handling the car at five miles per hour in parking lots. He was using all the main elements—the steering wheel, the brakes, the accelerator—he just used them in a limited context. That's your goal today. We're going to use Prolog to state some facts, make some rules, and do some basic queries. Like Io, Prolog is an extremely simple language syntactically. You can learn the syntax rules quickly. The real fun begins when you layer concepts in interesting ways. If this is your first exposure, I guarantee either you will change the way you think or you'll fail. We'll save the in-depth construction for a later day.

First things first. Get a working installation. I'm using GNU Prolog, version 1.3.1, for this book. Be careful. Dialects can vary. I'll do my best to stay on common ground, but if you choose a different version of Prolog, you'll need to do a little homework to understand where your dialect is different. Regardless of the version you choose, here's how you'll use it.

Basic Facts

In some languages, capitalization is entirely at the programmer's discretion, but in Prolog, the case of the first letter is significant. If a word begins with a lowercase character, it's an *atom*—a fixed value like a Ruby symbol. If it begins with an uppercase letter or an underscore, it's a *variable*. Variable values can change; atoms can't. Let's build a simple knowledge base with a few facts. Key the following into an editor:

prolog/friends.pl

```
likes(wallace, cheese).
likes(grommit, cheese).
likes(wendolene, sheep).

friend(X, Y) :- \+(X = Y), likes(X, Z), likes(Y, Z).
```

The previous file is a knowledge base with facts and rules. The first three statements are facts, and the last statement is a rule. Facts are direct observations of our world. Rules are logical inferences about our world. For now, pay attention to the first three lines. These lines are each facts. wallace, grommit, and wendolene are atoms. You can read them as wallace likes cheese, grommit likes cheese, and wendolene likes sheep. Let's put the facts into action.

Start your Prolog interpreter. If you're using GNU Prolog, type the command gprolog. Then, to load your file, enter the following:

```
| ?- ['friends.pl'].
compiling /Users/batate/prag/Book/code/prolog/friends.pl for byte code...
/Users/batate/prag/Book/code/prolog/friends.pl compiled, 4 lines read -
997 bytes written, 11 ms

yes

| ?-
```

Unless Prolog is waiting on an intermediate result, it will respond with yes or no. In this case, the file loaded successfully, so it returned yes. We can start to ask some questions. The most basic questions are yes and no questions about facts. Ask a few:

```
| ?- likes(wallace, sheep).

no
| ?- likes(grommit, cheese).

yes
```

These questions are pretty intuitive. Does wallace like sheep? (No.) Does grommit like cheese? (Yes.) These are not too interesting: Prolog is just parroting your facts back to you. It starts to get a little more exciting when you start to build in some logic. Let's take a look at inferences.

Basic Inferences and Variables

Let's try the friend rule:

```
| ?- friend(wallace, wallace).

no
```

So, Prolog is working through the rules we gave it and answering yes or no questions. There's more here than meets the eye. Check out the friend rule again:

In English, for X to be a friend of Y, X cannot be the same as Y. Look at the first part to the right of :-, called a *subgoal*. \+ does logical negation, so \+(X = Y) means X is not equal to Y.

Try some more queries:

```
| ?- friend(grommit, wallace).

yes
| ?- friend(wallace, grommit).

yes
```

In English, X is a friend of Y if we can prove that X likes some Z and Y likes that same Z. Both wallace and grommit like cheese, so these queries succeed.

Let's dive into the code. In these queries, X is not equal to Y, proving the first subgoal. The query will use the second and third subgoals, likes(X, Z) and likes(Y, Z). grommit and wallace like cheese, so we prove the second and third subgoals. Try another query:

```
| ?- friend(wendolene, grommit).

no
```

In this case, Prolog had to try several possible values for X, Y, and Z:

- wendolene, grommit, and cheese
- wendolene, grommit, and sheep

Neither combination satisfied both goals, that wendolene likes Z and grommit likes Z. None existed, so the logic engine reported no, they are not friends.

Let's formalize the terminology. This...

```
friend(X, Y) :- \+(X = Y), likes(X, Z), likes(Y, Z).
```

...is a Prolog rule with three variables, X, Y, and Z. We call the rule friend/2, shorthand for friend with two parameters. This rule has three subgoals, separated by commas. All must be true for the rule to be true. So, our rule means X is a friend of Y if X and Y are not the same and X and Y like the same Z.

Filling in the Blanks

We've used Prolog to answer some yes or no questions, but we can do more than that. In this section, we'll use the logic engine to find all possible matches for a query. To do this, you will specify a *variable* in your query.

Consider the following knowledge base:

prolog/food.pl

```
food_type(velveeta, cheese).
food_type(ritz, cracker).
food_type(spam, meat).
food_type(sausage, meat).
food_type(jolt, soda).
food_type(twinkie, dessert).

flavor(sweet, dessert).
flavor(savory, meat).
flavor(savory, cheese).
flavor(sweet, soda).

food_flavor(X, Y) :- food_type(X, Z), flavor(Y, Z).
```

We have a few facts. Some, such as food_type(velveeta, cheese), mean a food has a certain type. Others, such as flavor(sweet, dessert), mean a food type has a characteristic flavor. Finally, we have a rule called food_flavor that infers the flavor of food. A food X has a food_flavor Y if the food is of a food_type Z and that Z also has that characteristic flavor. Compile it:

```
| ?- ['code/prolog/food.pl'].
compiling /Users/batate/prag/Book/code/prolog/food.pl for byte code...
/Users/batate/prag/Book/code/prolog/food.pl compiled,
12 lines read - 1557 bytes written, 15 ms

(1 ms) yes
```

and ask some questions:

```
| ?- food_type(What, meat).

What = spam ? ;

What = sausage ? ;

no
```

Now, that's interesting. We're asking Prolog, "Find some value for What that satisfies the query food_type(What, meat)." Prolog found one, spam. When we typed the ;, we were asking Prolog to find another, and it returned sausage. They were easy values to find since the queries depended on basic facts. Then, we asked for another, and Prolog responded with no. This behavior can be slightly inconsistent. As a convenience, if Prolog can detect that there are no more alternatives remaining, you'll see a yes. If Prolog can't immediately determine whether there are more alternatives without doing more computation, it will prompt you for the next and return no. The feature is really a convenience. If Prolog can give you information sooner, it will. Try a few more:

```
| ?- food_flavor(sausage, sweet).

no

| ?- flavor(sweet, What).

What = dessert ? ;

What = soda

yes
```

No, sausage is not sweet. What food types are sweet? dessert and soda. These are all facts. But you can let Prolog connect the dots for you, too:

```
| ?- food_flavor(What, savory).

What = velveeta ? ;

What = spam ? ;

What = sausage ? ;

no
```

Remember, food_flavor(X, Y) is a rule, not a fact. We're asking Prolog to find all possible values that satisfy the query, "What foods have a savory flavor?" Prolog must tie together primitive facts about food, types, and flavors to reach the conclusion. The logic engine has to work through possible combinations that could make all the goals true.

Map Coloring

Let's use the same idea to do map coloring. For a more spectacular look at Prolog, take this example. We want to color a map of the southeastern United States. We'll cover the states shown in Figure 4.1, on the next page. We do not want two states of the same color to touch.

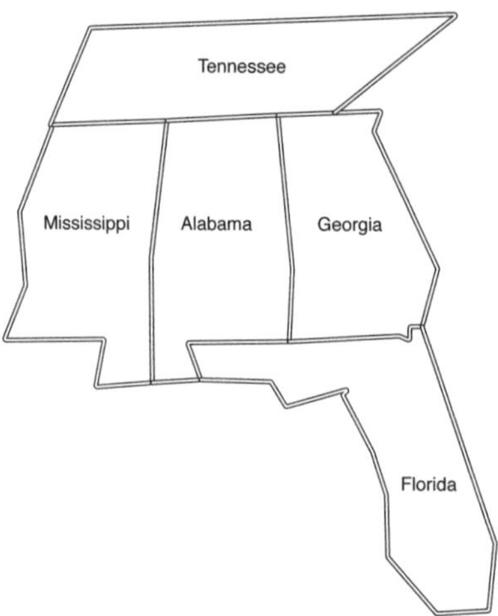

Figure 4.1: MAP OF SOME SOUTHEASTERN STATES

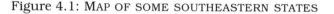

We code up these simple facts:

prolog/map.pl

```
different(red, green). different(red, blue).
different(green, red). different(green, blue).
different(blue, red). different(blue, green).

coloring(Alabama, Mississippi, Georgia, Tennessee, Florida) :-
  different(Mississippi, Tennessee),
  different(Mississippi, Alabama),
  different(Alabama, Tennessee),
  different(Alabama, Mississippi),
  different(Alabama, Georgia),
  different(Alabama, Florida),
  different(Georgia, Florida),
  different(Georgia, Tennessee).
```

We have three colors. We tell Prolog the sets of different colors to use in the map coloring. Next, we have a rule. In the coloring rule, we tell Prolog which states neighbor others, and we're done. Try it:

```
| ?- coloring(Alabama, Mississippi, Georgia, Tennessee, Florida).

Alabama = blue
Florida = green
Georgia = red
Mississippi = red
Tennessee = green ?
```

Sure enough, there is a way to color these five states with three colors. You can get the other possible combinations too by typing a. With a dozen lines of code, we're done. The logic is ridiculously simple—a child could figure it out. At some point, you have to ask yourself...

Where's the Program?

We have no algorithm! Try solving this problem in the procedural language of your choice. Is your solution easy to understand? Think through what you'd have to do to solve complex logic problems like this in Ruby or Io. One possible solution would be as follows:

1. Collect and organize your logic.
2. Express your logic in a program.
3. Find all possible solutions.
4. Put the possible solutions through your program.

And you would have to write this program over and over. Prolog lets you express the logic in facts and inferences and then lets you ask questions. You're not responsible for building any step-by-step recipe with this language. Prolog is not about writing algorithms to solve logical problems. Prolog is about describing your world as it is and presenting logical problems that your computer can try to solve.

Let the computer do the work!

Unification, Part 1

At this point, it's time to back up and provide a little more theory. Let's shine a little more light on unification. Some languages use variable assignment. In Java or Ruby, for example, x = 10 means assign 10 to the variable x. Unification across two structures tries to make both structures identical. Consider the following knowledge base:

prolog/ohmy.pl

```
cat(lion).
cat(tiger).

dorothy(X, Y, Z) :- X = lion, Y = tiger, Z = bear.
twin_cats(X, Y) :- cat(X), cat(Y).
```

In this example, = means unify, or make both sides the same. We have two facts: lions and tigers are cats. We also have two simple rules. In dorothy/3, X, Y, and Z are lion, tiger, and bear, respectively. In twin_cats/2,

X is a cat, and Y is a cat. We can use this knowledge base to shed a little light on unification.

First, let's use the first rule. I'll compile and then do a simple query with no parameters:

```
| ?- dorothy(lion, tiger, bear).

yes
```

Remember, unification means "Find the values that make both sides match." On the right side, Prolog binds X, Y, and Z to lion, tiger, and bear. These match the corresponding values on the left side, so unification is successful. Prolog reports yes. This case is pretty simple, but we can spice it up a little bit. Unification can work on both sides of the implication. Try this one:

```
| ?- dorothy(One, Two, Three).

One = lion
Three = bear
Two = tiger

yes
```

This example has one more layer of indirection. In the goals, Prolog unifies X, Y, and Z to lion, tiger, and bear. On the left side, Prolog unifies X, Y, and Z to One, Two, and Three and then reports the result.

Now, let's shift to the last rule, twin_cats/2. This rule says twin_cats(X, Y) is true if you can prove that X and Y are both cats. Try it:

```
| ?- twin_cats(One, Two).

One = lion
Two = lion ?
```

Prolog reported the first example. lion and lion are both cats. Let's see how it got there:

1. We issued the query twin_cats(One, Two). Prolog binds One to X and Two to Y. To solve these, Prolog must start working through the goals.

2. The first goal is cat(X).

3. We have two facts that match, cat(lion) and cat(tiger). Prolog tries the first fact, binding X to lion, and moves on to the next goal.

4. Prolog now binds Y to cat(Y). Prolog can solve this goal in exactly the same way as the first, choosing lion.

5. We've satisfied both goals, so the rule is successful. Prolog reports the values of One and Two that made it successful and reports yes.

So, we have the first solution that makes the rules true. Sometimes, one solution is enough. Sometimes, you need more than one. We can now step through solutions one by one by using ;, or we can get all of the rest of the solutions by pressing a.

```
Two = lion ? a

One = lion
Two = tiger

One = tiger
Two = lion

One = tiger
Two = tiger

(1 ms) yes
```

Notice that Prolog is working through the list of all combinations of X and Y, given the information available in the goals and corresponding facts. As you'll see later, unification also lets you do some sophisticated matching based on the structure of your data. That's enough for day 1. We're going to do a little more heavy lifting in day 2.

Prolog in Practice

It has to be a little disconcerting to see a "program" presented in this way. In Prolog, there's not often a finely detailed step-by-step recipe, only a description of the cake you'll take out of the pan when you're done. When I was learning Prolog, it helped me tremendously to interview someone who had used the language in practice. I talked to Brian Tarbox who used this logic language to create schedules for working with dolphins for a research project.

An Interview with Brian Tarbox, Dolphin Researcher

Bruce: *Can you talk about your experiences learning Prolog?*

Brian: *I learned Prolog back in the late 1980s when I was in graduate school at the University of Hawaii at Manoa. I was working at the Kewalo Basin Marine Mammal Laboratory doing research into the cognitive capabilities of bottlenosed dolphins. At the time I noticed that much* *of the discussion at the lab concerned people's theories about how the dolphins thought. We worked primarily with a dolphin named Akeakamai, or Ake for short. Many debates started with "Well, Ake probably sees the situation like this."*

I decided that my master's thesis would be to try to create an executable model that matched our beliefs about Ake's understanding of the world, or at least the tiny subset of it that we were doing research on. If our executable model predicted Ake's actual behavior, we would gain some confidence in our theories about her thinking.

Prolog is a wonderful language, but until you drink the Kool-Aid, it can give you some pretty weird results. I recall one of my first experiments with Prolog, writing something along the lines of x = x + 1. Prolog responded "no." Languages don't just say "no." They might give the wrong answer or fail to compile, but I had never had a language talk back to me. So, I called Prolog support and said that the language had said "no" when I tried to change the value of a variable. They asked me, "Why would you want to change the value of a variable?" I mean, what kind of language won't let you change the value of a variable? Once you grok Prolog, you understand that variables either have particular values or are unbound, but it was unsettling at the time.

Bruce: *How have you used Prolog?*

Brian: *I developed two main systems: the dolphin simulator and a laboratory scheduler. The lab would run four experiments a day with each of four dolphins. You have to understand that research dolphins are an incredibly limited resource. Each dolphin was working on different experiments, and each experiment required a different set of personnel. Some roles, such as the actual dolphin trainer, could be filled by only a few people. Other roles such as data recorder could be done by several people but still required training. Most experiments required a staff of six to a dozen people. We had graduate students, undergraduates, and Earthwatch volunteers. Every person had their own schedule and their own shift set of skills. Finding a schedule that utilized everyone and made sure all tasks were done had become a full-time job for one of the staff.*

I decided to try to build a Prolog-based schedule builder. It turned out to be a problem tailor-made for the language. I built a set of facts describing each person's skill set, each person's schedule, and each experiment's requirements. I could then basically tell Prolog "make it so." For each task listed in an experiment, the language would find an available person with that skill and bind them to the task. It would continue until it either satisfied the needs of the experiment or was unable to. If it could not find a valid binding, it would start undoing previous bindings and trying again with another combination. In the end, it would either find a valid schedule or declare that the experiment was over-constrained.

Bruce: *Are there some interesting examples of facts, rules, or assertions related to dolphins that would make sense to our readers?*

Brian: *There was one particular situation I remember where the simulated dolphin helped us understand Ake's actual behavior. Ake responded to a gestural sign language containing "sentences" such as "hoop through" or "right ball tail-touch." We would give her instructions, and she would respond.*

Part of my research was to try to teach new words such as "not." In this context, "touch not ball" meant touch anything but the ball. This was a hard problem for Ake to solve, but the research was proceeding well for a while. At one point, however, she started simply sinking underwater whenever we gave her the instruction. We didn't understand it all. This can be a very frustrating situation because you can't ask a dolphin why it did something. So, we presented the training task to the simulated dolphin and got an interesting result. Although dolphins are very smart, they will generally try to find the simplest answer to a problem. We had given the simulated dolphin the same heuristic. It turns out that Ake's gestural language included a "word" for one of the windows in the tank. Most trainers had forgotten about this word because it was rarely used. The simulated dolphin discovered the rule that "window" was a successful response to "not ball." It was also a successful response to "not hoop," "not pipe," and "not frisbee." We had guarded against this pattern with the other objects by changing the set of objects in the tank for any given trial, but obviously we could not remove the window. It turns out that when Ake was sinking to the bottom of the tank she was positioned next to the window, though I could not see the window!

Bruce: *What do you like about Prolog the most?*

Brian: *The declarative programming model is very appealing. In general, if you can describe the problem, you have solved the problem. In most languages I've found myself arguing with the computer at some point saying, "You know what I mean; just do it!" C and C++ compiler errors such as "semicolon expected" are symbolic of this. If you expected a semicolon, how about inserting one and seeing whether that fixes it?*

In Prolog, all I had to do in the scheduling problem was basically say, "I want a day that looks like this, so go make me one" and it would do it.

Bruce: *What gave you the most trouble?*

Brian: *Prolog seemed to be an all-or-nothing approach to problems, or at least to the problems I was working on. In the laboratory scheduling problem, the system would churn for 30 minutes and then either give us a beautiful schedule for the day or simply print "no." "No" in this case meant that we had over-constrained the day, and there was no full solution. It did not, however, give us a partial solution or much of any information about where the over-constraint was.*

What you see here is an extremely powerful concept. You don't have to describe the solution to a problem. You have only to describe the problem. And the language for the description of the problem is logic, only pure logic. Start from facts and inferences, and let Prolog do the rest. Prolog programs are at a higher level of abstraction. Schedules and behavior patterns are great examples of problems right in Prolog's wheelhouse.

What We Learned in Day 1

Today, we learned the basic building blocks of the Prolog language. Rather than encoding steps to guide Prolog to a solution, we encoded knowledge using pure logic. Prolog did the hard work of weaving that knowledge together to find solutions. We put our logic into knowledge bases and issued queries against them.

After we built a few knowledge bases, we then compiled and queried them. The queries had two forms. First, the query could specify a fact, and Prolog would tell us whether the facts were true or false. Second, we built a query with one or more variables. Prolog then computed all possibilities that made those facts true.

We learned that Prolog worked through rules by going through the clauses for a rule in order. For any clause, Prolog tried to satisfy each of the goals by going through the possible combinations of variables. All Prolog programs work this way.

In the sections to come, we're going to make more complex inferences. We're also going to learn to use math and more complex data structures such as lists, as well as strategies to iterate over lists.

Day 1 Self-Study

Find:

- Some free Prolog tutorials
- A support forum (there are several)
- One online reference for the Prolog version you're using

Do:

- Make a simple knowledge base. Represent some of your favorite books and authors.
- Find all books in your knowledge base written by one author.
- Make a knowledge base representing musicians and instruments. Also represent musicians and their genre of music.
- Find all musicians who play the guitar.

4.3 Day 2: Fifteen Minutes to Wapner

Grumpy Judge Wapner from *The People's Court* is an obsession of the central character in *Rain Man*. Like most autistics, Raymond obsesses over all things familiar. He latched on to Judge Wapner and *The People's Court*. As you're plowing through this enigmatic language, you might be ready for things to start to click. Now, you might be one of the lucky readers who has everything click for them right away, but if you don't, take heart. Today, there are definitely "fifteen minutes to Wapner." Sit tight. We will need a few more tools in the toolbox. You'll learn to use recursion, math, and lists. Let's get going.

Recursion

Ruby and Io were imperative programming languages. You would spell out each step of an algorithm. Prolog is the first of the declarative languages we'll look at. When you're dealing with collections of things such as lists or trees, you'll often use recursion rather than iteration. We'll look at recursion and use it to solve some problems with basic inferences, and then we'll apply the same technique to lists and math.

Take a look at the following database. It expresses the extensive family tree of the Waltons, characters in a 1963 movie and subsequent series. It expresses a father relationship and from that infers the ancestor relationship. Since an ancestor can mean a father, grandfather, or great grandfather, we will need to nest the rules or iterate. Since we're dealing with a declarative language, we're going to nest. One clause in the ancestor clause will use ancestor. In this case, ancestor(Z, Y) is a recursive subgoal. Here's the knowledge base:

prolog/family.pl

```
father(zeb,         john_boy_sr).
father(john_boy_sr, john_boy_jr).

ancestor(X, Y) :-
    father(X, Y).
ancestor(X, Y) :-
    father(X, Z), ancestor(Z, Y).
```

father is the core set of facts that enables our recursive subgoal. The rule ancestor/2 has two clauses. When you have multiple clauses that make up a rule, only one of them must be true for the rule to be true. Think of the commas between subgoals as and conditions and the periods between clauses as or conditions. The first clause says "X is the ancestor of Y if X is the father of Y." That's a straightforward relationship. We can try that rule like this:

```
| ?- ancestor(john_boy_sr, john_boy_jr).

true ?

no
```

Prolog reports true, john_boy_sr is an ancestor of john_boy_jr. This first clause depends on a fact.

The second clause is more complex: ancestor(X, Y) :- father(X, Z), ancestor(Z, Y). This clause says X is an ancestor of Y if we can prove that X is the father of Z and we can also prove that same Z is an ancestor of Y.

Whew. Let's use the second clause:

```
| ?- ancestor(zeb, john_boy_jr).

true ?
```

Yes, zeb is an ancestor of john_boy_jr. As always, we can try variables in a query, like this:

```
| ?- ancestor(zeb, Who).

Who = john_boy_sr ? a

Who = john_boy_jr

no
```

And we see that zeb is an ancestor for john_boy_jr and john_boy_sr. The ancestor predicate also works in reverse:

```
| ?- ancestor(Who, john_boy_jr).

Who = john_boy_sr ? a

Who = zeb

(1 ms) no
```

That's a beautiful thing, because we can use this rule in our knowledge base for two purposes, to find both ancestors and descendants.

A brief warning. When you use recursive subgoals, you need to be careful because each recursive subgoal will use stack space, and you can eventually run out. Declarative languages often solve this problem with a technique called *tail recursion optimization*. If you can position the recursive subgoal at the end of a recursive rule, Prolog can optimize the call to discard the call stack, keeping the memory use constant. Our call is tail recursive because the recursive subgoal, ancestor(Z, Y), is the last goal in the recursive rule. When your Prolog programs crash by running out of stack space, you'll know it's time to look for a way to optimize with tail recursion.

With that last bit of housekeeping out of the way, let's start to look at lists and tuples.

Lists and Tuples

Lists and tuples are a big part of Prolog. You can specify a list as [1, 2, 3] and a tuple as (1, 2, 3). Lists are containers of variable length, and tuples are containers with a fixed length. Both lists and tuples get much more powerful when you think of them in terms of unification.

Unification, Part 2

Remember, when Prolog tries to unify variables, it tries to make both the left and right sides match. Two tuples can match if they have the same number of elements and each element unifies. Let's take a look at a couple of examples:

```
| ?- (1, 2, 3) = (1, 2, 3).

yes
| ?- (1, 2, 3) = (1, 2, 3, 4).

no
```

```
| ?- (1, 2, 3) = (3, 2, 1).

no
```

Two tuples unify if all the elements unify. The first tuples were exact matches, the second tuples did not have the same number of elements, and the third set did not have the same elements in the same order. Let's mix in some variables:

```
| ?- (A, B, C) = (1, 2, 3).

A = 1
B = 2
C = 3

yes
| ?- (1, 2, 3) = (A, B, C).

A = 1
B = 2
C = 3

yes
| ?- (A, 2, C) = (1, B, 3).

A = 1
B = 2
C = 3

yes
```

It doesn't really matter which sides the variables are on. They unify if Prolog can make them the same. Now, for some lists. They can work like tuples:

```
| ?- [1, 2, 3] = [1, 2, 3].

yes
| ?- [1, 2, 3] = [X, Y, Z].

X = 1
Y = 2
Z = 3

yes
| ?- [2, 2, 3] = [X, X, Z].

X = 2
Z = 3

yes
```

```
| ?- [1, 2, 3] = [X, X, Z].

no
| ?- [] = [].
```

The last two examples are interesting. [X, X, Z] and [2, 2, 3] unified because Prolog could make them the same with X = 2. [1, 2, 3] = [X, X, Z] did not unify because we used X for both the first and second positions, and those values were different. Lists have a capability that tuples don't. You can deconstruct lists with [Head|Tail]. When you unify a list with this construct, Head will bind to the first element of the list, and Tail will bind to the rest, like this:

```
| ?- [a, b, c] = [Head|Tail].

Head = a
Tail = [b,c]

yes
```

[Head|Tail] won't unify with an empty list, but a one-element list is fine:

```
| ?- [] = [Head|Tail].

no
| ?- [a] = [Head|Tail].

Head = a
Tail = []

yes
```

You can get complicated by using various combinations:

```
| ?- [a, b, c] = [a|Tail].

Tail = [b,c]

(1 ms) yes
```

Prolog matched the a and unified the rest with Tail. Or we can split this tail into the head and tail:

```
| ?- [a, b, c] = [a|[Head|Tail]].

Head = b
Tail = [c]

yes
```

Or grab the third element:

```
| ?- [a, b, c, d, e] = [_, _|[Head|_]].

Head = c

yes
```

_ is a wildcard and unifies with anything. It basically means "I don't care what's in this position." We told Prolog to skip the first two elements and split the rest into head and tail. The Head will grab the third element, and the trailing _ will grab the tail, ignoring the rest of the list.

That should be enough to get you started. Unification is a powerful tool, and using it in conjunction with lists and tuples is even more powerful.

Now, you should have a basic understanding of the core data structures in Prolog and how unification works. We're now ready to combine these elements with rules and assertions to do some basic math with logic.

Lists and Math

In our next example, I thought I'd show you an example of using recursion and math to operate on lists. These are examples to do counting, sums, and averages. Five rules do all the hard work.

prolog/list_math.pl

```
count(0, []).
count(Count, [Head|Tail]) :- count(TailCount, Tail), Count is TailCount + 1.

sum(0, []).
sum(Total, [Head|Tail]) :- sum(Sum, Tail), Total is Head + Sum.

average(Average, List) :- sum(Sum, List), count(Count, List), Average is Sum/Count.
```

The simplest example is count. Use it like this:

```
| ?- count(What, [1]).

What = 1 ? ;

no
```

The rules are trivially simple. The count of an empty list is 0. The count of a list is the count of the tail plus one. Let's talk about how this works, step-by-step:

- We issue the query count(What, [1]), which can't unify with the first rule, because the list is not empty. We move on to satisfying the goals for the second rule, count(Count, [Head|Tail]). We unify, binding What to Count, Head to 1, and Tail to [].

- After unification, the first goal is count(TailCount, []). We try to prove that subgoal. This time, we unify with the first rule. That binds TailCount to 0. The first rule is now satisfied, so we can move on to the second goal.
- Now, we evaluate Count is TailCount + 1. We can unify variables. TailCount is bound to 0, so we bind Count to 0 + 1, or 1.

And that's it. We did not define a recursive process. We defined logical rules. The next example is adding up the elements of a list. Here's the code for those rules again:

```
sum(0, []).
sum(Total, [Head|Tail]) :- sum(Sum, Tail), Total is Head + Sum.
```

This code works precisely like the count rule. It also has two clauses, a base case and the recursive case. The usage is similar:

```
| ?- sum(What, [1, 2, 3]).

What = 6 ? ;

no
```

If you look at it imperatively, sum works exactly as you would expect in a recursive language. The sum of an empty list is zero; the sum of the rest is the Head plus the sum of the Tail.

But there's another interpretation here. We haven't really told Prolog how to compute sums. We've merely described sums as rules and goals. To satisfy some of the goals, the logic engine must satisfy some subgoals. The declarative interpretation is as follows: "The sum of an empty list is zero, and the sum of a list is Total if we can prove that the sum of the tail plus the head is Total." We're replacing recursion with the notion of proving goals and subgoals.

Similarly, the count of an empty list is zero; the count of a list is one for the Head plus the count of the Tail.

As with logic, these rules can build on each other. For example, you can use sum and count together to compute an average:

```
average(Average, List) :- sum(Sum, List), count(Count, List), Average is Sum/Count.
```

So, the average of List is Average if you can prove that

- the sum of that List is Sum,

- the count of that List is Count, and
- Average is Sum/Count.

And it works just as you'd expect:

```
| ?- average(What, [1, 2, 3]).

What = 2.0 ? ;

no
```

Using Rules in Both Directions

At this point, you should have a fairly good understanding of how recursion works. I'm going to shift gears a little bit and talk about a tight little rule called append. The rule append(List1, List2, List3) is true if List3 is List1 + List2. It's a powerful rule that you can use in a variety of ways.

That short little bit of code packs a punch. You can use it in many different ways. It's a lie detector:

```
| ?- append([oil], [water], [oil, water]).

yes
| ?- append([oil], [water], [oil, slick]).

no
```

It's a list builder:

```
| ?- append([tiny], [bubbles], What).

What = [tiny,bubbles]

yes
```

It does list subtraction:

```
| ?- append([dessert_topping], Who, [dessert_topping, floor_wax]).

Who = [floor_wax]

yes
```

And it computes possible permutations:

```
| ?- append(One, Two, [apples, oranges, bananas]).

One = []
Two = [apples,oranges,bananas] ? a

One = [apples]
```

```
Two = [oranges,bananas]

One = [apples,oranges]
Two = [bananas]

One = [apples,oranges,bananas]
Two = []

(1 ms) no
```

So, one rule gives you four. You may think that building such a rule will take a lot of code. Let's find out exactly how much. Let's rewrite the Prolog append, but we'll call it concatenate. We'll take it in several steps:

1. Write a rule called concatenate(List1, List2, List3) that can concatenate an empty list to List1.
2. Add a rule that concatenates one item from List1 onto List2.
3. Add a rule that concatenates two and three items from List1 onto List2.
4. See what we can generalize.

Let's get started. Our first step is to concatenate an empty list to List1. That's a fairly easy rule to write:

prolog/concat_step_1.pl

```
concatenate([], List, List).
```

No problem. concatenate is true if the first parameter is a list and the next two parameters are the same.

It works:

```
| ?- concatenate([], [harry], What).

What = [harry]

yes
```

Onto the next step. Let's add a rule that concatenates the first element of List1 to the front of List2:

prolog/concat_step_2.pl

```
concatenate([], List, List).
concatenate([Head|[]], List, [Head|List]).
```

For concatenate(List1, List2, List3), we break List1 into the head and tail, with the tail being an empty list. We'll break our third element into the head and tail, using List1's head and List2 as the tail. Remember to compile your knowledge base. It works just fine:

```
| ?- concatenate([malfoy], [potter], What).

What = [malfoy,potter]

yes
```

Now, we can define another couple of rules to concatenate lists of lengths 2 and 3. They work in the same way:

prolog/concat_step_3.pl

```
concatenate([], List, List).
concatenate([Head|[]], List, [Head|List]).
concatenate([Head1|[Head2|[]]], List, [Head1, Head2|List]).
concatenate([Head1|[Head2|[Head3|[]]]], List, [Head1, Head2, Head3|List]).
```

```
| ?- concatenate([malfoy, granger], [potter], What).

What = [malfoy,granger,potter]

yes
```

So, what we have is a base case and a strategy where each subgoal shrinks the first list and grows the third. The second stays constant. We now have enough information to generalize a result. Here's the concatenate using nested rules:

prolog/concat.pl

```
concatenate([], List, List).
concatenate([Head|Tail1], List, [Head|Tail2]) :-
  concatenate(Tail1, List, Tail2).
```

That terse little block of code has an incredibly simple explanation. The first clause says concatenating an empty list to List gives you that List. The second clause says concatenating List1 to List2 gives you List3 if the heads of List1 and List3 are the same, and you can prove that concatenating the tail of List1 with List2 gives you the tail of List3. The simplicity and elegance of this solution are a testament to the power of Prolog.

Let's see what it would do with the query concatenate([1, 2], [3], What). We'll walk through unification at each step. Keep in mind that we're nesting the rules, so each time we try to prove a subgoal, we'll have a different copy of the variables. I'll mark the important ones with a letter so you can keep them straight. With each pass, I'll show what happens when Prolog tries to prove the next subgoal.

- Start with this:

  concatenate([1, 2], [3], What)

- The first rule doesn't apply, because [1, 2] is not an empty list. We unify to this:

  concatenate([1|[2]], [3], [1|Tail2-A]) :- concatenate([2], [3], [Tail2-A])

  Everything unifies but the second tail. We now move on to the goals. Let's unify the right side.

- We try to apply the rule concatenate([2], [3], [Tail2-A]). That's going to give us this:

  concatenate([2|[ ]], [3], [2|Tail2-B]) :- concatenate([ ], [3], Tail2-B)

  Notice that Tail2-B is the tail of Tail2-A. It's not the same as the original Tail2. But now, we have to unify the right side again.

- concatenate([ ], [3], Tail2-C) :- concatenate([ ], [3], [3]) .

- So, we know Tail2-C is [3]. Now, we can work back up the chain. Let's look at the third parameter, plugging in Tail2 at each step. Tail2-C is [3], which means [2|Tail2-2] is [2, 3], and finally [1|Tail2] is [1, 2, 3]. What is [1, 2, 3].

Prolog is doing a lot of work for you here. Go over this list until you understand it. Unifying nested subgoals is a core concept for the advanced problems in this book.

Now, you've taken a deep look at one of the richest functions in Prolog. Take a little time to explore these solutions, and make sure you understand them.

What We Learned in Day 2

In this section, we moved into the basic building blocks that Prolog uses to organize data: lists and tuples. We also nested rules, allowing us to express problems that you might handle with iteration in other languages. We took a deeper look at Prolog unification and how Prolog works to match up both sides of a :- or =. We saw that when we're writing rules, we described logical rules instead of algorithms and let Prolog work its way through the solution.

We also used math. We learned to use basic arithmetic and nested subgoals to compute sums and averages.

Finally, we learned to use lists. We matched one or more variables within a list to variables, but more importantly, we matched the head of a list and the remaining elements with variables using the [Head|Tail] pattern. We used this technique to recursively iterate through lists. These building blocks will serve as the foundations of the complex problems we solve in day 3.

Day 2 Self-Study

Find:

- Some implementations of a Fibonacci series and factorials. How do they work?
- A real-world community using Prolog. What problems are they solving with it today?

If you're looking for something more advanced to sink your teeth into, try these problems:

- An implementation of the Towers of Hanoi. How does it work?
- What are some of the problems of dealing with "not" expressions? Why do you have to be careful with negation in Prolog?

Do:

- Reverse the elements of a list.
- Find the smallest element of a list.
- Sort the elements of a list.

4.4 Day 3: Blowing Up Vegas

You should be getting a better understanding of why I picked the Rain Man, the autistic savant, for Prolog. Though it's sometimes difficult to understand, it's amazing to think of programming in this way. One of my favorite points in *Rain Man* was when Ray's brother realized he could count cards. Raymond and his brother went to Vegas and just about broke the bank. In this section, you're going to see a side of Prolog that will leave you smiling. Coding the examples in this chapter was equal parts maddening and exhilarating. We're going to solve two famous puzzles that are right in Prolog's comfort zone, solving systems with constraints.

You may want to take a shot at some of these puzzles yourself. If you do, try describing the rules you know about each game rather than showing Prolog a step-by-step solution. We're going to start with a small Sudoku and then give you a chance to build up to a larger one in the daily exercises. Then, we'll move on to the classic Eight Queens puzzle.

Solving Sudoku

Coding the Sudoku was almost magical for me. A Sudoku is a grid that has rows, columns, and boxes. A typical puzzle is a nine-by-nine grid, with some spaces filled in and some blank. Each cell in the grid has a number, from 1–9 for a nine-by-nine square. Your job is to fill out the solution so that each row, column, and square has one each of all of the digits.

We're going to start with a four-by-four Sudoku. The concepts are exactly the same, though the solutions will be shorter. Let's start by describing the world, as we know it. Abstractly, we'll have a board with four rows, four columns, and four squares. The table shows squares 1–4:

```
1 1 2 2
1 1 2 2
3 3 4 4
3 3 4 4
```

The first task is to decide what the query will look like. That's simple enough. We'll have a puzzle and a solution, of the form `sodoku(Puzzle, Solution)`. Our users can provide a puzzle as a list, substituting underscores for unknown numbers, like this:

```
sodoku([_, _, 2, 3,
        _, _, _, _,
        _, _, _, _,
        3, 4, _, _],
        Solution).
```

If a solution exists, Prolog will provide the solution. When I solved this puzzle in Ruby, I had to worry about the algorithm for solving the puzzle. With Prolog, that's not so. I merely need to provide the rules for the game. These are the rules:

- For a solved puzzle, the numbers in the puzzle and solution should be the same.
- A Sudoku board is a grid of sixteen cells, with values from 1–4.

- The board has four rows, four columns, and four squares.
- A puzzle is valid if the elements in each row, column, and square has no repeated elements.

Let's start at the top. The numbers in the solution and puzzle should match:

prolog/sudoku4_step_1.pl

```
sudoku(Puzzle, Solution) :-
        Solution = Puzzle.
```

We've actually made some progress. Our "Sudoku solver" works for the case where there are no blanks:

```
| ?- sudoku([4, 1, 2, 3,
             2, 3, 4, 1,
             1, 2, 3, 4,
             3, 4, 1, 2], Solution).

Solution = [4,1,2,3,2,3,4,1,1,2,3,4,3,4,1,2]

yes
```

The format isn't pretty, but the intent is clear enough. We're getting sixteen numbers back, row by row. But we are a little too greedy:

```
| ?- sudoku([1, 2, 3], Solution).

Solution = [1,2,3]

yes
```

Now, this board isn't valid, but our solver reports that there is a valid solution. Clearly, we have to limit the board to sixteen elements. We have another problem, too. The values in the cells can be anything:

```
| ?- sudoku([1, 2, 3, 4, 5, 6, 7, 8, 9, 0, 1, 2, 3, 4, 5, 6], Solution).

Solution = [1,2,3,4,5,6,7,8,9,0,1,2,3,4,5,6]

yes
```

For a solution to be valid, it should have numbers from 1–4. This problem will impact us in two ways. First, we may allow some invalid solutions. Second, Prolog doesn't have enough information to test possible values for each cell. In other words, the set of results is not *grounded*. That means that we have not expressed rules that limit possible values of each cell, so Prolog will not be able to guess what the values are.

Let's solve these problems by solving the next rule to the game. Rule 2 says a board has sixteen cells, with values from 1–4. GNU Prolog has a built-in predicate to express possible values, called fd_domain(List, LowerBound, UpperBound). This predicate is true if all the values in List are between LowerBound and UpperBound, inclusive. We just need to make sure all values in Puzzle range from 1–4.

prolog/sudoku4_step_2.pl

```
sudoku(Puzzle, Solution) :-
        Solution = Puzzle,
        Puzzle = [S11, S12, S13, S14,
                  S21, S22, S23, S24,
                  S31, S32, S33, S34,
                  S41, S42, S43, S44],
        fd_domain(Puzzle, 1, 4).
```

We unified Puzzle with a list of sixteen variables, and we limited the domain of the cells to values from 1–4. Now, we fail if the puzzle is not valid:

```
| ?- sudoku([1, 2, 3], Solution).

no
```

```
| ?- sudoku([1, 2, 3, 4, 5, 6, 7, 8, 9, 0, 1, 2, 3, 4, 5, 6], Solution).

no
```

Now, we get to the main piece of the solution. Rule 3 says a board consists of rows, columns, and squares. We're going to carve the puzzle up into rows, columns, and squares. Now, you can see why we named the cells the way we did. It's a straightforward process to describe the rows:

```
Row1 = [S11, S12, S13, S14],
Row2 = [S21, S22, S23, S24],
Row3 = [S31, S32, S33, S34],
Row4 = [S41, S42, S43, S44],
```

Likewise for columns:

```
Col1 = [S11, S21, S31, S41],
Col2 = [S12, S22, S32, S42],
Col3 = [S13, S23, S33, S43],
Col4 = [S14, S24, S34, S44],
```

And squares:

```
Square1 = [S11, S12, S21, S22],
Square2 = [S13, S14, S23, S24],
Square3 = [S31, S32, S41, S42],
Square4 = [S33, S34, S43, S44].
```

Now that we've chopped the board into pieces, we can move on to the next rule. The board is valid if all rows, columns, and squares have no repeated elements. We'll use a GNU Prolog predicate to test for repeated elements. fd_all_different(List) succeeds if all the elements in List are different. We need to build a rule to test that all rows, columns, and squares are valid. We'll use a simple rule to accomplish this:

```
valid([]).
valid([Head|Tail]) :-
    fd_all_different(Head),
    valid(Tail).
```

This predicate is valid if all the lists in it are different. The first clause says that an empty list is valid. The second clause says that a list is valid if the first element's items are all different and if the rest of the list is valid.

All that remains is to invoke our valid(List) rule:

```
valid([Row1, Row2, Row3, Row4,
       Col1, Col2, Col3, Col4,
       Square1, Square2, Square3, Square4]).
```

Believe it or not, we're done. This solution can solve a four-by-four Sudoku:

```
| ?- sudoku([_, _, 2, 3,
             _, _, _, _,
             _, _, _, _,
             3, 4, _, _],
             Solution).

Solution = [4,1,2,3,2,3,4,1,1,2,3,4,3,4,1,2]

yes
```

Breaking that into a friendlier form, we have the solution:

```
4 1 2 3
2 3 4 1
1 2 3 4
3 4 1 2
```

Here's the completed program, beginning to end:

prolog/sudoku4.pl

```
valid([]).
valid([Head|Tail]) :-
    fd_all_different(Head),
    valid(Tail).


sudoku(Puzzle, Solution) :-
        Solution = Puzzle,

        Puzzle = [S11, S12, S13, S14,
                  S21, S22, S23, S24,
                  S31, S32, S33, S34,
                  S41, S42, S43, S44],

        fd_domain(Solution, 1, 4),

        Row1 = [S11, S12, S13, S14],
        Row2 = [S21, S22, S23, S24],
        Row3 = [S31, S32, S33, S34],
        Row4 = [S41, S42, S43, S44],

        Col1 = [S11, S21, S31, S41],
        Col2 = [S12, S22, S32, S42],
        Col3 = [S13, S23, S33, S43],
        Col4 = [S14, S24, S34, S44],

        Square1 = [S11, S12, S21, S22],
        Square2 = [S13, S14, S23, S24],
        Square3 = [S31, S32, S41, S42],
        Square4 = [S33, S34, S43, S44],

        valid([Row1, Row2, Row3, Row4,
               Col1, Col2, Col3, Col4,
               Square1, Square2, Square3, Square4]).
```

If you haven't had your Prolog moment, this example should give you a nudge in the right direction. Where's the program? Well, we didn't write a program. We described the rules of the game: a board has sixteen cells with digits from 1–4, and none of the rows, columns, or squares should repeat any of the values. The puzzle took a few dozen lines of code to solve and no knowledge of any Sudoku solving strategies. In the daily exercises, you'll get the chance to solve a nine-row Sudoku. It won't be too difficult.

This puzzle is a great example of the types of problems Prolog solves well. We have a set of constraints that are easy to express but hard to solve. Let's look at another puzzle involving highly constrained resources: the Eight Queens problem.

Eight Queens

To solve the Eight Queens problem, you put eight queens on a chess board. None can share the same row, column, or diagonal. It may appear to be a trivial problem on the surface. It's just a kid's game. But on another level, you can look at the rows, columns, and diagonals as constrained resources. Our industry is full of problems that solve constrained systems. Let's look at how we can solve this one in Prolog.

First, we'll look at what the query should look like. We can express each queen as (Row, Col), a tuple having a row and a column. A Board is a list of tuples. eight_queens(Board) succeeds if we have a valid board. Our query will look like this:

```
eight_queens([(1, 1), (3, 2), ...]).
```

Let's look at the goals we need to satisfy to solve the puzzle. If you want to take a shot at this game without looking at the solution, just look at these goals. I won't show the full solution until later in the chapter.

- A board has eight queens.
- Each queen has a row from 1–8 and a column from 1–8.
- No two queens can share the same row.
- No two queens can share the same column.
- No two queens can share the same diagonal (southwest to northeast).
- No two queens can share the same diagonal (northwest to southeast).

Rows and columns must be unique, but we must be more careful with diagonals. Each queen is on two diagonals, one running from the lower left (northwest) to the upper right (southeast) and the other running from the upper left to the lower right as in Figure 4.2, on the facing page. But these rules should be relatively easy to encode.

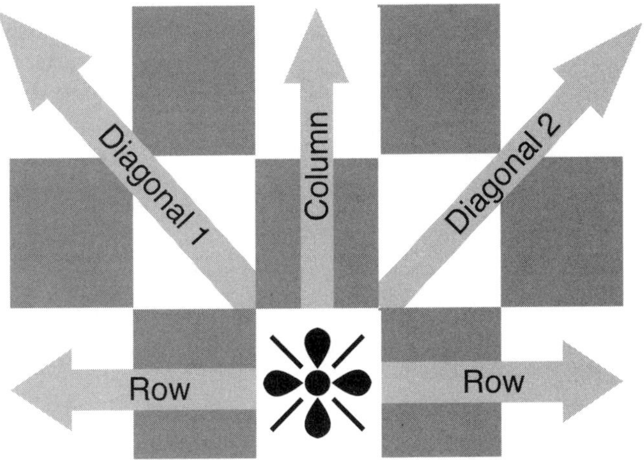

Figure 4.2: EIGHT QUEENS RULES

Once again, we'll start at the top of the list. A board has eight queens. That means our list must have a size of eight. That's easy enough to do. We can use the count predicate you saw earlier in the book, or we can simply use a built-in Prolog predicate called length. length(List, N) succeeds if List has N elements. This time, rather than show you each goal in action, I'm going to walk you through the goals we'll need to solve the whole problem. Here's the first goal, then:

```
eight_queens(List) :- length(List, 8).
```

Next, we need to make sure each queen from our list is valid. We build a rule to test whether a queen is valid:

```
valid_queen((Row, Col)) :-
    Range = [1,2,3,4,5,6,7,8],
    member(Row, Range), member(Col, Range).
```

The predicate member does just what you think; it tests for membership. A queen is valid if both the row and column are integers from 1–8. Next, we'll build a rule to check whether the whole board is made up of valid queens:

```
valid_board([]).
valid_board([Head|Tail]) :- valid_queen(Head), valid_board(Tail).
```

An empty board is valid, and a board is valid if the first item is a valid queen and the rest of the board is valid.

Moving on, the next rule is that two queens can't share the same row. To solve the next few constraints, we're going to need a little help. We will break down the program into pieces that can help us describe the problem: what are the rows, columns, and diagonals? First up is rows. We'll build a function called rows(Queens, Rows). This function should be true if Rows is the list of Row elements from all the queens.

```
rows([], []).
rows([(Row, _)|QueensTail], [Row|RowsTail]) :-
  rows(QueensTail, RowsTail).
```

This one takes a little imagination, but not much. rows for an empty list is an empty list, and rows(Queens, Rows) is Rows if the Row from the first queen in the list matches the first element of Rows and if rows of the tail of Queens is the tail of Rows. If it's confusing to you, walk through it with a few test lists. Luckily, columns works exactly the same way, but we're going to use columns instead of rows:

```
cols([], []).
cols([(_, Col)|QueensTail], [Col|ColsTail]) :-
  cols(QueensTail, ColsTail).
```

The logic works exactly the same as rows, but we match the second element of a queen tuple instead of the first.

Moving on, we're going to number diagonals. The easiest way to number them is to do some simple subtraction and addition. If north and west are 1, we're going to assign the diagonals that run from northwest to southeast a value of Col – Row. This is the predicate that grabs those diagonals:

```
diags1([], []).
diags1([(Row, Col)|QueensTail], [Diagonal|DiagonalsTail]) :-
  Diagonal is Col - Row,
  diags1(QueensTail, DiagonalsTail).
```

That rule worked just like rows and cols, but we had one more constraint: Diagonal is Col -- Row. Note that this is not unification! It's an is predicate, and it will make sure that the solution is fully grounded. Finally, we'll grab the southeast to northwest like this:

```
diags2([], []).
diags2([(Row, Col)|QueensTail], [Diagonal|DiagonalsTail]) :-
  Diagonal is Col + Row,
  diags2(QueensTail, DiagonalsTail).
```

The formula is a little bit tricky, but try a few values until you're satisfied that queens with the same sum of row and col are in fact on the same diagonal. Now that we have the rules to help us describe rows, columns, and diagonals, all that remains is to make sure rows, columns, and diagonals are all different.

So you can see it all in context, here's the entire solution. The tests for rows and columns are the last eight clauses.

prolog/queens.pl

```
valid_queen((Row, Col)) :-
    Range = [1,2,3,4,5,6,7,8],
    member(Row, Range), member(Col, Range).

valid_board([]).
valid_board([Head|Tail]) :- valid_queen(Head), valid_board(Tail).

rows([], []).
rows([(Row, _)|QueensTail], [Row|RowsTail]) :-
  rows(QueensTail, RowsTail).

cols([], []).
cols([(_, Col)|QueensTail], [Col|ColsTail]) :-
  cols(QueensTail, ColsTail).

diags1([], []).
diags1([(Row, Col)|QueensTail], [Diagonal|DiagonalsTail]) :-
  Diagonal is Col - Row,
  diags1(QueensTail, DiagonalsTail).

diags2([], []).
diags2([(Row, Col)|QueensTail], [Diagonal|DiagonalsTail]) :-
  Diagonal is Col + Row,
  diags2(QueensTail, DiagonalsTail).

eight_queens(Board) :-
  length(Board, 8),
  valid_board(Board),

  rows(Board, Rows),
  cols(Board, Cols),
  diags1(Board, Diags1),
  diags2(Board, Diags2),

  fd_all_different(Rows),
  fd_all_different(Cols),
  fd_all_different(Diags1),
  fd_all_different(Diags2).
```

At this point, you could run the program, and it would run... and run... and run. There are just too many combinations to efficiently sort through. If you think about it, though, we know that there will be one and only queen in every row. We can jump start the solution by providing a board that looks like this:

```
| ?- eight_queens([(1, A), (2, B), (3, C), (4, D), (5, E), (6, F), (7, G), (8, H)]).

A = 1
B = 5
C = 8
D = 6
E = 3
F = 7
G = 2
H = 4 ?
```

That works just fine, but the program is still working too hard. We can eliminate the row choices quite easily and simplify the API while we're at it. Here's a slightly optimized version:

prolog/optimized_queens.pl

```
valid_queen((Row, Col)) :- member(Col, [1,2,3,4,5,6,7,8]).

valid_board([]).
valid_board([Head|Tail]) :- valid_queen(Head), valid_board(Tail).

cols([], []).
cols([(_, Col)|QueensTail], [Col|ColsTail]) :-
  cols(QueensTail, ColsTail).

diags1([], []).
diags1([(Row, Col)|QueensTail], [Diagonal|DiagonalsTail]) :-
  Diagonal is Col - Row,
  diags1(QueensTail, DiagonalsTail).

diags2([], []).
diags2([(Row, Col)|QueensTail], [Diagonal|DiagonalsTail]) :-
  Diagonal is Col + Row,
  diags2(QueensTail, DiagonalsTail).

eight_queens(Board) :-
  Board = [(1, _), (2, _), (3, _), (4, _), (5, _), (6, _), (7, _), (8, _)],
  valid_board(Board),

  cols(Board, Cols),
  diags1(Board, Diags1),
  diags2(Board, Diags2),

  fd_all_different(Cols),
  fd_all_different(Diags1),
  fd_all_different(Diags2).
```

Philosophically, we've made one major change. We matched the Board with (1, _), (2, _), (3, _), (4, _), (5, _), (6, _), (7, _), (8, _) to reduce the total permutations significantly. We also removed all rules related to rows, and the results show. On my ancient MacBook, all solutions compute inside of three minutes.

Once again, the end result is quite pleasing. We built in very little knowledge of the solution set. We just described the rules to the game and applied a little logic to speed things up a little. Given the right problems, I could really find myself getting into Prolog.

What We Learned in Day 3

Today, you put together some of the ideas we've used in Prolog to solve some classic puzzles. The constraint-based problems have many of the same characteristics as classic industrial applications. List constraints, and crunch out a solution. We would never think of doing a SQL nine-table join imperatively, yet we don't even blink at solving logical problems in this way.

We started with a Sudoku puzzle. Prolog's solution was remarkably simple. We mapped sixteen variables onto rows, columns, and squares. Then, we described the rules of the game, forcing each row, column, and square to be unique. Prolog then methodically worked through the possibilities, quickly arriving at a solution. We used wildcards and variables to build an intuitive API, but we didn't provide any help at all for solution techniques.

Next, we used Prolog to solve the Eight Queens puzzle. Once again, we encoded the rules of the game and let Prolog work into a solution. This classic problem was computationally intensive, having 92 possible solutions, but even our simple approach could solve it within a handful of minutes.

I still don't know all of the tricks and techniques to solve advanced Sudokus, but with Prolog, I don't need to know them. I only need the rules of the game to play.

Day 3 Self-Study

Find:

- Prolog has some input/output features as well. Find print predicates that print out variables.
- Find a way to use the print predicates to print only successful solutions. How do they work?

Do:

- Modify the Sudoku solver to work on six-by-six puzzles (squares are 3x2) and 9x9 puzzles.
- Make the Sudoku solver print prettier solutions.

If you're a puzzle enthusiast, you can get lost in Prolog. If you want to dive deeper into the puzzles I've presented, Eight Queens is a good place to start.

- Solve the Eight Queens problem by taking a list of queens. Rather than a tuple, represent each queen with an integer, from 1–8. Get the row of a queen by its position in the list and the column by the value in the list.

4.5 Wrapping Up Prolog

Prolog is one of the older languages in this book, but the ideas are still interesting and relevant today. Prolog means programming with logic. We used Prolog to process rules, composed of clauses, which were in turn composed with a series of goals.

Prolog programming has two major steps. Start by building a knowledge base, composed of logical facts and inferences about the problem domain. Next, compile your knowledge base, and ask questions about the domain. Some of the questions can be assertions, and Prolog will respond with yes or no. Other queries have variables. Prolog fills in these gaps that makes those queries true.

Rather than simple assignment, Prolog uses a process called *unification* that makes variables on both sides of a system match. Sometimes, Prolog has to try many different possible combinations of variables to unify variables for an inference.

Strengths

Prolog is applicable for a wide variety of problems, from airline scheduling to financial derivatives. Prolog has a serious learning curve, but the demanding problems that Prolog solves tend to make the language, or others like it, worthwhile.

Think back to Brian Tarbox's work with the dolphins. He was able to make simple inferences about the world and make a breakthrough with a complex inference about dolphin behavior. He was also able to take highly constrained resources and use Prolog to find schedules that fit among them. These are some areas where Prolog is in active use today:

Natural-Language Processing

Prolog was perhaps first used to work with language recognition. In particular, Prolog language models can take natural language, apply a knowledge base of facts and inferences, and express that complex, inexact language in concrete rules appropriate for computers.

Games

Games are getting more complex, especially modeling the behavior of competitors or enemies. Prolog models can easily express the behavior of other characters in the system. Prolog can also build different behaviors into different types of enemies, making a more lifelike and enjoyable experience.

Semantic Web

The semantic Web is an attempt to attach meaning to the services and information on the Web, making it easier to satisfy requests. The resource description language (RDF) provides a basic description of resources. A server can compile these resources into a knowledge base. That knowledge, together with Prolog's natural-language processing, can provide a rich end user experience. Many Prolog packages exist for providing this sort of functionality in the context of a web server.

Artificial Intelligence

Artificial intelligence (AI) centers around building intelligence into machines. This intelligence can take different forms, but in every case, some "agent" modifies behavior based on complex rules. Prolog excels in this arena, especially when the rules are concrete, based on formal logic. For this reason, Prolog is sometimes called a *logic programming language*.

Scheduling

Prolog excels in working with constrained resources. Many have used Prolog to build operating system schedulers and other advanced schedulers.

Weaknesses

Prolog is a language that has held up over time. Still, the language is dated in many ways, and it does have significant limitations.

Utility

While Prolog excels in its core domain, it's a fairly focused niche, logic programming. It is not a general-purpose language. It also has some limitations related to language design.

Very Large Data Sets

Prolog uses a depth-first search of a decision tree, using all possible combinations matched against the set of rules. Various languages and compilers do a pretty good job of optimizing this process. Still, the strategy is inherently computationally expensive, especially as data sets get very large. It also forces Prolog users to understand how the language works to keep the size of data sets manageable.

Mixing the Imperative and Declarative Models

Like many languages in the functional family, particularly those that rely heavily on recursion, you must understand how Prolog will resolve recursive rules. You must often have tail-recursive rules to complete even moderately large problems. It's relatively easy to build Prolog applications that cannot scale beyond a trivial set of data. You must often have a deep understanding of how Prolog works to effectively design rules that will scale at acceptable levels.

Final Thoughts

As I worked through the languages in this book, I often kicked myself, knowing that through the years, I've driven many a screw with a sledgehammer. Prolog was a particularly poignant example of my evolving understanding. If you find a problem that's especially well suited for Prolog, take advantage. In such a setting, you can best use this rules-based language in combination with other general-purpose languages, just as you would use SQL within Ruby or Java. If you're careful with the way you tie them together, you're likely to come out ahead in the long run.

We are not sheep.
► Edward Scissorhands

Chapter 5

Scala

So far, I have introduced three languages and three different programming paradigms. Scala will be the fourth, sort of. It's a hybrid language, meaning that it intentionally tries to bridge the gaps between programming paradigms. In this case, the bridge is between object-oriented languages like Java and functional languages like Haskell. In this sense, Scala is a Frankenstein monster of sorts but not a monster. Think *Edward Scissorhands.*[1]

In this surreal Tim Burton movie, Edward was part boy, part machine, with scissors for hands, and was one of my favorite characters of all time. Edward was a fascinating character in a beautiful movie. He was often awkward, was sometimes amazing, but always had a unique expression. Sometimes, his scissors let him do incredible things. Other times, he was awkward and humiliated. As with anything new or different, he was often misunderstood, accused of "straying too far from the path of righteousness." But in one of his stronger moments, the shy kid offers, "We are not sheep." Indeed.

5.1 About Scala

As requirements for computer programs get more complex, languages, too, must evolve. Every twenty years or so, the old paradigms become inadequate to handle the new demands for organizing and expressing ideas. New paradigms must emerge, but the process is not a simple one.

1. *Edward Scissorhands*. DVD. Directed by Tim Burton. 1990; Beverly Hills, CA: 20th Century Fox, 2002.

Each new programming paradigm ushers in a wave of programming languages, not just one. The initial language is often strikingly productive and wildly impractical. Think Smalltalk for objects or Lisp for functional languages. Then, languages from other paradigms build in features that allow people to absorb the new concepts while users can live safely within the old paradigm. Ada, for example, allowed some core object-oriented ideas such as encapsulation to exist within a procedural language. At some point, some hybrid language offers just the right practical bridge between the old paradigm and the new, such as a C++. Next, we see a commercially adoptable language, such as Java or C#. Finally, we see some mature, pure implementations of the new paradigm.

Affinity with Java...

Scala is at least a bridge and maybe more. It offers tight integration into Java, offering a chance for people to protect their investment in many ways:

- Scala runs on the Java virtual machine, so Scala can run side-by-side with existing deployments.
- Scala can use Java libraries directly, so developers can leverage existing frameworks and legacy code.
- Like Java, Scala is statically typed, so the languages share a philosophical bond.
- Scala's syntax is relatively close to Java's, so developers can learn the basics quickly.
- Scala supports both object-oriented and functional programming paradigms, so programmers can gradually learn to apply functional programming ideas to their code.

Without Slavish Devotion

Some languages that embrace their ancestors go too far, extending the very limiting concepts that make the base inadequate. Although the similarities to Java are striking, Scala's design has some significant departures that will serve its community well. These important improvements represent important departures from the Java language:

- *Type inference.* In Java, you must declare the type of every variable, argument, or parameter. Scala infers variable types where possible.

- *Functional concepts.* Scala introduces important functional concepts to Java. Specifically, the new language allows you to use existing functions in many different ways to form new ones. Concepts you'll see in this chapter are code blocks, higher-order functions, and a sophisticated collection library. Scala goes far beyond some basic syntactical sugar.
- *Immutable variables.* Java does allow immutable variables but with a rarely used modifier. In this chapter, you'll see that Scala forces you to explicitly make a decision about whether a variable is mutable. These decisions will have a profound effect on how applications behave in a concurrent context.
- *Advanced programming constructs.* Scala uses the foundational language well, layering on useful concepts. In this chapter, we'll introduce you to actors for concurrency, Ruby-style collections with higher-order functions, and first-class XML processing.

Before we dive in, we should know about the motivations behind Scala. We'll spend some time with the creator, focusing on how he decided to tie two programming paradigms together.

An Interview with Scala's Creator, Martin Odersky

Martin Odersky, the creator of Scala, is a professor at École Polytechnique Fédérale de Lausanne (EPFL), one of two Swiss Federal Institutes of Technology. He has worked on the Java Generics specification and is the creator of the javac reference compiler. He is also the author of *Programming in Scala: A Comprehensive Step-by-Step Guide* [OSV08], one of the best Scala books available today. Here is what he had to say:

Bruce: *Why did you write Scala?*

Dr. Odersky: *I was convinced that unifying functional and object-oriented programming would have great practical value. I was frustrated both by the dismissive attitude of the functional programming community toward OOP and by the belief of object-oriented programmers that functional programming was just an academic exercise. So, I wanted to show that the two paradigms can be unified and that something new and powerful could result from that combination. I also wanted to create a language in which I would personally feel comfortable writing programs.*

Bruce: *What is the thing you like about it the most?*

Dr. Odersky: *I like that it lets programmers express themselves freely and that it feels lightweight, yet at the same time gives strong support through its type system.*

Bruce: *What kinds of problems does it solve the best?*

Dr. Odersky: *It's really general purpose. There's no problem I would not try to solve with it. That said, a particular strength of Scala relative to other mainstream languages is its support of functional programming. So, everywhere a functional approach is important Scala shines, be that concurrency and parallelism or web apps dealing with XML or implementing domain-specific languages.*

Bruce: *What is a feature that you would like to change, if you could start over?*

Dr. Odersky: *Scala's local type inference works generally well but has limitations. If I could start over, I'd try to use a more powerful constraint solver. Maybe it's still possible to do that, but the fact that we have to deal with a large installed base makes it more difficult.*

The buzz around Scala is growing, because Twitter has switched its core message processing from Ruby to Scala. The object-oriented features allow a pretty smooth transition from the Java language, but the ideas that are drawing attention to Scala are the functional programming features. Pure functional languages allow a style of programming that has strong mathematical foundations. A functional language has these characteristics:

- Functional programs are made up of functions.
- A function always returns a value.
- A function, given the same inputs, will return the same values.
- Functional programs avoid changing state or mutating data. Once you've set a value, you have to leave it alone.

Strictly speaking, Scala is not a pure functional programming language, just like C++ is not a pure object-oriented language. It allows mutable values, which can lead to functions with the same inputs but different outputs. (With most object-oriented languages, using getters and setters would break that rule.) But it offers tools that allow developers to use functional abstractions where they make sense.

Functional Programming and Concurrency

The biggest problem facing concurrency-minded programmers in object-oriented languages today is *mutable state*, meaning data that can change. Any variable that can hold more than one value, after initialization, is mutable. Concurrency is the Dr. Evil to mutable state's Austin Powers. If two different threads can change the same data at the same time, it's difficult to guarantee that the execution will leave the data in a valid state, and testing is nearly impossible. Databases deal with this problem with transactions and locking. Object-oriented programming languages deal with this problem by giving programmers the tools to control access to shared data. And programmers generally don't use those tools very well, even when they know how.

Functional programming languages can solve these problems by eliminating mutable state from the equation. Scala does not force you to completely eliminate mutable state, but it does give you the tools to code things in a purely functional style.

With Scala, you don't have to choose between making some Smalltalk and having a little Lisp. Let's get busy merging the object-oriented and functional worlds with some Scala code.

5.2 Day 1: The Castle on the Hill

In *Edward Scissorhands*, there's a castle on a hill that is, well, a little different. In a bygone era, the castle was a strange and enchanting place but is now showing signs of age and neglect. Broken windows let the weather in, and the rooms aren't all what they once were. The house that once felt so comfortable to its inhabitants is now cold and uninviting. The object-oriented paradigm, too, is showing some signs of age, especially the earlier object-oriented implementations. The Java language, with its dated implementations of static typing and concurrency, needs a face-lift. In this section, we're going to talk primarily about Scala in the context of that house on the hill, the object-oriented programming paradigm.

Scala runs on the Java virtual machine (JVM). I'm not going to offer an exhaustive overview of the Java language; that information is freely available elsewhere. You'll see some Java ideas creeping through to Scala, but I'll try to minimize their impact so you won't have to learn two languages at once. For now, install Scala. I'm using version 2.7.7.final for this book.

Scala Types

When you have Scala working, fire up the console with the command scala. If all is well, you won't get any error messages, and you will see a scala> prompt. You can then type a little code.

```
scala> println("Hello, surreal world")
Hello, surreal world

scala> 1 + 1
res8: Int = 2

scala> (1).+(1)
res9: Int = 2

scala> 5 + 4 * 3
res10: Int = 17

scala> 5.+(4.*(3))
res11: Double = 17.0

scala> (5).+((4).*(3))
res12: Int = 17
```

So, integers are objects. In Java, I've pulled out my fair share of hair converting between Int (primitives) and Integer (objects). In fact, everything is an object in Scala, with some small exceptions. That's a significant departure from most statically typed object oriented languages. Let's see how Scala handles strings:

```
scala> "abc".size
res13: Int = 3
```

So a string, too, is a first-class object, with a little syntactic sugar mixed in. Let's try to force a type collision:

```
scala> "abc" + 4
res14: java.lang.String = abc4

scala> 4 + "abc"
res15: java.lang.String = 4abc

scala> 4 + "1.0"
res16: java.lang.String = 41.0
```

Hm...that's not quite what we were looking for. Scala is coercing those integers into strings. Let's try a little harder to force a mismatch:

```
scala> 4 * "abc"
<console>:5: error: overloaded method value * with alternatives (Double)Double
<and> (Float)Float <and> (Long)Long <and> (Int)Int <and> (Char)Int
<and> (Short)Int <and> (Byte)Int cannot be applied to (java.lang.String)
       4 * "abc"
         ^
```

Ah. That's the ticket. Scala is actually strongly typed. Scala will use type inference, so most of the time, it will understand the types of variables through syntactical clues, but unlike Ruby, Scala can do that type checking at compile time. Scala's console actually compiles lines of code and runs each one piecemeal.

On a side note, I know you're getting back Java strings. Most Scala articles and books go into this topic in more detail, but we can't do so and still dive into the programming constructs that I think will be most interesting to you. I'll point you to a few books that will go into the Java integration in detail. For now, I'm going to tell you that in many places, Scala has a strategy for managing types across two languages. Part of that is using simple Java types where they make sense, like java.lang.String. Please trust me, and accept these oversimplifications.

Expressions and Conditions

Now we're going to move through some basic syntax quickly and strictly by example. Here are a few Scala true/false expressions:

```
scala> 5 < 6
res27: Boolean = true

scala> 5 <= 6
res28: Boolean = true

scala> 5 <= 2
res29: Boolean = false

scala> 5 >= 2
res30: Boolean = true

scala> 5 != 2
res31: Boolean = true
```

There's nothing too interesting going on there. This is the C-style syntax that you're familiar with from several of the languages we've talked about so far. Let's use an expression in an if statement:

```
scala> val a = 1
a: Int = 1

scala> val b = 2
b: Int = 2

scala> if ( b < a) {
     |   println("true")
     | } else {
     |   println("false")
     | }
false
```

We assign a couple of variables and compare them in an if/else statement. Take a closer look at the variable assignment. First, notice that you didn't specify a type. Unlike Ruby, Scala binds types at compile time. But unlike Java, Scala can infer the type, so you don't have to type val a : Int = 1, though you can if you want.

Next, notice that these Scala variable declarations start with the val keyword. You can also use the var keyword. val is immutable; var is not. We'll talk more about this later.

In Ruby, 0 evaluated to true. In C, 0 was false. In both languages, nil evaluated to false. Let's see how Scala handles them:

```
scala> Nil
res3: Nil.type = List()

scala> if(0) {println("true")}
<console>:5: error: type mismatch;
 found   : Int(0)
 required: Boolean
       if(0) {println("true")}
          ^

scala> if(Nil) {println("true")}
<console>:5: error: type mismatch;
 found   : Nil.type (with underlying type object Nil)
 required: Boolean
       if(Nil) {println("true")}
          ^
```

So, a Nil is an empty list, and you can't even test Nil or 0. This behavior is consistent with Scala's strong, static typing philosophy. Nils and numbers are not booleans, so don't treat them like booleans. With simple expressions and the most basic decision construct behind us, let's move on to loops.

Loops

As the next couple of programs get more complex, we're going to run them as scripts rather than in the console. Like Ruby and Io, you'll run them with scala path/to/program.scala.

You'll see a number of ways to iterate over result sets in day 2 when we attack code blocks. For now, we'll focus on the imperative programming style of loops. You'll see that these look a lot like the Java-style loop structures.

My Inner Battle with Static Typing

Some novice programming language enthusiasts confuse the ideas of strong typing and static typing. Loosely speaking, strong typing means the language detects when two types are compatible, throwing an error or coercing the types if they are not. On the surface, Java and Ruby are both strongly typed. (I realize this idea is an oversimplification.) Assembly language and C compilers, on the other hand, are weakly typed. The compiler doesn't necessarily care whether the data in a memory location is an integer, a string, or just data.

Static and dynamic typing is another issue. Statically typed languages enforce polymorphism based on the structure of the types. Is it a duck by the genetic blueprint (static), or is it a duck because it quacks or walks like one? Statically typed languages benefit because compilers and tools know more about your code to trap errors, highlight code, and refactor. The cost is having to do more work and living with some restrictions. Your history as a developer will often determine how you feel about the trade-offs of static typing.

My first OO development was in Java. I saw one framework after another try to break free from the chains of Java's static typing. The industry invested hundreds of millions of dollars in three versions of Enterprise Java Beans, Spring, Hibernate, JBoss, and aspect-oriented programming to make certain usage models more malleable. We were making Java's typing model more dynamic, and the battles at every step of the way were intense, feeling more like rival cults than programming environments. My books took the same journey, from increasingly dynamic frameworks to dynamic languages.

So, my bias against static typing was shaped by the Java wars. Haskell and its great static type system are helping me recover but slowly. My conscience is clear. You've invited a closet politician to this casual dinner, but I'll try my hardest to keep the conversation light and unbiased.

First is the basic while loop:

scala/while.scala

```
def whileLoop {
    var i = 1
    while(i <= 3) {
        println(i)
        i += 1
    }
}

whileLoop
```

We define a function. As a side note, Java developers will notice that you don't have to specify public. In Scala, public is the default visibility, meaning this function will be visible to all.

Within the method, we declare a simple while loop that counts to three. i changes, so we declare it with var. Then, you see a Java-style declaration of a while statement. As you can see, the code inside braces executes unless the condition is false. You can run the code like this:

```
batate$ scala code/scala/while.scala
1
2
3
```

The for loop works a lot like Java's and C's but with a slightly different syntax:

scala/for_loop.scala

```
def forLoop {
    println( "for loop using Java-style iteration" )
    for(i <- 0 until args.length) {
        println(args(i))
    }
}

forLoop
```

The argument is a variable, followed by the <- operator, followed by a range for the loop in the form of initialValue until endingValue. In this case, we're iterating over the incoming command-line arguments:

```
batate$ scala code/scala/forLoop.scala its all in the grind
for loop using Java-style iteration
its
all
in
the
grind
```

As with Ruby, you can also use loops to iterate over a collection. For now, we'll start with foreach, which is reminiscent of Ruby's each:

scala/ruby_for_loop.scala

```
def rubyStyleForLoop {
    println( "for loop using Ruby-style iteration" )
    args.foreach { arg =>
        println(arg)
    }
}

rubyStyleForLoop
```

args is a list with the inbound command-line arguments. Scala passes each element into this block, one by one. In our case, arg is one argument from the inbound args list. In Ruby, the same code would be args.each {|arg| println(arg) }. The syntax for specifying each argument is slightly different, but the idea is the same. Here's the code in action:

```
batate$ scala code/scala/ruby_for_loop.scala freeze those knees chickadees
for loop using Ruby-style iteration
freeze
those
knees
chickadees
```

Later, you'll find yourself using this method of iteration much more often than the other imperative loops. But since we're concentrating on the house on the hill, we'll delay that part of the conversation for a little while.

Ranges and Tuples

Like Ruby, Scala supports first-class ranges. Start the console, and enter these code snippets:

```
scala> val range = 0 until 10
range: Range = Range(0, 1, 2, 3, 4, 5, 6, 7, 8, 9)

scala> range.start
res2: Int = 0

scala> range.end
res3: Int = 10
```

That all makes sense. It works like Ruby's range. You can also specify increments:

```
scala> range.step
res4: Int = 1
```

```
scala> (0 to 10) by 5
res6: Range = Range(0, 5, 10)

scala> (0 to 10) by 6
res7: Range = Range(0, 6)
```

The equivalent of Ruby's range, 1..10, is 1 to 10, and the equivalent of Ruby's range, 1...10, is 1 until 10. to is inclusive:

```
scala> (0 until 10 by 5)
res0: Range = Range(0, 5)
```

You can also specify direction with this:

```
scala> val range = (10 until 0) by -1
range: Range = Range(10, 9, 8, 7, 6, 5, 4, 3, 2, 1)
```

But the direction is not inferred:

```
scala> val range = (10 until 0)
range: Range = Range()

scala> val range = (0 to 10)
range: Range.Inclusive = Range(0, 1, 2, 3, 4, 5, 6, 7, 8, 9, 10)
```

1 is the default step, regardless of the endpoints that you express for your range. You are not limited to integers:

```
scala> val range = 'a' to 'e'
range: RandomAccessSeq.Projection[Char] = RandomAccessSeq.Projection(a, b, c, d, e)
```

Scala will do some implicit type conversions for you. In fact, when you specified a for statement, you were actually specifying a range.

Like Prolog, Scala offers tuples. A tuple is a fixed-length set of objects. You'll find this pattern in many other functional languages as well. The objects in a tuple can all have different types. In purely functional languages, programmers often express objects and their attributes with tuples. Try this example:

```
scala> val person = ("Elvis", "Presley")
person: (java.lang.String, java.lang.String) = (Elvis,Presley)

scala> person._1
res9: java.lang.String = Elvis

scala> person._2
res10: java.lang.String = Presley

scala> person._3
<console>:6: error: value _3 is not a member of (java.lang.String, java.lang.String)
       person._3
              ^
```

Scala uses tuples rather than lists to do multivalue assignments:

```
scala> val (x, y) = (1, 2)
x: Int = 1
y: Int = 2
```

Since tuples have a fixed length, Scala can do static type checking based on each of the tuple values:

```
scala> val (a, b) = (1, 2, 3)
<console>:15: error: constructor cannot be instantiated to expected type;
 found   : (T1, T2)
 required: (Int, Int, Int)
       val (a, b) = (1, 2, 3)
           ^
<console>:15: error: recursive value x$1 needs type
       val (a, b) = (1, 2, 3)
            ^
```

With these foundations out of the way, let's put it all together. We'll create some object-oriented class definitions.

Classes in Scala

The simplest classes, those with attributes but no methods or constructors, are simple, one-line definitions in Scala:

```
class Person(firstName: String, lastName: String)
```

You don't have to specify any body to specify a simple value class. The Person class will be public and have firstName and lastName attributes. And you can use that class in the console:

```
scala> class Person(firstName: String, lastName: String)
defined class Person

scala> val gump = new Person("Forrest", "Gump")
gump: Person = Person@7c6d75b6
```

But you're looking for a little more. Object-oriented classes mix data and behavior. Let's build a full object-oriented class in Scala. We'll call this class Compass. The compass orientation will start with north. We'll tell the compass to turn 90 degrees left or right and update the direction accordingly. Here's what the Scala code looks like, in its entirety:

scala/compass.scala

```
class Compass {

  val directions = List("north", "east", "south", "west")
  var bearing = 0
```

```
  print("Initial bearing: ")
  println(direction)

  def direction() = directions(bearing)

  def inform(turnDirection: String) {
    println("Turning " + turnDirection + ". Now bearing " + direction)
  }

  def turnRight() {
    bearing = (bearing + 1) % directions.size
    inform("right")
  }

  def turnLeft() {
    bearing = (bearing + (directions.size - 1)) % directions.size
    inform("left")
  }
}

val myCompass = new Compass

myCompass.turnRight
myCompass.turnRight

myCompass.turnLeft
myCompass.turnLeft
myCompass.turnLeft
```

The syntax is relatively straightforward, with a couple of notable peculiarities. The constructor is responsible for defining instance variables (at least, those you don't pass into the constructor) and methods. Unlike Ruby, all method definitions have parameter types and names. And the initial block of code isn't in any method definition at all. Let's take it apart:

```
class Compass {

  val directions = List("north", "east", "south", "west")
  var bearing = 0

  print("Initial bearing: ")
  println(direction)
```

The whole block of code following the class definition is actually the constructor. Our constructor has a List of directions and a bearing, which is simply an index for the directions. Later, turning will manipulate the bearing. Next, there are a couple of convenience methods to show the user of the class the current direction, in English:

```
def direction() = directions(bearing)
```

```
def inform(turnDirection: String) {
  println("Turning " + turnDirection + ". Now bearing " + direction)
}
```

The constructor continues with method definitions. The direction method just returns the element of directions at the index of bearing. Scala conveniently allows an alternate syntax for one-line methods, omitting the braces around the method body.

The inform method prints a friendly message whenever the user turns. It takes a simple parameter, the direction of the turn. This method doesn't return a value. Let's look at the methods to handle turns.

```
def turnRight() {
  bearing = (bearing + 1) % directions.size
  inform("right")
}

def turnLeft() {
  bearing = (bearing + (directions.size - 1)) % directions.size
  inform("left")
}
```

The turns method changes the bearing based on the direction of the turn. The % operator is modular division. (This operator does a division operation, discarding the quotient and returning only the remainder.) The result is that right turns add one to the bearing and left turns subtract one, wrapping the result accordingly.

Auxiliary Constructors

You've seen how the basic constructor works. It's a code block that initializes classes and methods. You can have alternate constructors as well. Consider this Person class, with two constructors:

scala/constructor.scala

```
class Person(first_name: String) {
  println("Outer constructor")
  def this(first_name: String, last_name: String) {
    this(first_name)
    println("Inner constructor")
  }
  def talk() = println("Hi")

}

val bob = new Person("Bob")
val bobTate = new Person("Bob", "Tate")
```

The class has a constructor with one parameter, firstName, and a method called talk. Notice the this method. That's the second constructor. It takes two parameters, firstName and lastName. Initially, the method invokes this with the primary constructor, with only the firstName parameter.

The code after the class definition instantiates a person in two ways, first with the primary constructor, then next with the auxiliary constructor:

```
batate$ scala code/scala/constructor.scala
Outer constructor
Outer constructor
Inner constructor
```

That's all there is to it. Auxiliary constructors are important because they allow for a broad array of usage patterns. Let's look at how to create class methods.

Extending Classes

So far, the classes have been pretty vanilla. We created a couple of basic classes with nothing more than attributes and methods. In this section, we'll look at some of the ways that classes can interact.

Companion Objects and Class Methods

In Java and Ruby, you create both class methods and instance methods within the same body. In Java, class methods have the static keyword. Ruby uses def self.class_method. Scala uses neither of these strategies. Instead, you will declare instance methods in the class definitions. When there's something that can have only one instance, you'll define it with the object keyword instead of the class keyword. Here's an example:

scala/ring.scala

```
object TrueRing {
 def rule = println("To rule them all")
}

TrueRing.rule
```

The TrueRing definition works exactly like any class definition, but it creates a singleton object. In Scala, you can have both an object definition and a class definition with the same name. Using this scenario, you can create class methods within the singleton object declaration and instance methods within the class declaration. In our example, the method rule is a class method. This strategy is called *companion objects*.

Inheritance

Inheritance in Scala is pretty straightforward, but the syntax must be exact. Here's an example of extending a Person class with Employee. Notice that the Employee has an additional employee number in the id field. Here's the code:

scala/employee.scala

```
class Person(val name: String) {
  def talk(message: String) = println(name + " says " + message)
  def id(): String = name
}


class Employee(override val name: String,
                        val number: Int) extends Person(name) {
  override def talk(message: String) {
    println(name + " with number " + number + " says " + message)
  }
  override def id():String = number.toString
}

val employee = new Employee("Yoda", 4)
employee.talk("Extend or extend not. There is no try.")
```

In this example, we're extending the Person base class with Employee. We're adding a new instance variable called number in Employee, and we're also overriding the talk message to add some new behavior. Most of the tricky syntax is around the class constructor definition. Notice that you must specify the complete parameter list for Person, though you can omit the types.

The override keyword, both in the constructor and for any methods you want to extend from the base class, is mandatory. This keyword will keep you from inadvertently introducing new methods with misspellings. All in all, there are no major surprises here, but at times, I do feel a bit like Edward trying to pet a fragile baby bunny. Moving on....

Traits

Every object-oriented language must solve the problem that one object can have several different roles. An object can be a persistent, serializable shrubbery. You don't want your shrubbery to have to know how to push binary data into MySQL. C++ uses multiple inheritance, Java uses interfaces, Ruby uses mixins, and Scala uses traits. A Scala trait is like a Ruby mixin, implemented with modules. Or, if you prefer, a trait is like a Java interface plus an implementation. Look at a trait as a partial-class implementation. Ideally, it should implement one critical concern. Here's an example that adds the trait Nice to Person:

scala/nice.scala

```
class Person(val name:String)

trait Nice {
  def greet() = println("Howdily doodily.")
}

class Character(override val name:String) extends Person(name) with Nice

val flanders = new Character("Ned")
flanders.greet
```

The first element you see is Person. It is a simple class with a single attribute called name. The second element is the trait called Nice. That is the mixin. It has a single method called greet. The final element, a class called Character, mixes in the Nicetrait. Clients can now use the greet method on any instance of Character. The output is what you would expect:

```
batate$ scala code/scala/nice.scala
Howdily doodily.
```

There's nothing too complicated here. We can take our trait called Nice with a method called greet and mix it into any Scala class to introduce the greet behavior.

What We Learned in Day 1

We covered a tremendous amount of territory in day 1 because we have to fully develop two different programming paradigms in one language. Day 1 showed that Scala embraces object-oriented concepts, running in the JVM side-by-side with existing Java libraries. Scala's syntax is similar to that of Java and is also strongly and statically typed. But Martin Odersky wrote Scala to bridge two paradigms: object-oriented programming and functional programming. These functional programming concepts that we'll introduce in day 2 will make it easier to design concurrent applications.

Scala's static typing is also inferred. Users do not always need to declare types for all variables in all situations because Scala can often infer those types from syntactical clues. The compiler can also coerce types, such as integers to strings, allowing implicit type conversions when they make sense.

Scala's expressions work much like they do in other languages, but they are a little more strict. Most conditionals must take a boolean type, and 0 or Nil will not work at all; they can substitute for neither true nor false. But there's nothing dramatically different about Scala's looping or control structures. Scala does support some more advanced types, like tuples (fixed-length lists with heterogeneous types) and ranges (a fixed, all-inclusive ordered sequence of numbers).

Scala classes work much like they do in Java, but they don't support class methods. Instead, Scala uses a concept called *companion objects* to mix class and instance methods on the same class. Where Ruby uses mixins and Java uses interfaces, Scala uses a structure like a mixin called a Trait.

In day 2, we'll take a full pass through Scala's functional features. We'll cover code blocks, collections, immutable variables, and some advanced built-in methods like foldLeft.

Day 1 Self-Study

The first day of Scala covered a lot of ground, but it should be mostly familiar territory. These object-oriented concepts should be familiar to you. These exercises are a little advanced compared to the earlier exercises in the book, but you can handle it.

Find:

- The Scala API
- A comparison of Java and Scala
- A discussion of val versus var

Do:

- Write a game that will take a tic-tac-toe board with X, O, and blank characters and detect the winner or whether there is a tie or no winner yet. Use classes where appropriate.
- Bonus problem: Let two players play tic-tac-toe.

5.3 Day 2: Clipping Bushes and Other New Tricks

In *Edward Scissorhands*, a magical moment happens when Edward realizes that he's come far from the house on the hill and his unique abilities may give him a special place in the existing society.

Anyone with an eye for programming language history has seen this fable played out before. When the object-oriented paradigm was new, the masses could not accept Smalltalk because the paradigm was too new. We needed a language that would let them continue to do procedural programming and experiment with object-oriented ideas. With C++, the new object-oriented tricks could live safely beside the existing C procedural features. The result was that people could start using the new tricks in an old context.

Now, it's time to put Scala through its paces as a functional language. Some of this will seem awkward at first, but the ideas are powerful and important. They will form the foundation for the concurrency constructs you'll see later in day 3. Let's start from the beginning, with a simple function:

```
scala> def double(x:Int):Int = x * 2
double: (Int)Int

scala> double(4)
res0: Int = 8
```

Defining a function looks a whole lot like it does with Ruby. The def keyword defines both a function and a method. The parameters and their types come next. After that, you can specify an optional return type. Scala can often infer the return type.

To invoke the function, just use the name and the argument list. Notice that unlike Ruby, the parentheses are not optional in this context.

This is a one-line method definition. You can also specify a method definition in block form:

```
scala> def double(x:Int):Int = {
     |   x * 2
     | }
double: (Int)Int

scala> double(6)
res3: Int = 12
```

That = after the Int return type is mandatory. Forgetting it will cause you trouble. These are the major forms of function declarations. You'll see minor variations, such as omitting parameters, but these are the forms you'll see most often.

Let's move on to the variables that you'll use within a function. You'll want to pay careful attention to the life cycle of the variable if you want to learn the pure functional programming model.

var versus val

Scala is based on the Java virtual machine and has a tight relationship with Java. In some ways, these design goals limit the language. In other ways, Scala can take advantage of the last fifteen or twenty years of programming language development. You'll see an increased emphasis on making Scala friendly for concurrent programming. But all the concurrency features in the world won't help you if you don't follow basic design principles. Mutable state is bad. When you declare variables, you should make them immutable whenever you can to avoid conflicting state. In Java, that means using the final keyword. In Scala, immutable means using val instead of var:

```
scala> var mutable = "I am mutable"
mutable: java.lang.String = I am mutable

scala> mutable = "Touch me, change me..."
mutable: java.lang.String = Touch me, change me...

scala> val immutable = "I am not mutable"
immutable: java.lang.String = I am not mutable

scala> immutable = "Can't touch this"
<console>:5: error: reassignment to val
       immutable = "Can't touch this"
                 ^
```

So, var values are mutable; val values are not. In the console, as a convenience, you can redefine a variable several times even if you use val. Once you step outside of the console, redefining a val will generate an error.

In some ways, Scala had to introduce the var-style variables to support the traditional imperative programming style, but while you're learning Scala, it's best to avoid var when you can for better concurrency. This basic design philosophy is the key element that differentiates functional programming from object-oriented programming: *mutable state limits concurrency*.

Let's move on to some of my favorite areas within functional languages, dealing with collections.

Collections

Functional languages have a long history of spectacularly useful features for collections. One of the earliest functional languages, Lisp, was built around the idea of dealing with lists. The very name stands for

LISt Processing. Functional languages make it easy to build complex structures containing data and code. Scala's primary collections are lists, sets, and maps.

Lists

As with most functional languages, the bread-and-butter data structure is the list. Scala's lists, of type List, are ordered collections of like things with random access. Enter these lists into the console:

```
scala> List(1, 2, 3)
res4: List[Int] = List(1, 2, 3)
```

Notice the first return value: List[Int] = List(1, 2, 3). This value not only shows the type of the overall list but also shows the type of the data structures within the list. A list of Strings looks like this:

```
scala> List("one", "two", "three")
res5: List[java.lang.String] = List(one, two, three)
```

If you're seeing a little Java influence here, you're right. Java has a feature called Generics that allows you to type the items within a data structure like a list or array. Let's see what happens when you have a list combining Strings and Ints:

```
scala> List("one", "two", 3)
res6: List[Any] = List(one, two, 3)
```

You get the data type Any, which is the catchall data type for Scala. Here's how you'd access an item of a list:

```
scala> List("one", "two", 3)(2)
res7: Any = 3

scala> List("one", "two", 3)(4)
java.util.NoSuchElementException: head of empty list
        at scala.Nil$.head(List.scala:1365)
        at scala.Nil$.head(List.scala:1362)
        at scala.List.apply(List.scala:800)
        at .<init>(<console>:5)
        at .<clinit>(<console>)
        at RequestResult$.<init>(<console>:3)
        at RequestResult$.<clinit>(<console>)
        at RequestResult$result(<console>)
        at sun.reflect.NativeMethodAccessorImpl.invoke0(Native Met...
```

You use the () operator. List access is a function, so you use () instead of []. Scala's index for list starts with 0, as it does with Java and Ruby. Unlike Ruby, accessing an item out of range will throw an exception.

You can try to index with a negative number. Earlier versions return the first element:

```
scala> List("one", "two", 3)(-1)
res9: Any = one

scala> List("one", "two", 3)(-2)
res10: Any = one

scala> List("one", "two", 3)(-3)
res11: Any = one
```

Since that behavior is a little inconsistent with the NoSuchElement exception for an index that's too large, version 2.8.0 corrects that behavior, returning java.lang.IndexOutOfBoundsException.

One final note. Nil in Scala is an empty list:

```
scala> Nil
res33: Nil.type = List()
```

We'll use this list as a basic building block when we cover code blocks, but for now, bear with me. I'm going to introduce a couple of other types of collections first.

Sets

A set is like a list, but sets do not have any explicit order. You specify a set with the Set keyword:

```
scala> val animals = Set("lions", "tigers", "bears")
animals: scala.collection.immutable.Set[java.lang.String] =
    Set(lions, tigers, bears)
```

Adding or subtracting from that set is easy:

```
scala> animals + "armadillos"
res25: scala.collection.immutable.Set[java.lang.String] =
    Set(lions, tigers, bears, armadillos)

scala> animals - "tigers"
res26: scala.collection.immutable.Set[java.lang.String] = Set(lions, bears)

scala> animals + Set("armadillos", "raccoons")
<console>:6: error: type mismatch;
 found   : scala.collection.immutable.Set[java.lang.String]
 required: java.lang.String
       animals + Set("armadillos", "raccoons")
                 ^
```

Keep in mind that set operations are not destructive. Each set operation builds a new set rather than modifying the old ones. By default, sets are immutable. As you can see, adding or removing a single element is a piece of cake, but you can't use the + or - to combine sets, as you would in Ruby. In Scala, you want to use ++ and -- for set union and set difference:

```
scala> animals ++ Set("armadillos", "raccoons")
res28: scala.collection.immutable.Set[java.lang.String] =
  Set(bears, tigers, armadillos, raccoons, lions)

scala> animals -- Set("lions", "bears")
res29: scala.collection.immutable.Set[java.lang.String] = Set(tigers)
```

You can also perform set intersection (elements in two sets that are the same) with **[2]:

```
scala> animals ** Set("armadillos", "raccoons", "lions", "tigers")
res1: scala.collection.immutable.Set[java.lang.String] = Set(lions, tigers)
```

Unlike a List, a Set is independent of order. This rule will mean that equality for sets and lists is different:

```
scala> Set(1, 2, 3) == Set(3, 2, 1)
res36: Boolean = true

scala> List(1, 2, 3) == List(3, 2, 1)
res37: Boolean = false
```

That's enough set manipulation for now. Let's move on to maps.

Maps

A Map is a key-value pair, like a Ruby Hash. The syntax should be familiar to you:

```
scala> val ordinals = Map(0 -> "zero", 1 -> "one", 2 -> "two")
ordinals: scala.collection.immutable.Map[Int,java.lang.String] =
  Map(0 -> zero, 1 -> one, 2 -> two)

scala> ordinals(2)
res41: java.lang.String = two
```

Like a Scala List or Set, you specify a Map with the Map keyword. You separate the elements of the map with the -> operator. You just used some syntactic sugar that makes it easy to create a Scala map. Let's use another form of the hash map and specify the types of the key and value:

```
scala> import scala.collection.mutable.HashMap
import scala.collection.mutable.HashMap
```

2. Use & beginning in Scala 2.8.0, because ** is deprecated.

```
scala> val map = new HashMap[Int, String]
map: scala.collection.mutable.HashMap[Int,String] = Map()

scala> map += 4 -> "four"

scala> map += 8 -> "eight"

scala> map
res2: scala.collection.mutable.HashMap[Int,String] =
  Map(4 -> four, 8 -> eight)
```

First, we import the Scala libraries for a mutable HashMap. That means the values within the hash map can change. Next, we declare an immutable variable called map. That means that the *reference* to the map cannot change. Notice that we're also specifying the types of the key-value pairs. Finally, we add some key-value pairs and return the result.

Here's what would happen if you specified the wrong types:

```
scala> map += "zero" -> 0
<console>:7: error: overloaded method value += with alternatives (Int)map.MapTo
    <and> ((Int, String))Unit cannot be applied to ((java.lang.String, Int))
       map += "zero" -> 0
           ^
```

As expected, you get a typing error. The type constraints are enforced where possible at compile time but also at run time. So now that you've seen the basics for collections, let's dive into some of the finer details.

Any and Nothing

Before we move on to anonymous functions, let's talk a little bit more about the class hierarchy in Scala. When you're using Scala with Java, you will often be more concerned about the Java class hierarchy. Still, you should know a little bit about the Scala types. Any is the root class in the Scala class hierarchy. It's often confusing, but know that any Scala type will inherit from Any.

Similarly, Nothing is a subtype of every type. That way, a function, say for a collection, can return Nothing and conform to the return value for the given function. It is all laid out in Figure 5.1, on the next page. Everything inherits from Any, and Nothing inherits from everything.

There are a few different nuances when you're dealing with nil concepts. Null is a Trait, and null is an instance of it that works like Java's null, meaning an empty value. An empty collection is Nil. By contrast, Nothing is a trait that is a subtype of everything. Nothing has no instance, so

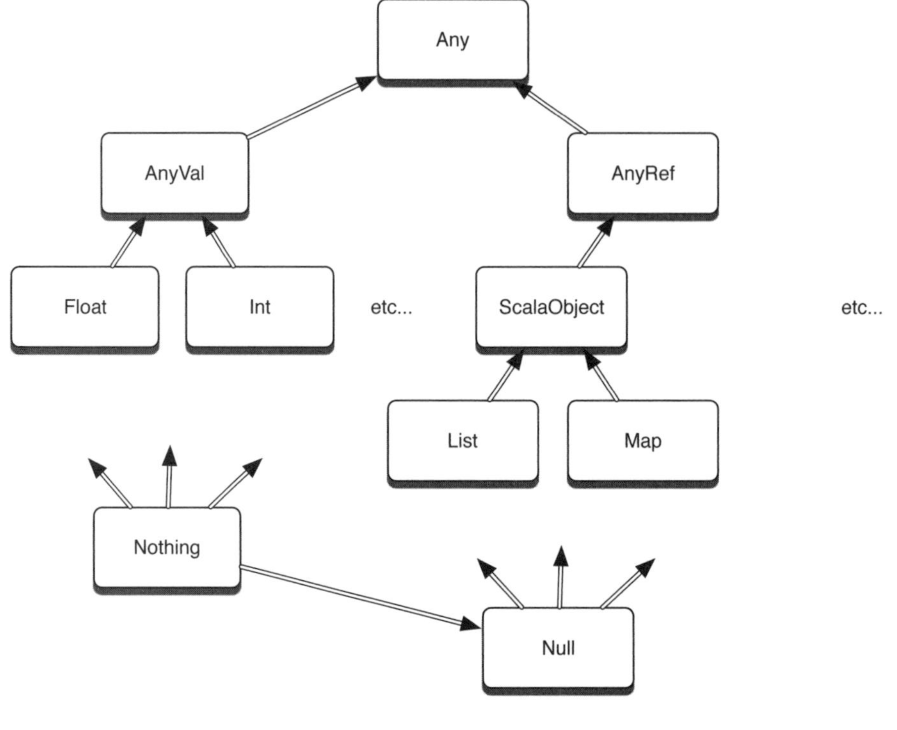

Figure 5.1: ANY AND NOTHING

you can't dereference it like Null. For example, a method that throws an Exception has the return type Nothing, meaning no value at all.

Keep those rules in the back of your mind, and you'll be fine. Now, you're ready to do a little bit more with collections using higher-order functions.

Collections and Functions

As we start on languages that have a stronger functional foundation, I want to formalize some of the concepts we've been working with all along. The first such concept is *higher-order functions*.

As with Ruby and Io, Scala collections get a whole lot more interesting with higher-order functions. Just as Ruby used each and Io used foreach, Scala will let you pass functions into foreach. The underlying concept that you've been using all along is the higher-order function. In layman's terms, a higher-order function is one that produces or consumes functions. More specifically, a higher-order function is one that takes other functions as input parameters or returns functions as output. Composing functions that use other functions in this way is a critical concept for the functional family of languages and one that will shape the way you code in other languages as well.

Scala has powerful support for higher-order functions. We don't have time to look at some of the advanced topics such as partially applied functions or currying, but we will learn to pass simple functions, often called *code blocks*, as parameters into collections. You can take a function and assign it to any variable or parameter. You can pass them into functions and return them from functions. We're going to focus on anonymous functions as input parameters to a few of the more interesting methods on collections.

foreach

The first function we're going to examine is foreach, the iteration workhorse in Scala. As with Io, the foreach method on a collection takes a code block as a parameter. In Scala, you'll express that code block in the form variableName => yourCode like this:

```
scala> val list = List("frodo", "samwise", "pippin")
list: List[java.lang.String] = List(frodo, samwise, pippin)

scala> list.foreach(hobbit => println(hobbit))
frodo
samwise
pippin
```

hobbit => println(hobbit) is an anonymous function, meaning a function without a name. The declaration has the arguments to the left of the =>, and the code is to the right. foreach calls the anonymous function, passing in each element of the list as an input parameter. As you might have guessed, you can use the same technique for sets and maps too, though the order won't be guaranteed:

```
val hobbits = Set("frodo", "samwise", "pippin")
hobbits: scala.collection.immutable.Set[java.lang.String] =
  Set(frodo, samwise, pippin)

scala> hobbits.foreach(hobbit => println(hobbit))
frodo
samwise
pippin

scala> val hobbits = Map("frodo" -> "hobbit",
  "samwise" -> "hobbit", "pippin" -> "hobbit")
```

```
hobbits: scala.collection.immutable.Map[java.lang.String,java.lang.String] =
  Map(frodo -> hobbit, samwise -> hobbit, pippin -> hobbit)

scala> hobbits.foreach(hobbit => println(hobbit))
(frodo,hobbit)
(samwise,hobbit)
(pippin,hobbit)
```

Of course, maps will return tuples instead of elements. As you recall, you can access either end of the tuple, like this:

```
scala> hobbits.foreach(hobbit => println(hobbit._1))
frodo
samwise
pippin

scala> hobbits.foreach(hobbit => println(hobbit._2))
hobbit
hobbit
hobbit
```

With these anonymous functions, you can do far more than just iterate. I'm going to walk you through some basics and then a few of the other interesting ways Scala uses functions in conjunction with collections.

More List Methods

I'm going to take a brief diversion to introduce a few more methods on List. These basic methods provide the features you'll need to do manual iteration or recursion over lists. First, here are the methods to test for the empty state or check the size:

```
scala> list
res23: List[java.lang.String] = List(frodo, samwise, pippin)

scala> list.isEmpty
res24: Boolean = false

scala> Nil.isEmpty
res25: Boolean = true

scala> list.length
res27: Int = 3

scala> list.size
res28: Int = 3
```

Notice that you can check the size of a list with both length and size. Also, remember that the implementation of Nil is an empty list. As with Prolog, it's useful to be able to grab the head and tail of a list for recursion.

```
scala> list.head
res34: java.lang.String = frodo

scala> list.tail
res35: List[java.lang.String] = List(samwise, pippin)

scala> list.last
res36: java.lang.String = pippin

scala> list.init
res37: List[java.lang.String] = List(frodo, samwise)
```

There's a surprise. You can use head and tail to recurse head first, or last and init to recurse tail first. We'll do a little more with recursion later. Let's wrap up the basics with a few interesting convenience methods:

```
scala> list.reverse
res29: List[java.lang.String] = List(pippin, samwise, frodo)

scala> list.drop(1)
res30: List[java.lang.String] = List(samwise, pippin)

scala> list
res31: List[java.lang.String] = List(frodo, samwise, pippin)

scala> list.drop(2)
res32: List[java.lang.String] = List(pippin)
```

These do just about what you'd expect. reverse returns the list with inverted ordering, and drop(n) returns the list with the first n elements removed, without modifying the original list.

count, map, filter, and Others

As with Ruby, Scala has many other functions that manipulate lists in various ways. You can filter the list to match a given condition, sort a list using whatever criteria you want, create other lists using each element as an input, and create aggregate values:

```
scala> val words = List("peg", "al", "bud", "kelly")
words: List[java.lang.String] = List(peg, al, bud, kelly)

scala> words.count(word => word.size > 2)
res43: Int = 3

scala> words.filter(word => word.size > 2)
res44: List[java.lang.String] = List(peg, bud, kelly)

scala> words.map(word => word.size)
res45: List[Int] = List(3, 2, 3, 5)
```

```
scala> words.forall(word => word.size > 1)
res46: Boolean = true

scala> words.exists(word => word.size > 4)
res47: Boolean = true

scala> words.exists(word => word.size > 5)
res48: Boolean = false
```

We start with a Scala list. Then, we count all the words with a size greater than two. count will call the code block word => word.size > 2, evaluating the expression word.size > 2 for each element in the list. The count method counts all the true expressions.

In the same way, words.filter(word => word.size > 2) returns a list of all words that have a size greater than two, much like Ruby's select. Using the same pattern, map builds a list of the sizes of all the words in the list, forall returns true if the code block returns true for all items in the set, and exists returns true if the code block returns true for any item in the set.

Sometimes, you can generalize a feature using code blocks to make something more powerful. For example, you may want to sort in the traditional way:

```
scala> words.sort((s, t) => s.charAt(0).toLowerCase < t.charAt(0).toLowerCase)
res49: List[java.lang.String] = List(al, bud, kelly, peg)
```

This code uses a code block that takes two parameters, s and t. Using sort,[3] you can compare the two arguments any way you want. In the previous code, we convert the characters to lowercase[4] and compare them. That will yield a case-insensitive search. We can also use the same method to sort the list by the size of the words:

```
scala> words.sort((s, t) => s.size < t.size)
res50: List[java.lang.String] = List(al, bud, peg, kelly)
```

By using a code block, we can sort[5] based on any policy that we want. Let's take a look at a more complex example, foldLeft.

foldLeft

The foldLeft method in Scala is much like the inject method in Ruby. You'll supply an initial value and a code block. foldLeft will pass to the

3. In version 2.8.0, sort is deprecated. Use sortWith instead.
4. In version 2.8.0, toLowerCase is deprecated. Use toLower instead.
5. In version 2.8.0, sort is deprecated. Use sortWith instead.

code block each element of the array and another value. The second value is either the initial value (for the first invocation) or the result from the code block (for subsequent invocations). There are two versions of the method. The first version, /:, is an operator with initialValue /: codeBlock. Here's the method in action:

```
scala> val list = List(1, 2, 3)
list: List[Int] = List(1, 2, 3)

scala> val sum = (0 /: list) {(sum, i) => sum + i}
sum: Int = 6
```

We walked through this sequence for Ruby, but it may help you to see it again. Here's how it works:

- We invoke the operator with a value and a code block. The code block takes two arguments, sum and i.

- Initially, /: takes the initial value, 0, and the first element of list, 1, and passes them into the code block. sum is 0, i is 1, and the result of 0 + 1 is 1.

- Next, /: takes 1, the result returned from the code block, and folds it back into the calculation as sum. So, sum is 1; i is the next element of list, or 2; and the result of the code block is 3.

- Finally, /: takes 3, the result returned from the code block, and folds it back into the calculation as sum. So, sum is 3; i is the next element of list, or 3; and sum + i is 6.

The syntax of the other version of foldLeft will seem strange to you. It uses a concept called *currying*. Functional languages use currying to transform a function with multiple parameters to several functions with their own parameter lists. We'll see more currying in Chapter 8, *Haskell*, on page 255. Just understand that what's going on under the covers is a composition of functions rather than a single function. Though the mechanics and syntax are different, the result is exactly the same:

```
scala> val list = List(1, 2, 3)
list: List[Int] = List(1, 2, 3)

scala> list.foldLeft(0)((sum, value) => sum + value)
res54: Int = 6
```

Notice that the function call list.foldLeft(0)((sum, value) => sum + value) has two parameter lists. That's the currying concept that I mentioned earlier. You'll see versions of this method with all the rest of the languages in this book.

What We Learned in Day 2

Day 1 was encumbered with working through the object-oriented features that you already know. Day 2 introduced Scala's primary reason for being: functional programming.

We started with a basic function. Scala has flexible syntax with function definitions. The compiler can often infer the return type, the function body has one-line and code-block forms, and the parameter list can vary.

Next, we looked at various collections. Scala supports three: lists, maps, and sets. A set is a collection of objects. A list is an ordered collection. Finally, maps are key-value pairs. As with Ruby, you saw the powerful combinations of code blocks and collections of various kinds. We looked at some collection APIs that are indicative of functional programming paradigms.

For lists, we could also use Lisp-style head and tail methods, just like Prolog, to return the first element of the list or the rest. We also used count, empty, and first methods for obvious purposes. But the most powerful methods took function blocks.

We iterated with foreach and used filter to selectively return various elements of the lists. We also learned to use foldLeft to accumulate results as we iterated through a collection to do things such as keeping a running total.

Much of functional programming is learning to manipulate collections with higher-level constructs instead of Java-style iteration. We will put these skills through their paces in day 3, when we will learn to use concurrency, do some XML, and work a simple practical example. Stay tuned.

Day 2 Self-Study

Now that we've gotten deeper into Scala, you're starting to see some of its functional aspects. Whenever you deal with functions, the collections are a great place to start. These exercises will let you use some of the collections, as well as some functions.

Find:

- A discussion on how to use Scala files
- What makes a closure different from a code block

Do:

- Use foldLeft to compute the total size of a list of strings.
- Write a Censor trait with a method that will replace the curse words *Shoot* and *Darn* with *Pucky* and *Beans* alternatives. Use a map to store the curse words and their alternatives.
- Load the curse words and alternatives from a file.

5.4 Day 3: Cutting Through the Fluff

Just before the climax of *Edward Scissorhands*, Edward learns to wield his scissors as an artist in everyday life. He molds shrubs into dinosaurs, crafts spectacular hair with the effortless skill of Vidal Sassoon, and even carves the family roast. With Scala, we've encountered some awkward moments, but when this language feels right, it's borderline spectacular. Hard things, like XML and concurrency, become almost routine. Let's take a look.

XML

Modern programming problems meet Extensible Markup Language (XML) with increasing regularity. Scala takes the dramatic step of elevating XML to a first-class programming construct of the language. You can express XML just as easily as you do any string:

```
scala> val movies =
     | <movies>
     |     <movie genre="action">Pirates of the Caribbean</movie>
     |     <movie genre="fairytale">Edward Scissorhands</movie>
     | </movies>
movies: scala.xml.Elem =
<movies>
           <movie genre="action">Pirates of the Caribbean</movie>
           <movie genre="fairytale">Edward Scissorhands</movie>
       </movies>
```

After you've defined the movies variable with XML, you can access different elements directly.

For example, to see all the inner text, you would simply type this:

```
scala> movies.text
res1: String =

            Pirates of the Caribbean
            Edward Scissorhands
```

You see all the inner text from the previous example. But we're not limited to working with the whole block at once. We can be more selective. Scala builds in a query language that's much like XPath, an XML search language. But since the // keyword in Scala is a comment, Scala will use \ and \\. To search the top-level nodes, you'd use one backslash, like this:

```
scala> val movieNodes = movies \ "movie"
movieNodes: scala.xml.NodeSeq =
  <movie genre="action">Pirates of the Caribbean</movie>
  <movie genre="fairytale">Edward Scissorhands</movie>
```

In that search, we looked for XML movie elements. You can find individual nodes by index:

```
scala> movieNodes(0)
res3: scala.xml.Node = <movie genre="action">Pirates of the Caribbean</movie>
```

We just found element number zero, or Pirates of the Caribbean. You can also look for attributes of individual XML nodes by using the @ symbol. For example, to find the genre attribute of the first element in the document, we'd do this search:

```
scala> movieNodes(0) \ "@genre"
res4: scala.xml.NodeSeq = action
```

This example just scratches the surface with what you can do, but you get the idea. If we mix in Prolog-style pattern matching, things get a little more exciting. Next, we'll walk through an example of pattern matching with simple strings.

Pattern Matching

Pattern matching lets you conditionally execute code based on some piece of data. Scala will use pattern matching often, such as when you parse XML or pass messages between threads.

Here's the simplest form of pattern matching:

scala/chores.scala

```
def doChore(chore: String): String = chore match {
    case "clean dishes" => "scrub, dry"
    case "cook dinner" => "chop, sizzle"
    case _ => "whine, complain"
  }
  println(doChore("clean dishes"))
  println(doChore("mow lawn"))
```

We define two chores, clean dishes and cook dinner. Next to each chore, we have a code block. In this case, the code blocks simply return strings. The last chore we define is _, a wildcard. Scala executes the code block associated with the first matching chore, returning "whine, complain" if neither chore matches, like this:

```
>> scala chores.scala
scrub, dry
whine, complain
```

Guards

Pattern matching has some embellishments too. In Prolog, the pattern matching often had associated conditions. To implement a factorial in Scala, we specify a condition in a guard for each match statement:

scala/factorial.scala

```
def factorial(n: Int): Int = n match {
    case 0 => 1
    case x if x > 0 => factorial(n - 1) * n
}

println(factorial(3))
println(factorial(0))
```

The first pattern match is a 0, but the second guard has the form case x if x > 0. It matches any x for x > 0. You can specify a wide variety of conditions in this way. Pattern matching can also match regular expressions and types. You'll see an example later that defines empty classes and uses them as messages in our concurrency examples later.

Regular Expressions

Scala has first-class regular expressions. The .r method on a string can translate any string to a regular expression. On the next page is an example of a regular expression that can match uppercase or lowercase F at the beginning of a string.

```
scala> val reg = """^(F|f)\w*""".r
reg: scala.util.matching.Regex = ^(F|f)\w*

scala> println(reg.findFirstIn("Fantastic"))
Some(Fantastic)

scala> println(reg.findFirstIn("not Fantastic"))
None
```

We start with a simple string. We use the """ delimited form of a string, allowing multiline string and eliminating evaluation. The .r method converts the string to a regular expression. We then use the method findFirstIn to find the first occurrence.

```
scala> val reg = "the".r
reg: scala.util.matching.Regex = the

scala> reg.findAllIn("the way the scissors trim the hair and the shrubs")
res9: scala.util.matching.Regex.MatchIterator = non-empty iterator
```

In this example, we build a regular expression and use the findAllIn method to find all occurrences of the word the in the string "the way the scissors trim the hair and the shrubs". If we wanted, we could iterate through the entire list of matches with foreach. That's really all there is to it. You can match with regular expressions just as you would use a string.

XML with Matching

An interesting combination in Scala is the XML syntax in combination with pattern matching. You can go through an XML file and conditionally execute code based on the various XML elements that come back. For example, consider the following XML movies file:

scala/movies.scala

```
val movies = <movies>
    <movie>The Incredibles</movie>
    <movie>WALL E</movie>
    <short>Jack Jack Attack</short>
    <short>Geri's Game</short>
</movies>

(movies \ "_").foreach { movie =>
    movie match {
        case <movie>{movieName}</movie> => println(movieName)
        case <short>{shortName}</short> => println(shortName + " (short)")
    }
}
```

It queries for all nodes in the tree. Then, it uses pattern matching to match shorts and movies. I like the way Scala makes the most common tasks trivial by working in XML syntax, pattern matching, and the XQuery-like language. The result is almost effortless.

So, that's a basic tour of pattern matching. You'll see it in practice in the concurrency section next.

Concurrency

One of the most important aspects of Scala is the way it handles concurrency. The primary constructs are actors and message passing. Actors have pools of threads and queues. When you send a message to an actor (using the ! operator), you place an object on its queue. The actor reads the message and takes action. Often, the actor uses a pattern matcher to detect the message and perform the appropriate message. Consider the kids program:

scala/kids.scala

```
import scala.actors._
import scala.actors.Actor._

case object Poke
case object Feed

class Kid() extends Actor {
  def act() {
    loop {
      react {
        case Poke => {
          println("Ow...")
          println("Quit it...")
        }
        case Feed => {
          println("Gurgle...")
          println("Burp...")
        }
      }
    }
  }
}

val bart = new Kid().start
val lisa = new Kid().start
println("Ready to poke and feed...")
bart ! Poke
lisa ! Poke
bart ! Feed
lisa ! Feed
```

In this program, we create two empty, trivial singletons called Poke and Feed. They don't do anything. They simply serve as messages. The meat of the program is the Kid class. Kid is an actor, meaning it will run from a pool of threads and get messages in a queue. It will process each message and move on to the next. We start a simple loop. Within that is a react construct. react receives an actor's messages. The pattern match lets us match the appropriate message, which will always be Poke or Feed.

The rest of the script creates a couple of kids and manipulates them by sending them Poke or Feed messages. You can run it like this:

```
batate$ scala code/scala/kids.scala
Ready to poke and feed...
Ow...
Quit it...
Ow...
Quit it...
Gurgle...
Burp...
Gurgle...
Burp...

batate$ scala code/scala/kids.scala
Ready to poke and feed...
Ow...
Quit it...
Gurgle...
Burp...
Ow...
Quit it...
Gurgle...
Burp...
```

I run the application a couple of times to show that it is actually concurrent. Notice that the order is different. With actors, you can also react with a timeout (reactWithin), which will time out if you don't receive the message within the specified time. Additionally, you can use receive (which blocks a thread) and receiveWithin (which blocks a thread with a timeout).

Concurrency in Action

Since there's only a limited market for simulated Simpsons, let's do something a little more robust. In this application called sizer, we're computing the size of web pages. We hit a few pages and then compute the size. Since there's a lot of waiting time, we would like to get all of the pages concurrently using actors. Take a look at the overall program, and then we'll look at some individual sections:

scala/sizer.scala

```
import scala.io._
import scala.actors._
import Actor._

object PageLoader {
 def getPageSize(url : String) = Source.fromURL(url).mkString.length
}

val urls = List("http://www.amazon.com/",
               "http://www.twitter.com/",
               "http://www.google.com/",
               "http://www.cnn.com/" )

def timeMethod(method: () => Unit) = {
 val start = System.nanoTime
 method()
 val end = System.nanoTime
 println("Method took " + (end - start)/1000000000.0 + " seconds.")
}

def getPageSizeSequentially() = {
 for(url <- urls) {
   println("Size for " + url + ": " + PageLoader.getPageSize(url))
 }
}

def getPageSizeConcurrently() = {
 val caller = self

 for(url <- urls) {
   actor { caller ! (url, PageLoader.getPageSize(url)) }
 }

 for(i <- 1 to urls.size) {
   receive {
     case (url, size) =>
       println("Size for " + url + ": " + size)
   }
 }
}

println("Sequential run:")
timeMethod { getPageSizeSequentially }

println("Concurrent run")
timeMethod { getPageSizeConcurrently }
```

So, let's start at the top. We do a few basic imports to load the libraries for actors and io so we can do concurrency and HTTP requests. Next, we will compute the size of a page, given a URL:

```
object PageLoader {
 def getPageSize(url : String) = Source.fromURL(url).mkString.length
}
```

Next, we create a val with a few URLs. After that, we build a method to time each web request:

```
def timeMethod(method: () => Unit) = {
 val start = System.nanoTime
 method()
 val end = System.nanoTime
 println("Method took " + (end - start)/1000000000.0 + " seconds.")
}
```

Then, we do the web requests with two different methods. The first is sequentially, where we iterate through each request in a forEach loop.

```
def getPageSizeSequentially() = {
 for(url <- urls) {
   println("Size for " + url + ": " + PageLoader.getPageSize(url))
 }
}
```

Here's the method to do things asynchronously:

```
def getPageSizeConcurrently() = {
 val caller = self

 for(url <- urls) {
   actor { caller ! (url, PageLoader.getPageSize(url)) }
 }

 for(i <- 1 to urls.size) {
   receive {
     case (url, size) =>
       println("Size for " + url + ": " + size)
   }
 }
}
```

In this actor, we know we'll be receiving a fixed set of messages. Within a forEach loop, we send four asynchronous requests. This happens more or less instantly. Next, we simply receive four messages with receive. This method is where the real work happens. Finally, we're ready to run the script that invokes the test:

```
println("Sequential run:")
timeMethod { getPageSizeSequentially }
```

```
println("Concurrent run")
timeMethod { getPageSizeConcurrently }
```

And here's the output:

```
>> scala sizer.scala
Sequential run:
Size for http://www.amazon.com/: 81002
Size for http://www.twitter.com/: 43640
Size for http://www.google.com/: 8076
Size for http://www.cnn.com/: 100739
Method took 6.707612 seconds.
Concurrent run
Size for http://www.google.com/: 8076
Size for http://www.cnn.com/: 100739
Size for http://www.amazon.com/: 84600
Size for http://www.twitter.com/: 44158
Method took 3.969936 seconds.
```

As expected, the concurrent loop is faster. That's an overview of an interesting problem in Scala. Let's review what we learned.

What We Learned in Day 3

What day 3 lacked in size, it made up in intensity. We built a couple of different concurrent programs and worked in direct XML processing, distributed message passing with actors, pattern matching, and regular expressions.

Over the course of the chapter, we learned four fundamental constructs that built on one another. First, we learned to use XML directly in Scala. We could query for individual elements or attributes using an XQuery-like syntax.

We then introduced Scala's version of pattern matching. At first, it looked like a simple case statement, but as we introduced guards, types, and regular expressions, their power became readily apparent.

Next, we shifted to concurrency. We used the actor concept. Actors are objects built for concurrency. They usually have a loop statement wrapped around a react or receive method, which does the dirty work of receiving queued messages to the object. Finally, we had an inner pattern match. We used raw classes as messages. They are small, light, robust, and easy to manipulate. If we needed parameters within the message, we could just add naked attributes to our class definitions, as we did with the URL within the sizer application.

Like all of the languages in this book, Scala is far more robust than you've seen here. The interaction with Java classes is far deeper than I've shown you here, and I've merely scratched the surface on complex concepts such as currying. But you have a good foundation should you choose to explore further.

Day 3 Self-Study

So, now you've seen some of the advanced features Scala has to offer. Now, you can try to put Scala through its paces yourself. As always, these exercises are more demanding.

Find.

- For the sizer program, what would happen if you did not create a new actor for each link you wanted to follow? What would happen to the performance of the application?

Do:

- Take the sizer application and add a message to count the number of links on the page.
- Bonus problem: Make the sizer follow the links on a given page, and load them as well. For example, a sizer for "google.com" would compute the size for Google and all of the pages it links to.

5.5 Wrapping Up Scala

We've covered Scala more exhaustively than the other languages so far because Scala strongly supports two programming paradigms. The object-oriented features firmly position Scala as a Java alternative. Unlike Ruby and Io, Scala has a static typing strategy. Syntactically, Scala borrows many elements from Java, including curly braces and constructor usage.

Scala also offers strong support for functional concepts and immutable variables. The language has a strong focus on concurrency and XML, fitting a wide variety of enterprise applications currently implemented in the Java language.

Scala's functional capabilities go beyond what I've covered in this chapter. I haven't covered constructs such as currying, full closures, multiple parameter lists, or exception processing, but they are all worthy concepts that add to the power and flexibility of Scala.

Let's look at some of Scala's core strengths and weaknesses.

Core Strengths

Most of Scala's strengths are centered around an advanced programming paradigm that integrates well with the Java environment and some core well-designed features. In particular, actors, pattern matching, and the XML integration are important and well-designed. Let's get right to the list.

Concurrency

Scala's treatment of concurrency represents a significant advance in concurrent programming. The actor model and the thread pool are welcome improvements, and the ability to design applications without mutable state is absolutely huge.

The actor paradigm that you've seen in Io and now Scala is easy to understand for developers and well studied by the academic community. Both Java and Ruby could use some improvement in this area.

The concurrency model is only part of the story. When objects share state, you must strive for immutable values. Io and Scala get this at least partially right, allowing mutable state but also offering libraries and keywords that support immutability. Immutability is the single most important thing you can do to improve code design for concurrency.

Finally, the message-passing syntax you see in Scala is much like you will see in the next chapter on Erlang. It is a significant improvement over the standard Java threading libraries.

Evolution of Legacy Java

Scala starts with a strong, built-in user base: the Java community. Scala applications can use Java libraries directly, and through the use of code generation of proxy objects when necessary, the interoperability is excellent. Inferred typing is a much-needed advance over the archaic Java typing system. The best way to establish a new programming community is to fully embrace an existing one. Scala does a good job offering a more concise Java, and that idea has value.

Scala also offers new features to the Java community. Code blocks are a first-class language construct, and they work well with the core collection libraries. Scala also offers first-class mixins in the form of traits. Pattern matching is also a significant improvement. With these and other features, Java developers can have an advanced programming language without even touching the more advanced functional paradigms.

Throw in the functional constructs, and you can have significantly improved applications. Scala applications will usually have a fraction of the total lines of code than an equivalent Java app would have, and that's extremely important. A better programming language should allow you to express more complex ideas with fewer lines of code, with minimal overhead. Scala delivers on this promise.

Domain-Specific Languages

Scala's flexible syntax and operator overloading make it an ideal language for developing Ruby-style domain-specific languages. Remember, as in Ruby, operators are simply method declarations, and you can override them in most cases. Additionally, optional spaces, periods, and semicolons let the syntax take many different forms. Together with robust mixins, these are the tools that a DSL developer seeks.

XML

Scala has integrated XML support. The pattern matching makes parsing blocks of disparate XML structures easy to use. The integration of the XPath syntax for diving deep into complex XML leads to simple and readable code. This advance is welcome and important, especially to the XML-heavy Java community.

Bridging

The emergence of each new programming paradigm needs a bridge. Scala is well-positioned to be that bridge. The functional programming model is important because it handles concurrency well, and evolving processor designs are much more concurrent. Scala offers an iterative way to take developers there.

Weaknesses

Although I like many of the Scala ideas in concept, I find the syntax demanding and academic. Although syntax is a matter of taste, Scala does have a higher burden than most other languages, at least to these old eyes. I also recognize that some of the compromises that make Scala such an effective bridge also will undercut its value. I only see three weaknesses, but they are big ones.

Static Typing

Static typing is a natural fit for functional programming languages, but Java-style static typing for object-oriented systems is a deal with the devil. Sometimes, you must satisfy a compiler's requirements by putting more of a burden on your developers. With static typing, the burden is much more than you ever expect. The impact on code, syntax, and program design are profound. As I learned Scala, I found myself in a fairly constant battle with the language syntax and in program design. Traits eased this burden somewhat, but I found the trade-off between programmer flexibility and compile-time checking wanting.

Later in this book, you'll see what a purely functional strong, static type system looks like with Haskell. Without the burden of two programming paradigms, the type system becomes much more fluid and productive, providing better support for polymorphism and requiring less rigor from programmers for similar benefit.

Syntax

I do find Scala's syntax to be a little academic and hard on the eyes. I hesitate to put this in print because syntax can be so subjective, but some elements are a little baffling. Sometimes, Scala keeps Java conventions, such as constructors. You'd use `new Person` rather than `Person.new`. At other times, Scala introduces a new convention, as with argument types. In Java, you'd use `setName(String name)` versus Scala's `setName(name: String)`. Return types shift to the end of the method declaration versus the beginning, as they are with Java. These little differences keep me thinking about syntax rather than code. The problem is that moving back and forth between Scala and Java will take more effort than it should.

Mutability

When you build a bridge language, you must factor in compromises. One significant compromise in Scala is the introduction of mutability. With `var`, Scala opens Pandora's box in some ways, because the mutable state allows a wide variety of concurrency bugs. But such compromises are unavoidable if you want to bring home the special kid who lived in the house on the hill.

Final Thoughts

All in all, my experience with Scala was mixed. The static typing threw me. At the same time, the Java developer in me greatly appreciates the improved concurrency models, inferred typing, and XML. Scala represents a significant jump in the state of the art.

I would use Scala to improve my productivity if I had a significant investment in Java programs or programmers. I'd also consider Scala for an application that has significant scalability requirements that would require concurrency. Commercially, this Frankenstein has a good shot because it represents a bridge and fully embraces a significant programming community.

Do you hear that, Mr. Anderson? That is the sound of inevitability.

► Agent Smith

Chapter 6

Erlang

Few languages have the mystique of Erlang, the concurrency language that makes hard things easy and easy things hard. Its virtual machine, called *BEAM*, is rivaled only by the Java virtual machine for robust enterprise deployment. You could call it efficient, even brutally so, but Erlang's syntax lacks the beauty and simplicity of, say, a Ruby. Think Agent Smith of *The Matrix*.[1]

The Matrix was a 1999 science-fiction classic that painted our current world as a virtual world, created and maintained with computers, as an illusion. Agent Smith was an artificial intelligence program in the matrix that had an amazing ability to take any form and bend the rules of reality to be in many places at once. He was unavoidable.

6.1 Introducing Erlang

The name is strange, but the acronym for Ericsson Language that shares a name with a Danish mathematician somehow fits. Agner Karup Erlang was a huge name in the math behind telephone network analysis.

In 1986, Joe Armstrong developed the first version at Ericsson, continuing to develop and polish it through the last half of the decade. Through the 1990s, it grew in fits and starts and gained still more traction in the 2000s. It is the language behind CouchDB and SimpleDB, popular databases for cloud-based computing. Erlang also powers Facebook's chat. The buzz for Erlang is growing steadily because it

1. *The Matrix*. DVD. Directed by Andy Wachowski, Lana Wachowski. 1999; Burbank, CA: Warner Home Video, 2007.

provides what many other languages can't: scalable concurrency and reliability.

Built for Concurrency

Erlang is a product of years of research from Ericsson to develop near-real-time fault-tolerant distributed applications for telecom applications. The systems often could not be taken down for maintenance, and software development was prohibitively expensive. Ericsson studied programming languages through the 1980s and found that, for one reason or another, existing languages were inadequate for their needs. These requirements eventually led to the development of an entirely new language.

Erlang is a functional language—one with many reliability features cooked in. Erlang can support insanely reliable systems. You can't take a phone switch down for maintenance, and you don't have to take Erlang down to replace entire modules. Some of its applications have run for years without ever coming down for maintenance. But the key Erlang capability is concurrency.

Concurrency experts do not always agree on the best approaches. One common debate is whether threads or processes lead to better concurrency. Many threads make up a process. Processes have their own resources; threads have their own execution path but share resources with other threads in the same process. Usually, a thread is lighter weight than a process, though implementations vary.

No Threading

Many languages, like Java and C, take a threading approach to concurrency. Threads take fewer resources, so theoretically, you should be able to get better performance from them. The downside to threads is that shared resources can lead to complex, buggy implementations and the need for locks that form bottlenecks. To coordinate control between two applications sharing resources, threading systems require semaphores, or operating system level locks. Erlang takes a different approach. It tries to make processes as lightweight as possible.

Lightweight Processes

Rather than wade through the quagmire of shared resources and resource bottlenecks, Erlang embraces the philosophy of lightweight processes. Erlang's creators spent effort to simplify the creation, management, and communication within applications with many processes.

Distributed message passing is a basic language-level construct, eliminating the need for locking and improving concurrency.

Like Io, Armstrong's creation uses actors for concurrency, so message passing is a critical concept. You'll recognize Scala's message passing syntax, which is similar to Erlang's message passing. In Scala, an actor represents an object, backed by a thread pool. In Erlang, an actor represents a lightweight process. The actor reads inbound messages from a queue and uses pattern matching to decide how to process it.

Reliability

Erlang does have traditional error checking, but in a traditional application, you'll see far less error handling than you would in a traditional fault-tolerant application. The Erlang mantra is "Let it crash." Since Erlang makes it easy to monitor the death of a process, killing related processes and starting new ones are trivial exercises.

You can also hot-swap code, meaning you can replace pieces of your application without stopping your code. This capability allows far simpler maintenance strategies than similar distributed applications. Erlang combines the robust "Let it crash" error strategies with hot-swapping and lightweight processes that you can start with minimal overhead. It's easy to see how some applications run for years at a time without downtime.

So, the Erlang concurrency story is compelling. The important primitives—message passing, spawning a process, monitoring a process—are all there. The processes that you spawn are lightweight, so you don't have to worry about constrained resources in this area. The language is heavily slanted to remove side effects and mutability, and monitoring the death of a process is simple, even trivial. The combined package is compelling.

Interview with Dr. Joe Armstrong

Through writing this book, I've had the chance to meet some of the people who I respect the most, at least, through email. Dr. Joe Armstrong, creator of Erlang and author of *Programming Erlang: Software for a Concurrent World* [Arm07], is high on that list for me. I finally got to have several conversations with Erlang's first implementor, who hails from Stockholm, Sweden.

Bruce: *Why did you write Erlang?*

Dr. Armstrong: *By accident. I didn't set out to invent a new programming language. At the time we wanted to find a better way of writing the control software for a telephone exchange. I started fiddling around with Prolog. Prolog was fantastic but didn't do exactly what I wanted. So, I started messing around with Prolog. I thought, "I wonder what would happen if I changed the way Prolog does things?" So, I wrote a Prolog meta-interpreter that added parallel processes to Prolog, and then I added error handling mechanisms, and so on. After a while, this set of changes to Prolog acquired a name, Erlang, and a new language was born. Then more people joined the project, the language grew, we figured out how to compile it, we added more stuff and got some more users, and ....*

Bruce: *What do you like about it the most?*

Dr. Armstrong: *The error handling and on-the-fly code upgrade mechanisms and the bit-level pattern matching. Error handling is one of the least understood parts of the language and the part where it most differs from other languages. The whole notion of "nondefensive" programming and "Let It Crash," which is the mantra of Erlang programming, is completely the opposite of conventional practice, but it leads to really short and beautiful programs.*

Bruce: *What is a feature you most would want to change, if you could do it all over again? (Alternatively, you could answer, what are the greatest limitations of Erlang?)*

Dr. Armstrong: *This is a difficult question; I'd probably give different answers on different days of the week. It would be nice to add mobility to the language so we could send computations over the Net. We can do this in library code, but it's not supported in the language. Right now I think it would be really nice to go back to the roots of Erlang and add Prolog-like predicate logic to the language, a kind of new mixture of predicate logic plus message passing.*

Then there are a number of small changes that are desirable, adding hash maps, higher-order modules, and so on.

If I were to do it all over again, I'd probably give a lot more thought to how we fit things together, such as how we run big projects with lots of code—how we manage versions of code, how we find things, how things evolve. When lots of code has been written, the programmer's job changes from writing fresh code to finding and integrating existing code, so finding things and fitting things together becomes increasingly important. It would be nice to integrate ideas from things like GIT and Mercurial and type systems into the language itself so that we could understand how code evolves in a controlled manner.

Bruce: *What's the most surprising place you've ever seen Erlang used in production?*

Dr. Armstrong: *Well, I wasn't actually surprised since I knew this was going to happen. When I upgraded my version of Ubuntu to Karmic Koala, I found a rather well-hidden Erlang ticking away in the background. This was to support CouchDB, which was also running live on my machine. This kind of sneaked in Erlang under the radar to 10 million machines.*

In this chapter, we're going to cover some Erlang basics. Then, we'll put Erlang through its paces as a functional language. Finally, we'll spend some time with concurrency and some cool reliability features. Yes, friends, reliability can be cool.

6.2 Day 1: Appearing Human

Agent Smith is as a program that kills other programs, or simulated people, that disrupt the simulated reality known as the Matrix. The most basic trait that makes him dangerous is his ability to appear human. In this section, we're going to look at Erlang's ability to build general-purpose applications. I'm going to try my best to give you "normal." It's not going to be easy.

If you started this book as a pure object-oriented programmer, you may struggle a little bit, but don't fight it. You've already seen code blocks in Ruby, actors in Io, pattern matching in Prolog, and distributed message passing in Scala. These are foundational principles in Erlang. This chapter will start with another important concept. Erlang is the first of our functional languages. (Scala is a hybrid functional/object-oriented language.) To you, that means the following:

- Your programs are going to be built entirely out of functions, with no objects anywhere.
- Those functions will usually return the same values, given the same inputs.

- Those functions will not usually have side effects, meaning they will not modify program state.
- You will only be able to assign any variable once.

Living by the first rule is mildly challenging. Living by the next three can knock you down, at least for a little while. Know that you can learn to code this way, and the result will be programs that are built from the inside out for concurrency. When you remove mutable state from the equation, concurrency gets dramatically simpler.

If you paid close attention, you caught the word *usually* in the second and third rules. Erlang is not a pure functional language; it does allow a few exceptions. Haskell is the only pure functional language in this book. But you will get a strong flavor of functional-style programming, and you will code to these rules more often than not.

Getting Started

I'm working with Erlang version R13B02, but the basic stuff in this chapter should work OK on any reasonable version. You'll get to the Erlang shell by typing erl (werl on some Windows systems) at the command line, like this:

```
batate$ erl
Erlang (BEAM) emulator version 5.4.13 [source]

Eshell V5.4.13  (abort with ^G)
1>
```

We'll do most of our work there, early on, as with other chapters. Like Java, Erlang is a compiled language. You'll compile a file with c(filename). (you need the period at the end). You can break out of the console, or a loop, with Control+C. Let's get started.

Comments, Variables, and Expressions

Let's get some of the basic syntax out of the way. Crack open the console, and type the following:

```
1> % This is a comment
```

That was simple enough. Comments start with a % and eat everything until the end of a line. Erlang parses a comment as a single space.

```
1> 2 + 2.
4
2> 2 + 2.0.
4.0
```

```
3> "string".
"string"
```

Each statement ends in a period. These are some of the basic types: strings, integers, and floats. Now, for a list:

```
4> [1, 2, 3].
[1,2,3]
```

As with the Prolog family of languages, lists are in square brackets. Here's a little surprise:

```
4> [72, 97, 32, 72, 97, 32, 72, 97].
"Ha Ha Ha"
```

So, a String is really a List, and Agent Smith just laughed at your mamma. Oh, those social skills. 2 + 2.0 tells us that Erlang does some basic type coercion. Let's try to break a line of code with a bad type:

```
5> 4 + "string".
** exception error: bad argument in an arithmetic expression
 in operator  +/2
    called as 4 + "string"
```

Unlike Scala, there's no coercion between strings and ints. Let's assign a variable:

```
6> variable = 4.
** exception error: no match of right hand side value 4
```

Ah. Here, you see the ugly side of the comparison between agents and Erlang. Sometimes, this pesky language has more brain than soul. This error message is really a reference to Erlang's pattern matching. It's breaking because variable is an atom. Variables must start with an uppercase letter.

```
7> Var = 1.
1
8> Var = 2.

=ERROR REPORT==== 8-Jan-2010::11:47:46 ===
Error in process <0.39.0> with exit value: {{badmatch,2},[{erl_eval,expr,3}]}

** exited: {{badmatch,2},[{erl_eval,expr,3}]} **
8> Var.
1
```

As you can see, variables begin with a capital letter, and they are immutable. You can assign each value only once. This concept gives most first-time programmers trouble within a functional language. Let's introduce some data types with more complexity.

Atoms, Lists, and Tuples

In functional languages, symbols become more important. They are the most primitive data element and can represent anything you want to name. You've encountered symbols in each of the other programming languages in this book. In Erlang, a symbol is called an *atom* and begins with a lowercase character. They are atomic values that you can use to represent something. You'll use them like this:

```
9> red.
red
10> Pill = blue.
blue
11> Pill.
blue
```

red and blue are atoms—arbitrary names that we can use to symbolize real-world things. We first return a simple atom called red. Next, we assign the atom called blue to the variable called Pill. Atoms get more interesting as you attach them to more robust data structures that we'll see a little later. For now, let's build on the primitives by looking at the list. You'll represent lists with square brackets:

```
13> [1, 2, 3].
[1,2,3]
14> [1, 2, "three"].
[1,2,"three"]
15> List = [1, 2, 3].
[1,2,3]
```

So, the list syntax is familiar. Lists are heterogeneous and can be any length. You can assign them to variables, just as you would a primitive. Tuples are fixed-length heterogeneous lists:

```
18> {one, two, three}.
{one,two,three}
19> Origin = {0, 0}.
{0,0}
```

There are no surprises here. You can see the strong Prolog influence here. Later, when we cover pattern matching, you will notice that when you match a tuple, the size will matter. You can't match a three-tuple to a two-tuple. When you match a list, the length can vary, just as it did in Prolog.

In Ruby, you use hash maps to associate names with values. In Erlang, you'll often see tuples used as you would use maps or hashes:

```
20> {name, "Spaceman Spiff"}.
{name,"Spaceman Spiff"}
21> {comic_strip, {name, "Calvin and Hobbes"}, {character, "Spaceman Spiff"}}.
{comic_strip,{name,"Calvin and Hobbes"},
        {character,"Spaceman Spiff"}}
```

We've represented a hash for a comic strip. We use atoms for the hash keys and use strings for the values. You can mix lists and tuples as well, such as a list of comics, represented by tuples. So, how do you access the individual elements? If Prolog is fresh in your mind, you're already thinking in the right direction. You'll use pattern matching.

Pattern Matching

If you worked through the Prolog chapter, you got a pretty solid foundation of pattern matching. I want to point out one major difference. In Prolog, when you defined a rule, you matched all the values in the database, and Prolog worked through all the combinations. Erlang works like Scala. A match will work against a single value. Let's use pattern matching to extract the values from a tuple. Say we have a person:

```
24> Person = {person, {name, "Agent Smith"}, {profession, "Killing programs"}}.
                {person,{name,"Agent Smith"},
                        {profession,"Killing programs"}}
```

Let's say we want to assign the name to Name, and the profession to Profession. This match would do the trick:

```
25> {person, {name, Name}, {profession, Profession}} = Person.
{person,{name,"Agent Smith"},
        {profession,"Killing programs"}}
26> Name.
"Agent Smith"
27> Profession.
"Killing programs"
```

Erlang will match up the data structures, assigning variables to the values in the tuples. An atom will match itself, so the only work to be done is to match the variable Name to "Agent Smith" and the variable Profession to "Killing programs". This feature works much like it does in Prolog and will be the fundamental decision-making construct that you use.

If you are used to Ruby or Java-style hashes, it may seem strange to have the initial atom of person. In Erlang, you'll often have multiple matching statements and multiple kinds of tuples. By designing your data structures this way, you can quickly match all person tuples, leaving the others behind.

List pattern matching is similar to Prolog's:

```
28> [Head | Tail] = [1, 2, 3].
[1,2,3]
29> Head.
1
30> Tail.
[2,3]
```

Easy as one, two, three. You can bind to more than one variable at the head of a list, too:

```
32> [One, Two|Rest] = [1, 2, 3].
[1,2,3]
33> One.
1
34> Two.
2
35> Rest.
[3]
```

If there are not enough elements in the list, the pattern won't match:

```
36> [X|Rest] = [].
** exception error: no match of right hand side value []
```

Now, some of the other error messages make a little more sense. Let's say you forget to start your variables with an uppercase letter. You'll get this error message:

```
31> one = 1.
** exception error: no match of right hand side value 1
```

As you've seen before, the = statement is not a simple assignment. It is actually a pattern match. You're asking Erlang to match the integer 1 with the atom one, and it can't.

Bit Matching

Sometimes, you need to access data at the bit level. If you're cramming more data into less space or dealing with predefined formats such as JPEGs or MPEGs, the location of each bit matters. Erlang lets you pack several pieces of data into one byte quite easily. To do these two things, you need two operations: pack and unpack. In Erlang, a bitmap works just like other types of collections. To pack a data structure, you'll just tell Erlang how many bits to take for each item, like this:

```
1> W = 1.
1
2> X = 2.
2
3>
3> Y = 3.
3
4> Z = 4.
4
5> All = <<W:3, X:3, Y:5, Z:5>>.
<<"(d">>
```

The << and >> bracket binary patterns in this constructor. In this case, it means take 3 bits for the variable W, 3 bits for X, 5 bits for Y, and 5 bits for Z. Next, we need to be able to unpack. You can probably guess the syntax:

```
6> <<A:3, B:3, C:5, D:5>> = All.
<<"(d">>
7> A
7> .
1
8> D.
4
```

Just like tuples and lists, we just supply the same syntax and let pattern matching do the rest. With these bitwise operations, Erlang is surprisingly powerful for low-level tasks.

We're covering a lot of ground pretty quickly, because you've already been introduced to all the major concepts in the chapter. Believe it or not, we're almost through the first day of the Erlang chapter, but we first need to introduce the most important concept, the function.

Functions

Unlike Scala, Erlang is dynamically typed. You won't have to worry too much about assigning types to data elements. Like Ruby, Erlang typing is dynamic. Erlang will bind types at run time, based on syntactic clues such as quotes or decimal points. At this point, I'm going to crack open a fresh copy of the console. Let me introduce a few terms. You're going to write functions in a file with an .erl extension. The file contains code for a module, and you have to compile it to run it. After you've compiled a file, it produces a .beam executable. The .beam compiled module will run in a virtual machine called the beam.

With the housekeeping out of the way, it's time to create some basic functions.

I'm going to enter a file that looks like this:

erlang/basic.erl

```
-module(basic).
-export([mirror/1]).

mirror(Anything) -> Anything.
```

The first line defines the name of the module. The second line defines a function that you want to use outside of the module. The function is called mirror, and the /1 means it has one parameter. Finally, you get to the function itself. You can see the influence of the Prolog-style rule. The function definition names the function and determines the arguments. Afterward, you have the -> symbol, which simply returns the first argument.

With a function definition complete, I'll fire up the console from the same directory that has the code file. I can then compile it like this:

```
4> c(basic).
{ok,basic}
```

We compiled basic.erl, and you will find a basic.beam file in the same directory. You can run it like this:

```
5> mirror(smiling_mug).
** exception error: undefined shell command mirror/1
6> basic:mirror(smiling_mug).
smiling_mug
6> basic:mirror(1).
1
```

Notice that it is not enough to have the function name alone. You also need to include the module name, followed by a colon. This function is dead simple.

Notice one thing. We were able to bind Anything to two different types. Erlang is dynamically typed, and to me, it feels good. After Scala's strong typing, I'm coming home from a weekend in Siberia, or at least Peoria.

Let's look at a function that's slightly more complicated. This one defines several matching alternatives.

You can create a matching_function.erl file like this:

erlang/matching_function.erl

```
-module(matching_function).
-export([number/1]).

number(one)   -> 1;
number(two)   -> 2;
number(three) -> 3.
```

And you can execute it like this:

```
8> c(matching_function).
{ok,matching_function}
9> matching_function:number(one).
1
10> matching_function:number(two).
2
11> matching_function:number(three).
3
12> matching_function:number(four).
** exception error: no function clause matching matching_function:number(four)
```

This is the first function I've introduced with multiple matching possibilities. Each possible match has the function name, the argument to match, and the code to execute after the -> symbol. In each case, Erlang just returns an integer. Terminate the last statement with . and all others with ;.

Just as with Io, Scala, and Prolog, recursion will play a big role. Like Prolog, Erlang is optimized for tail recursion. Here is the obligatory factorial:

erlang/yet_again.erl

```
-module(yet_again).
-export([another_factorial/1]).
-export([another_fib/1]).

another_factorial(0) -> 1;
another_factorial(N) -> N * another_factorial(N-1).

another_fib(0) -> 1;
another_fib(1) -> 1;
another_fib(N) -> another_fib(N-1) + another_fib(N-2).
```

So, it's another factorial, and it's defined recursively just like all the others. While I was at it, I may as well include a Fibonacci series, too.

Let me try to make it worth your while this time:

```
18> c(yet_again).
{ok,yet_again}
19> yet_again:another_factorial(3).
6
20> yet_again:another_factorial(20).
2432902008176640000
21> yet_again:another_factorial(200).
788657867364790503552363213932185062295135977687173263294742533244359
449963403342920304284011984623904177212138919638830257642790242637105
061926624952829931113462857270763317237396988943922445621451664240254
033291864131227428294853277524242407573903240321257405579568660226031
904170324062351700858796178922222789623703897374720000000000000000000
000000000000000000000000000000
22> yet_again:another_factorial(2000).
3316275092450633241175393380576324038281117208105780394571935437060380
7790560082240027323085973259225540235294122583410925808481741529379613
1386633526343688905634058556163940605117252571870647856393544045405243
9574670376741087229704346841583437524315808775336451274879954368592474
... and on and on...
0000000000000000000000000000000000000000000000000000000000000000000000
```

Ooooh-kaaay. That was certainly different. Now, you're starting to see the butt-kicking side of the Agent Smith/Erlang comparison. If you didn't take the time to run it, let me assure you, the results are absolutely instantaneous. I don't know what the maximum integer size is, but I'm going to go out on a limb and say it's big enough for me.

That's a pretty good starting point. You've created some simple functions and seen them work. It's a good time to wrap up day 1.

What We Learned in Day 1

Erlang is a functional language. It is strongly, dynamically typed. There is not a lot of syntax, but what is there is not at all like the typical object-oriented languages.

Like Prolog, Erlang has no notion of an object. However, Erlang does have a strong connection to Prolog. The pattern matching constructs and multiple function entry points should look familiar to you, and you handle some problems in the same way, through recursion. The functional language has no notion of mutable state or even side effects. Maintaining program state is awkward, but you will learn a new bag of tricks. You'll soon see the other side of the coin. Eliminating state and side effects will have a dramatic impact on how you will manage concurrency.

In the first day, you worked both in the console and with the compiler. Primarily, you focused on the basics. You created basic expressions. You also created simple functions. Like Prolog, Erlang lets a function have multiple entry points. You used basic pattern matching.

You also used basic tuples and lists. Tuples took the place of Ruby hashes and formed the foundation of data structures. You learned to pattern match across lists and tuples. These ideas will allow you to quickly attach behavior to tuples or interprocess messages in later chapters.

In day 2, I'm going to expand the basic functional concepts. We'll learn how to build code that will work in a concurrent world, but we won't actually go there yet. Take a little time to do some self-study to practice what you've learned so far.

Day 1 Self-Study

The online community for Erlang is growing rapidly. A conference in San Francisco is picking up momentum. And unlike Io and C, you should be able to use Google to find what you need.

Find:

- The Erlang language's official site
- Official documentation for Erlang's function library
- The documentation for Erlang's OTP library

Do:

- Write a function that uses recursion to return the number of words in a string.
- Write a function that uses recursion to count to ten.
- Write a function that uses matching to selectively print "success" or "error: message" given input of the form `{error, Message}` or `success`.

6.3 Day 2: Changing Forms

In this section, you're going to begin to appreciate Agent Smith's power. The agents in *The Matrix* have super-human strength. They can dodge bullets and punch through concrete. Functional languages are at a higher level of abstraction than object-oriented languages. Though they are more difficult to understand, you can express bigger ideas with less code.

Agent Smith can also take the form of any other person in the matrix. That's an important capability in a functional language. You're going to learn to apply functions to lists that can quickly shape the list into exactly what you need. Do you want to turn a shopping list into a list of prices? What about turning a list of URLs into tuples containing content and URLs? These are the problems that functional languages simply devour.

Control Structures

Let's start with a few mundane pieces of Erlang: basic control structures. You'll notice that this section of the book is much shorter than Scala's. Often, you'll see programs with plenty of case statements, because they will interpret which message to process when you're writing concurrent applications. ifs are less prevalent.

Case

Let's start with a case. Most of the time, you think of a pattern match in the context of function invocation. Think of this control structure as a pattern match that you can use anywhere. For example, say you have a variable called Animal. You want to conditionally execute the code based on the value:

```
1> Animal = "dog".
2> case Animal of
2>     "dog" -> underdog;
2>     "cat" -> thundercat
2> end.
underdog
```

So, in this example, the string matched the first clause and returned the atom underdog. As with Prolog, you can use the underscore (_) to match anything, like this (note: Animal is still "dog"):

```
3> case Animal of
3>     "elephant" -> dumbo;
3>     _ -> something_else
3> end.
something_else
```

The animal was not "elephant", so it matched the last clause. You can also use underscores in any other Erlang match. I'd like to point out a basic syntactic wart here. Notice that all case clauses but the last end in a semicolon. That means if you want to edit your statement to reorder your clauses, you must adjust the syntax accordingly, though it would have been pretty easy to allow an optional semicolon after the last clause. Sure, the syntax is logical: the semicolon is a separator for the case clauses. It's just not very convenient. Agent Smith just kicked sand all over my kid nephew, and I think I heard him laugh. He has to brush up on those public relations if he wants to win Agent of the Month. Let's move on to the basic if.

If

The case statement uses pattern matching, and the if statement uses *guards*. In Erlang, a guard is a condition that must be satisfied for a match to succeed. Later, we'll introduce guards on pattern matches, but the most basic form of a guard is in an if statement. You start with the if keyword and then follow it with several guard -> expression clauses. Here's the idea:

```
if
  ProgramsTerminated > 0 ->
    success;
  ProgramsTerminated < 0 ->
    error
end.
```

What happens if there is no match?

```
8> X = 0.
0
9> if
9>   X > 0 -> positive;
9>   X < 0 -> negative
9> end.
** exception error: no true branch found when evaluating an if expression
```

Unlike Ruby or Io, one of the statements must be true, because if is a function. Each case must return a value. If you truly want an else, make the last guard true, like this:

```
9> if
9>   X > 0 -> positive;
9>   X < 0 -> negative;
9>   true  -> zero
9> end.
```

That's really it for control structures. You're going to get much more out of higher-order functions and pattern matching to accomplish your goals, so let's leave these control statements behind and dive in deeper into functional programming. We're going to work with higher-order functions and use them to process lists. We'll learn to solve progressively more complex problems with functions.

Anonymous Functions

As you recall, higher-order functions either return functions or take functions as arguments. Ruby used code blocks for higher-order functions, with special attention to passing code blocks to iterate over lists. In Erlang, you can assign arbitrary functions to variables and pass them around like any other data types.

You've seen some of these concepts before, but we're going to lay some of the foundations in Erlang and then build some higher-level abstractions. It all starts with anonymous functions. Here's how you'd assign a function to a variable:

```
16> Negate = fun(I) -> -I end.
#Fun<erl_eval.6.13229925>
17> Negate(1).
-1
18> Negate(-1).
1
```

Line 16 uses a new keyword called fun. That keyword defines an anonymous function. In this case, the function takes a single argument called I and returns the negation, -I. We assign that anonymous function to Negate. To be clear, Negate is not the value returned by the function. It actually *is* the function.

Two significant ideas are happening here. First, we're assigning a function to a variable. This concept allows us to pass around behaviors just as we would any other data. Second, we can easily invoke the underlying function, just by specifying an argument list. Notice the dynamic typing. We don't have to concern ourselves with the return type of the function, so we're protected from some of the invasive syntax you see with, say, Scala. The downside is that these functions can fail. I'll show you some of the ways Erlang lets you compensate for that limitation.

Let's use some of this newfound power. We'll use anonymous functions to handle the each, map, and inject concepts that you initially encountered with Ruby.

Lists and Higher-Order Functions

As you've seen, lists and tuples are the heart and soul of functional programming. It's no accident that the first functional language started with lists, and everything built on that foundation. In this section, you'll start to apply higher-order functions to lists.

Applying Functions to Lists

By now, the idea should be pretty clear to you. We're going to use functions to help us manage lists. Some, like ForEach, will iterate over lists. Others, like filter or map, will return lists, either filtered or mapped onto other functions. Still more, like foldl or foldr, will process lists, rolling up results along the way, like Ruby's inject or Scala's FoldLeft. Open a fresh console, define a list or two, and get cracking.

First, we'll handle basic iteration. The lists:foreach method takes a function and a list. The function can be anonymous, like this:

```
1> Numbers = [1, 2, 3, 4].
[1,2,3,4]
2> lists:foreach(fun(Number) -> io:format("~p~n", [Number]) end, Numbers).
1
2
3
4
ok
```

The syntax of line 2 is a little tricky, so we'll walk through it. We start by invoking a function called lists:foreach. The first argument is the anonymous function fun(Number) -> io:format("~p~n", [Number]) end. That function has one argument and prints the value of whatever you pass in with the io:format function.[2] Finally, the second argument to foreach is Numbers, the list we defined on line 1. We could simplify this by defining the function in a separate line:

```
3> Print = fun(X) -> io:format("~p~n", [X]) end.
```

Now, Print is bound to the io:format function. We can simplify the code like this:

```
8> lists:foreach(Print, Numbers).
1
2
3
4
ok
```

That's basic iteration. Let's move on to a function that maps. The map function works like Ruby's collect, passing each value of a list to a

2. ~p pretty prints an argument, ~n is a newline, and [Number] is a list of arguments to print.

function and building a list with the results. Like lists:foreach, lists:map takes a function and a list. Let's use map with our list of numbers, increasing each value by one:

```
10> lists:map(fun(X) -> X + 1 end, Numbers).
[2,3,4,5]
```

That was easy. This time, our anonymous function was fun(X) -> X + 1 end. It increased each value by one, and lists:map built a list with the results.

Defining map is really easy:

```
map(F, [H|T]) -> [F(H) | map(F, T)];
map(F, [])    -> [].
```

Simple enough. The map of F over a list is F(head) plus map(F, tail). We'll look at a more concise version when we look at list comprehensions.

Moving on, we can filter lists with a boolean. Let's define an anonymous function and assign it to Small:

```
11> Small = fun(X) -> X < 3 end.
#Fun<erl_eval.6.13229925>
12> Small(4).
false
13> Small(1).
true
```

Now, we can take that function and use it to filter the list. The function lists:filter will build a list of all the elements that satisfy Small or those less than three:

```
14> lists:filter(Small, Numbers).
[1,2]
```

You can see that Erlang is making it very easy to code in this way. Alternatively, we can use the Small function to test lists with all and any. lists:all returns true only if all the items in a list satisfy the filter, like this:

```
15> lists:all(Small, [0, 1, 2]).
true
16> lists:all(Small, [0, 1, 2, 3]).
false
```

Alternatively, lists:any returns true if any of the items in the list satisfies the filter:

```
17> lists:any(Small, [0, 1, 2, 3]).
true
18> lists:any(Small, [3, 4, 5]).
false
```

Let's see what happens with empty lists:

```
19> lists:any(Small, []).
false
20> lists:all(Small, []).
true
```

As you'd expect, all returns true (meaning all of the items present in the list satisfy the filter, though there are no items in the list), and any returns false (meaning no element in the empty list satisfies the filter). In these cases, it doesn't matter what the filter is.

You can also make a list of all the elements at the head of a list that match a filter or discard all the items at the front of a list that satisfy the filter:

```
22> lists:takewhile(Small, Numbers).
[1,2]
23> lists:dropwhile(Small, Numbers).
[3,4]
24> lists:takewhile(Small, [1, 2, 1, 4, 1]).
[1,2,1]
25> lists:dropwhile(Small, [1, 2, 1, 4, 1]).
[4,1]
```

These tests are useful to do things such as process or discard headers of messages. Let's finish this whirlwind with foldl and foldr.

foldl

I realize that you've seen these concepts before. If you're Neo and you've mastered this part of the matrix, read the basic example and fight on. For some, foldl takes a little while to master, so I'm going to teach it a few different ways.

Remember, these functions are useful for rolling up the results of a function across a list. One of the arguments serves as an accumulator, and the other represents each item. lists:foldl takes a function, the initial value of the accumulator, and the list:

```
28> Numbers.
[1,2,3,4]
29> lists:foldl(fun(X, Sum) -> X + Sum end, 0, Numbers).
10
```

To simplify a little bit, let's break that anonymous function into a variable and make our intentions clear with better variable names:

```
32> Adder = fun(ListItem, SumSoFar) -> ListItem + SumSoFar end.
#Fun<erl_eval.12.113037538>
```

```
33> InitialSum = 0.
0
34> lists:foldl(Adder, InitialSum, Numbers).
10
```

Ah, that's better. So, we are going to keep a running sum. We're going to pass the SumSoFar and each number from Numbers into a function called Adder, one at a time. Each time, the sum will get bigger, and the lists:foldl function will remember the running total and pass it back into Adder. Ultimately, the function will return the last running sum.

So far, all you've seen are functions that work on existing lists. I haven't shown you how to build a list a piece at a time. Let's shift gears toward list building.

Advanced List Concepts

All of the list concepts I've introduced are extensions of the ideas you've seen in the other languages. But we can get a little more sophisticated. We haven't yet talked about building lists, and we've only used pretty basic abstractions with simple code blocks.

List Construction

On the surface, it may seem difficult to build lists without mutable state. With Ruby or Io, you would continually add items to a list. There's another way. You can return a new list with the list item added. Often, you'll add items to a list headfirst. You'll use the [H|T] construct but in the right side of a match instead. This program uses the list construction technique to double each item of a list:

erlang/double.erl

```
-module(double).
-export([double_all/1]).

double_all([]) -> [];
double_all([First|Rest]) -> [First + First|double_all(Rest)].
```

The module exports one function, called double_all. That function has two distinct clauses. The first says that double_all for an empty list returns an empty list. This rule stops the recursion.

The second rule uses the [H|T] construct, but in the predicate of the match as well as the function definition. You've already seen something like [First|Rest] on the left side of a match. It lets you break a list into the first element and the rest of the list.

Using it on the right side does list construction instead of destruction. In this case, [First + First|double_all(Rest)] means build a list with First + First as the first element and double_all(Rest) as the rest of the list.

You can compile and run the program as usual:

```
8> c(double).
{ok,double}
9> double:double_all([1, 2, 3]).
[2,4,6]
```

Let's take another look at list construction with | from the console:

```
14> [1| [2, 3]].
[1,2,3]
15> [[2, 3] | 1].
[[2,3]|1]
16> [[] | [2, 3]].
[[],2,3]
17> [1 | []].
[1]
```

There should be no surprises in there. The second argument must be a list. Whatever is on the left side will be added as the first element of a new list.

Let's look at a more advanced Erlang concept, called *list comprehensions*. They combine some of the concepts we have been talking about so far.

List Comprehensions

One of the most important functions in just about any functional language is map. With it, your lists can mutate, just like *The Matrix* enemies. Since the feature is so important, Erlang provides a more powerful form that is concise and allows you to do multiple transformations at once.

Let's start things off with a fresh console. We'll do a map the old-fashioned way:

```
1> Fibs = [1, 1, 2, 3, 5].
[1,1,2,3,5]
2> Double = fun(X) -> X * 2 end.
#Fun<erl_eval.6.13229925>
3> lists:map(Double, Fibs).
[2,2,4,6,10]
```

We have a list of numbers called Fibs and an anonymous function called Double that will double whatever you pass in. Then, we called lists:map to call Double on each element and build a list out of the result. That's a great tool, but it's used often enough that Erlang provides a much more concise way to provide the same syntax. The construct is called a *list comprehension*. Here's the equivalent to what we just typed, with a list comprehension:

```
4> [Double(X) || X <- Fibs].
[2,2,4,6,10]
```

In English, we're saying compute the Double of X for each X taken from the list called Fibs. If you'd prefer, we can cut out the middleman:

```
5> [X * 2 || X <- [1, 1, 2, 3, 5]].
[2,2,4,6,10]
```

The concept is the same. We're computing X * 2 for each X taken from the list called [1, 1, 2, 3, 5]. This feature is a bit more than syntactic sugar. Let's build some more sophisticated list comprehensions. We will start with a more concise definition of map:

```
map(F, L) -> [ F(X) || X <- L].
```

In English, the map of some function F over some list L is the collection of F(X) for each X that is a member of L. Now, let's use a list comprehension to work with a catalog having a product, quantity, and price:

```
7> Cart = [{pencil, 4, 0.25}, {pen, 1, 1.20}, {paper, 2, 0.20}].
[{pencil,4,0.25},{pen,1,1.2},{paper,2,0.2}]
```

Say that I need to add a tax that is eight cents on the dollar. I can add a simple list comprehension to roll up the new cart with tax with a single list comprehension, like this:

```
8> WithTax = [{Product, Quantity, Price, Price * Quantity * 0.08} ||
8>    {Product, Quantity, Price} <- Cart].
[{pencil,4,0.25,0.08},{pen,1,1.2,0.096},{paper,2,0.2,0.032}]
```

All the earlier Erlang concepts you've learned still apply: there's pattern matching going on here! So in English, we're returning a list of tuples having a Product, Price, Quantity, and tax (Price * Quantity * 0.08), for each tuple of {Product, Quantity, Price} taken from the list called Cart. This code is absolutely beautiful to me. This syntax allows me to change the form of my list, literally on demand.

As another example, say I have a catalog and I want to provide a similar catalog to my preferred customers with a 50 percent discount. The catalog could look something like this. I'll just take the catalog from the cart, ignoring quantity:

```
10> Cat = [{Product, Price} || {Product, _, Price} <- Cart].
[{pencil,0.25},{pen,1.2},{paper,0.2}]
```

In English, give me tuples with Product and Price for each tuple of Product, and Price (ignoring the second attribute) taken from the Cart list. Now, I can provide my discount:

```
11> DiscountedCat = [{Product, Price / 2} || {Product, Price} <- Cat].
[{pencil,0.125},{pen,0.6},{paper,0.1}]
```

It's concise, readable, and powerful. It's a beautiful abstraction.

In truth, I've showed you only part of the power of a list comprehension. The full form can be even more powerful:

- A list comprehension takes the form of [Expression || Clause1, Clause2, ..., ClauseN].
- List comprehensions can have an arbitrary number of clauses.
- The clauses can be generators or filters.
- A filter can be a boolean expression or a function returning a boolean.
- A generator, of the form Match <-List, matches a pattern on the left to the elements of a list on the right.

Really, it's not too hard. Generators add, and filters remove. There's a lot of Prolog influence here. Generators determine the possible values, and filters trim the list down to the specified conditions. Here are a couple of examples:

```
[X || X  <- [1, 2, 3, 4], X < 4, X > 1].
[2,3]
```

In English, return X, where X is taken from [1, 2, 3, 4], X is less than four, and X is greater than one. You can also have multiple generators:

```
23> [{X, Y} || X  <- [1, 2, 3, 4], X < 3, Y <- [5, 6]].
[{1,5},{1,6},{2,5},{2,6}]
24>
```

This one makes a tuple {X, Y} by combining X values from [1, 2, 3, 4] that are less than 3 with Y values from [5, 6]. You wind up with two X values and two Y values, and Erlang computes a Cartesian product.

And that's the whole story. You've learned to use Erlang to do sequential programming. Let's take a break to wrap up and put this stuff into practice.

What We Learned in Day 2

Admittedly, we didn't go into deep detail about Erlang expressions or the library, but you are now armed with enough information to write functional programs. You started the day with some mundane control structures, but we picked up the pace quickly.

Next, we covered higher-order functions. You used higher-order functions within lists to iterate through lists, filter them, and modify them. You also learned to use foldl to roll up results, just as you did with Scala.

Finally, we moved on to advanced list concepts. We used [H|T] on the left side of a match to deconstruct a list into the first element of the list and the rest. We used [H|T] on the right side of a match, or solo, to construct lists, headfirst. We then moved on to list comprehensions, an elegant and powerful abstraction that can quickly transform lists with generators and filters.

The syntax was a mixed bag. You could cruise through the higher concepts with very little typing, thanks to Erlang's dynamic typing strategy. Still, there were some awkward moments, especially with the semicolons after the various pieces of case and if clauses.

In the next section, we'll learn what all of the fuss was about. We'll tackle concurrency.

Day 2 Self-Study

Do:

- Consider a list of keyword-value tuples, such as [{erlang, "a functional language"}, {ruby, "an OO language"}]. Write a function that accepts the list and a keyword and returns the associated value for the keyword.

- Consider a shopping list that looks like [{item quantity price}, ...]. Write a list comprehension that builds a list of items of the form [{item total_price}, ...], where total_price is quantity times price.

Bonus problem:

- Write a program that reads a tic-tac-toe board presented as a list or a tuple of size nine. Return the winner (x or o) if a winner has been determined, cat if there are no more possible moves, or no_winner if no player has won yet.

6.4 Day 3: The Red Pill

Most of you have heard it before. In the matrix, take the blue pill, and you can continue to live in blissful ignorance. Take the red pill, and your eyes are open to reality. Sometimes, reality hurts.

We have a whole industry slamming blue pills like a preacher's kid in Amsterdam. Concurrency is hard, so we punt. We add mutable state, so our programs collide when we run them concurrently. Our functions and methods have side effects, so we can't prove correctness or predict their outcomes. We use threads with shared state rather than shared-nothing processes for performance, so we have to do extra work to protect each piece of code.

The result is chaos. Concurrency hurts, not because it is inherently difficult but because we've been using the wrong programming model!

Earlier in the chapter, I said Erlang made some easy things hard. Without side effects and mutable state, you'll have to change the way you approach coding altogether. You'll have to put up with a Prolog-based syntax that seems alien to many. But now, you'll get the payoff. That red pill, concurrency and reliability, will seem like candy to you. Let's find out how.

Basic Concurrency Primitives

Your three basic primitives for concurrency will be sending a message (using `!`), spawning a process (with `spawn`), and receiving a message (with `receive`). In this section, I'll show you how to use these three primitives to send and receive a message and to wrap them in a basic client-server idiom.

A Basic Receive Loop

We'll start with a translation process. If you send the process a string in Spanish, it will reply with an English translation. In general, your strategy will be to spawn a process that receives and processes the message in a loop.

Here's what a basic receive loop looks like:

erlang/translate.erl

```
-module(translate).
-export([loop/0]).

loop() ->
    receive
        "casa" ->
            io:format("house~n"),
            loop();

        "blanca" ->
            io:format("white~n"),
            loop();

        _ ->
            io:format("I don't understand.~n"),
            loop()

end.
```

That's longer than our other examples so far, so we'll break it down. The first two lines just define the module called translate and export the function called loop. The next block of code is the function called loop():

```
loop() ->
    ...
end.
```

Notice that the code inside calls loop() three times, without any returns. That's OK: Erlang is optimized for tail recursion, so there's very little overhead, as long as the last thing in any receive clause is a loop(). We're basically defining an empty function and looping forever. Moving on to the receive:

```
receive ->
    ...
```

This function will receive a message from another process. receive works like the other pattern matching constructs in Erlang, the case and the function definitions. You'll follow receive with several pattern matching constructs. Moving on to the individual matches:

```
"casa" ->
    io:format("house~n"),
    loop();
```

This is a matching clause. The syntax is nicely consistent with case statements. If the inbound message matches the string "casa", Erlang will execute the following code. Separate lines are delimited with a , character, and you'll terminate the clause with a ; character. This code displays the word *house* and then calls loop. (Remember, there's no overhead on the stack, because loop is the last function called.) All of the other matching clauses look the same.

Now, we have a module with a receive loop in it. It's time to put it to use.

Spawning a Process

First, we compile this module:

```
1> c(translate).
{ok,translate}
```

To spawn a process, you'll use the function spawn, which takes a function. That function will be started in a new lightweight process. spawn returns a process ID (PID). We'll pass in the function from our translate module, like this:

```
2> Pid = spawn(fun translate:loop/0).
<0.38.0>
```

You can see that Erlang returned the process ID of <0.38.0>. In the console, you'll see process IDs enclosed in angle brackets. We're going to cover only the primitive version of process spawning, but you should know about a few others too. You can register processes by name, so other processes can find, say, common services by name rather than process ID. You can also use another version of spawn for code that you want to be able to change on the fly, or hot-swap. If you were spawning a remote process, you would use spawn(Node, function) instead. These topics are beyond the scope of this book.

So now, we've coded a module with a code block, and we've spawned it as a lightweight process. The last step is to pass messages to it. That is the third Erlang primitive.

Sending Messages

As you saw in Scala, you will pass distributed messages to Erlang with the ! operator. The form is Pid ! message. The Pid is any process identifier. message can be any value, including primitives, lists, or tuples. Let's send a few messages:

```
3> Pid ! "casa".
"house"
"casa"
```

```
4> Pid ! "blanca".
"white"
"blanca"
5> Pid ! "loco".
"I don't understand."
"loco"
```

Each line sends a message. The io:format in our receive clauses prints a message, and then the console prints the return value of the expression, which is the message you sent.

If you were sending a distributed message to a named resource, you'd use the syntax node@server ! message instead. Setting up a remote server is beyond the scope of this book, but with very little self-study, you can easily get a distributed server going.

This example illustrates the basic primitives and how you'd weave them together to form a basic asynchronous service. You may have noticed that there is no return value. In the next section, we'll explore how to send synchronous messages.

Synchronous Messaging

Some concurrent systems work asynchronously, like phone chats. The sender transmits a message and goes on, without waiting for a response. Others work synchronously, like the Web. We ask for a page, and the web server sends it while we wait for the response. Let's turn the translation service that prints return values into a service that actually returns the translated string to the user.

To change our messaging model from asynchronous to synchronous, we'll have a three-part strategy:

- Each receive clause in our messaging service will need to match a tuple having the ID of the process requesting the translation and the word to translate. Adding this ID will allow us to send a response.
- Each receive clause will need to send a response to the sender instead of printing the result.
- Instead of using the simple ! primitive, we'll write a simple function to send the request and await the response.

Now that you know the background, take a look at the pieces of the implementation.

Receiving Synchronously

The first order of business is to modify our receive clauses to take additional parameters. That means we're going to have to use tuples. Pattern matching makes it easy. Each receive clause looks like this:

```
receive
    {Pid, "casa"} ->
        Pid ! "house",
        loop();
        ...
```

We match any element (this should always be a process ID), followed by the word *casa*. We then send the word *house* to the receiver and loop back to the top.

Note the pattern match. This is a common form for a receive, where the ID of the sending process is the first element of a tuple. Otherwise, the only major difference is sending the result rather than printing it. Sending a message gets a little more complicated, though.

Sending Synchronously

The other side of the equation needs to send a message and then immediately wait for a response. Given a process ID in Receiver, sending a synchronous message will look something like this:

```
Receiver !  "message_to_translate",
    receive
        Message -> do_something_with(Message)
    end
```

Since we'll be sending messages so often, we'll simplify the service by encapsulating a request to the server. In our case, that simple remote procedure call looks like this:

```
translate(To, Word) ->
    To ! {self(), Word},
    receive
        Translation -> Translation
    end.
```

When you put it all together, you get a concurrent program that's only marginally more complicated.

erlang/translate_service.erl

```
-module(translate_service).
-export([loop/0, translate/2]).

loop() ->
    receive
        {From, "casa"} ->
            From ! "house",
            loop();

        {From, "blanca"} ->
            From ! "white",
            loop();

        {From, _} ->
            From ! "I don't understand.",
            loop()

end.

translate(To, Word) ->
    To ! {self(), Word},
    receive
        Translation -> Translation
    end.
```

The usage model looks like this:

```
1> c(translate_service).
{ok,translate_service}
2> Translator = spawn(fun translate_service:loop/0).
<0.38.0>
3> translate_service:translate(Translator, "blanca").
"white"
4> translate_service:translate(Translator, "casa").
"house"
```

We simply compile the code, spawn the loop, and then request a synchronous service through the helper function we wrote. As you can see, the Translator process now returns the translated value for the word. And now, you have a synchronous message.

Now, you can see the structure of a basic receive loop. Each process has a mailbox. The receive construct just picks messages off the queue and matches them to some function to execute. Processes communicate between one another with message passing. It's no accident that Dr. Armstrong calls Erlang a true object-oriented language! It gives you message passing and encapsulation of behavior. We're just losing mutable state and inheritance, though it's possible to simulate inheritance, and more, through higher-order functions.

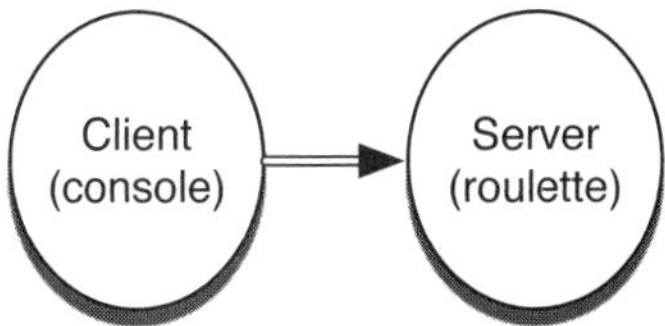

Figure 6.1: SIMPLE CLIENT-SERVER DESIGN

So far, we've worked in basic, sterile conditions with no error recovery capability. Erlang does provide checked exceptions, but I want to walk you through another way of handling errors instead.

Linking Processes for Reliability

In this section, we're going to look at ways to link processes for better reliability. In Erlang, you can link two processes together. Whenever a process dies, it sends an exit signal to its linked twin. A process can then receive that signal and react accordingly.

Spawning a Linked Process

To see how linking processes works, let's first create a process that can easily die. I've created a Russian roulette game. It has a gun with six chambers. To fire a chamber, you just send a number 1–6 to the gun process. Enter the wrong number, and the process kills itself. Here's the code:

erlang/roulette.erl

```
-module(roulette).
-export([loop/0]).

% send a number, 1-6
loop() ->
    receive
        3 -> io:format("bang.~n"), exit({roulette,die,at,erlang:time()});
        _ -> io:format("click~n"), loop()
end.
```

The implementation is pretty easy. We have a message loop. Matching 3 executes the code io:format("bang~n"), exit({roulette,die,at,erlang:time()};, killing the process. Anything else just prints a message and goes back to the top of the loop.

We really have a simple client-server program. The client is the console, and the server is the roulette process, as shown in Figure 6.1.

And here's what the execution looks like:

```
1> c(roulette).
{ok,roulette}
2> Gun = spawn(fun roulette:loop/0).
<0.38.0>
3> Gun ! 1.
"click"
1
4> Gun ! 3.
"bang"
3
5> Gun ! 4.
4
6> Gun ! 1.
1
```

The problem is that after a 3, the gun process is dead, and further messages do nothing. We can actually tell whether the process is alive:

```
7> erlang:is_process_alive(Gun).
false
```

The process is definitely dead. It's time to get on the cart. We can do a little bit better. Let's build a monitor that will tell us whether the process dies. I guess that's more of a coroner than a monitor. We're only interested in death.

Here's what the code looks like:

erlang/coroner.erl

```
-module(coroner).
-export([loop/0]).

loop() ->
    process_flag(trap_exit, true),
    receive
        {monitor, Process} ->
            link(Process),
            io:format("Monitoring process.~n"),
            loop();

        {'EXIT', From, Reason} ->
            io:format("The shooter ~p died with reason ~p.", [From, Reason]),
                        io:format("Start another one.~n"),
            loop()
        end.
```

As usual, we're building a receive loop. Before we do anything else, the program must register the process as one that will trap exits. You won't receive EXIT messages without it.

Then, we process a receive. The receive gets two types of tuples: those beginning with the atom monitor and those beginning with the string 'EXIT'. Let's look at each in more detail.

```
{monitor, Process} ->
    link(Process),
    io:format("Monitoring process.~n"),
    loop();
```

This code links the coroner process to any process with a PID of Process. You can also spawn a process with the links already in place with spawn_link. Now, if the monitored process should die, it will send an exit message to this coroner. Moving on to trapping the error:

```
{'EXIT', From, Reason} ->
    io:format("The shooter died. Start another one.~n"),
    loop()
end.
```

This is the code that matches the exit message. It will be a three-tuple with 'EXIT', followed by the PID from the dying process as From and the reason for failure. We print the PID of the dying process and the reason. Here's the overall flow:

```
1> c(roulette).
{ok,roulette}
2> c(coroner).
{ok,coroner}
3> Revolver=spawn(fun roulette:loop/0).
<0.43.0>
4> Coroner=spawn(fun coroner:loop/0).
<0.45.0>
5> Coroner ! {monitor, Revolver}.
Monitoring process.
{monitor,<0.43.0>}
6> Revolver ! 1.
click
1
7> Revolver ! 3.
bang.
3
The shooter <0.43.0> died with reason
{roulette,die,at,{8,48,1}}. Start another one.
```

Now, we're getting more sophisticated than client-server. We've added a monitor process, as in Figure 6.2, on the following page, so we can tell when the process dies.

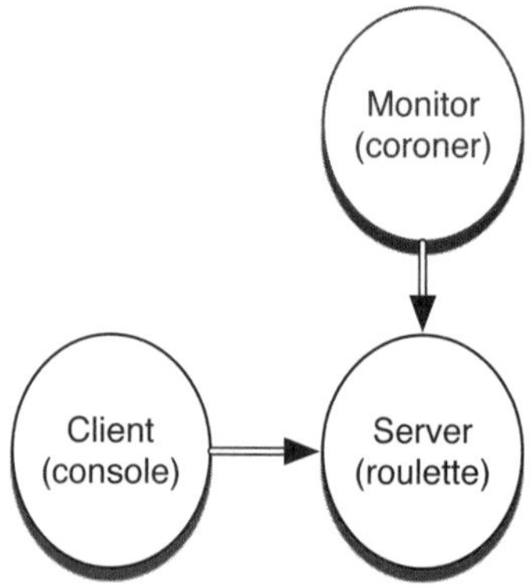

Figure 6.2: ADDING MONITORING

From Coroner to Doctor

We can do better. If we register the gun (gun pun intended), game players will no longer have to know the PID of the gun to play. Then, we can push the gun creation into the coroner. Finally, the coroner can restart the process whenever the process dies. And we've achieved much better reliability and without excessive error reporting. At this point, the coroner is not just a coroner. He's a doctor, and one that's capable of raising the dead. Here's the new doctor:

erlang/doctor.erl

```
-module(doctor).
-export([loop/0]).

loop() ->
    process_flag(trap_exit, true),
    receive
        new ->
            io:format("Creating and monitoring process.~n"),
            register(revolver, spawn_link(fun roulette:loop/0)),
            loop();

        {'EXIT', From, Reason} ->
            io:format("The shooter ~p died with reason ~p.", [From, Reason]),
                        io:format(" Restarting. ~n"),
            self() ! new,
            loop()
        end.
```

The receive block now matches two messages: new and the same EXIT tuple. They are both a little different from the coroner predecessor. This is the magic line of code in the new block:

```
register(revolver, spawn_link(fun roulette:loop/0)),
```

Working from the inside out, we spawn a process with spawn_link. That version of spawn will link the processes so the doctor will get notified whenever a roulette process dies. We then register the PID, associating it with the revolver atom. Now, users can send messages to this process by using revolver ! message. We no longer need the PID. The EXIT match block is also smarter. Here's the new line of code:

```
self() ! new,
```

We send a message to ourself, spawning and registering a new gun. The game is much easier to play, too:

```
2> c(doctor).
{ok,doctor}
3> Doc = spawn(fun doctor:loop/0).
<0.43.0>
4> revolver ! 1.
** exception error: bad argument
     in operator  !/2
        called as revolver ! 1
```

As expected, we have not created the process yet, so we get an error. Now, we'll create and register one:

```
5> Doc ! new.
Creating and monitoring process.
new
6> revolver ! 1.
click
1
7> revolver ! 3.
bang.
3
The shooter <0.47.0> died with reason {roulette,die,at,{8,53,40}}.
    Restarting.
Creating and monitoring process.
8> revolver ! 4.
click
4
```

We now take the incongruous step of creating the revolver through the Doctor. We interact with the revolver by sending messages through the revolver atom instead of the Gun PID. You can also see after line 8 that we in fact create and register a new revolver. The overall topology is generally the same as it was in Figure 6.2, on page 202, with the doctor playing a more active role than the coroner did.

We've just scratched the surface, but I hope that you can see how Erlang can make it easy to create much more robust concurrent systems. You don't see much error handling here at all. When something crashes, we just start a new one. It's relatively simple to build monitors that watch each other. In fact, the base libraries have plenty of tools to build monitoring services and keep-alives that Erlang restarts automatically upon any kind of failure.

What We Learned in Day 3

In day 3, you started to get a pretty good feel for what you can do with Erlang. We started with the concurrency primitives: send, receive, and spawn. We built the natural asynchronous version of a translator to illustrate how basic message-passing works. Then, we built a simple helper function that encapsulated a send and a receive together to simulate a remote procedure call with a send and receive.

Next, we linked processes together to show how one process notifies another when it dies. We also learned to monitor one process with another for better reliability. Our system was not fault tolerant, though the ideas that we used could be used to build fault-tolerant systems. Erlang distributed communication works exactly like interprocess communication. We could link two processes, on separate computers, so that a standby monitored the master and took over in the event of a problem.

Let's put some of what you've learned to work.

Day 3 Self-Study

These exercises are relatively easy, but I did add some bonus questions to stretch you a little bit.

Open Telecom Platform (OTP) is a powerful package with much of what you'll need to build a distributed, concurrent service.

Find:

- An OTP service that will restart a process if it dies
- Documentation for building a simple OTP server

Do:

- Monitor the translate_service and restart it should it die.
- Make the Doctor process restart itself if it should die.
- Make a monitor for the Doctor monitor. If either monitor dies, restart it.

The following bonus questions will take a little bit of research to complete:

- Create a basic OTP server that logs messages to a file.
- Make the translate_service work across a network.

6.5 Wrapping Up Erlang

At the beginning of this chapter, I said that Erlang made hard things easy and easy things hard. The Prolog-style syntax is alien to those familiar with the broad family of C-style languages, and the functional programming paradigm has its own set of challenges.

But Erlang has some core capabilities that will be tremendously important as new hardware designs make programming for concurrency more important. Some of the capabilities are philosophical. The lightweight processes run counter to Java's thread and process models. The "Let it crash" philosophy simplifies code tremendously but also requires base support at the virtual machine level that just doesn't exist in other systems. Let's break down the core advantages and disadvantages.

Core Strengths

Erlang is all about concurrency and fault tolerance, from the inside out. As processor designers look to distributed cores, the state of the art in programming must evolve. Erlang's strengths are in the most important areas that this generation of programmers will face.

Dynamic and Reliable

First and foremost, Erlang is built for reliability. The core libraries have been tested, and Erlang applications are among the most reliable and available in the world. Most impressively, the language designers achieved this reliability without sacrificing the dynamic typing strategies that make Erlang so productive. Rather than depend on the compiler for an artificial safety net, Erlang depends on the ability to link concurrent processes, reliably and simply. I was astounded about how easy it was to build dependable monitors without relying on operating system kludges.

I think the set of compromises that you find in Erlang is compelling and unique. The Java language and virtual machine does not provide the right set of primitives to duplicate Erlang performance or reliability. The libraries built on the BEAM also reflect this philosophy, so it's relatively easy to build reliable, distributed systems.

Lightweight, Share-Nothing Processes

Another place Erlang shines is the underlying process model. Erlang processes are light, so Erlang programmers use them often. Erlang builds on a philosophy of enforcing immutability, so programmers build systems that are inherently less likely to fail by conflicting with one another. The message-passing paradigm and primitives make it easy to code applications with a level of separation that you rarely find in object-oriented applications.

OTP, the Enterprise Libraries

Since Erlang grew up in a telecom company with high requirements for availability and reliability, it has twenty years worth of libraries that support this style of development. The primary library is Open Telecom Platform (OTP). You can find libraries that help you build monitored, keep-alive processes; link to databases; or build distributed applications. OTP has a full web server and many tools for binding to telecom applications.

The nice thing about the set of libraries is that fault tolerance, scalability, transactional integrity, and hot-swapping are all built in. You don't have to worry about them. You can build your own server processes that take advantage of these features.

Let It Crash

When you're dealing with parallel processes and no side effects, "Let it crash" works—you're not as worried about why individual processes crash because you can restart them. The functional programming model amplifies the benefits of Erlang's distribution strategy.

Like all the other languages in this book, Erlang is tainted. Only the nature of the problems changes. These are the places that Agent Smith may not always play so nice.

Core Weaknesses

Erlang's fundamental problems with adoption come from roots firmly planted in a niche language. The syntax is alien to the vast majority of programmers. Also, the functional programming paradigm is different enough that it will cause problems with widespread adoption. Finally, by far the best implementation is on the BEAM and not the Java virtual machine. Let's dig in a little deeper.

Syntax

Like a movie, syntax is subjective. Beyond this problem, though, Erlang has some problems that even the impartial will notice. Let's look at two of them.

Interestingly, some of Erlang's core strengths come from the Prolog foundations, as well as its weaknesses. To most of the programming population, Prolog is obscure, and the syntax comes off as awkward and alien. A little syntactic sugar to ease the transition could go a long way.

In the chapter, I mentioned the problems with `if` and `case` constructs. The syntactic rules are logical—use a separator between statements—but not practical because you can't change the order of `case`, `if`, or `receive` blocks without having to change your punctuation. These restrictions are unnecessary. And there are other oddities, such as the conditional presentation of an array of numbers as strings. Cleaning these up would help Erlang tremendously.

Integration

As with the Prolog heritage, not being on the JVM has been a double-edged sword. Recently, a JVM-based VM called Erjang has made progress but is not yet to the level of the best JVM alternatives. The JVM does come with baggage, such as a process and threading model that's inadequate for Erlang's needs. But being on the JVM has a set of advantages as well, too, including the wealth of Java libraries and the hundreds of thousands of potential deployment servers.

Final Thoughts

The success of a programming language is a fickle thing. Erlang faces some serious obstacles on the marketing side, and having to lure Java programmers over to a Lisp-style programming paradigm and a Prolog-style syntax won't be easy. Erlang does seem to be gathering momentum because it solves the right problems in the right way at the right time. In this battle between Anderson and Agent Smith, I give Agent Smith an even-money chance at success.

Do or do not...there is no try.

► Yoda

Chapter 7 Clojure

Clojure is Lisp on the JVM. Perplexing and powerful, Lisp is one of the first programming languages and one of the latest too. Dozens of dialects tried to launch Lisp into the mainstream and failed. The syntax and programming model so far have been too much for a typical developer to absorb. Yet, there's something special about Lisp that's worth revisiting, so the new dialects continue to emerge. Some of the best programming universities lead with the Lisp language to form young minds while they are still open.

In many ways, Clojure is the wise kung fu master, the oracle on the hill, or the enigmatic Jedi trainer. Think Yoda. In *Star Wars Episode V: The Empire Strikes Back*,[1] Yoda was introduced as a cute character with little significance. His communication style is often inverted and hard to understand, like Lisp prefix notation (understand me later you will). He seems too small to make a difference, like the Lisp syntactic rules with little more than parentheses and symbols. But it quickly becomes apparent that there is more to Yoda than meets the eye. As with Lisp, he is old, with wisdom (like the quote above) that has been honed by time and tried under fire. Like Lisp's macros and higher-order constructs, he has an inner power that others can't seem to master. In many ways, Lisp started it all. Before diving in too deeply, let's talk a little bit about Lisp and then shift gears to what's exciting about Clojure.

1. *Star Wars Episode V: The Empire Strikes Back*. Directed by George Lucas. 1980; Beverly Hills, CA: 20th Century Fox, 2004.

7.1 Introducing Clojure

When all is said and done, Clojure is yet another Lisp dialect. It will have the same language limitations and many of the same considerable strengths. Understanding Clojure starts with understanding Lisp.

All Lisp

After Fortran, Lisp is the oldest commercially active language. It's a functional language but not a pure functional language. The acronym stands for LISt Processing, and early on, you'll see why. Lisp has some interesting characteristics:

- Lisp is a language of lists. A function call uses the first list element as the function and the rest as the arguments.
- Lisp uses its own data structures to express code. Lisp followers call this strategy *data as code*.

When you combine these two ideas, you get a language that's ideal for metaprogramming. You can arrange your code as named methods in a class. You could arrange those objects into a tree, and you have a basic object model. You could also build a prototype-based code organization with slots for data and behavior. You can build a pure-functional implementation. It's this flexibility that allows Lisp to morph the language into just about any programming paradigm you want.

In *Hackers and Painters* [Gra04], Paul Graham chronicles the story of how a small development team used Lisp and its powerful programming model to defeat much larger companies. They believed Lisp provided a significant programming advantage. In fact, they paid more attention to start-ups posting jobs requiring Lisp and other higher-level languages.

The primary Lisp dialects are Common Lisp and Scheme. Scheme and Clojure are from the same family of dialects called lisp-1, and Common Lisp is a lisp-2 dialect. The primary difference between the dialect families has to do with the way namespaces work. Common Lisp uses a separate namespace for functions and variables, while Scheme uses the same namespace for both. With the Lisp side of the equation behind us, let's move on to the Java side.

On the JVM

Every Lisp dialect caters to its audience. For Clojure, one of the most important characteristics is the JVM. With Scala, you saw that having a commercially successful deployment platform can make all the difference in the world. You don't have to sell a Clojure server to your deployment people to use it. Though the language is relatively new, you can access the tens of thousands of Java libraries to do just about anything you need.

Throughout this chapter, you'll see evidence of the JVM, in the way you invoke it, in the libraries we use, and in artifacts we create. But you'll also see liberation, too. Clojure is functional, so you'll be able to apply advanced concepts to your code. Clojure is dynamically typed, so your code will be more concise, easier to read, and more fun to write. And Clojure has the expressiveness of Lisp.

Clojure and Java desperately need each other. Lisp needs the market place that the Java virtual machine can offer, and the Java community needs a serious update and an injection of fun.

Updated for a Concurrent World

The last piece of the equation for this language is the set of libraries. Clojure is a functional language, with emphasis on functions without side effects. But when you do use mutable state, the language supports a number of concepts to help. Transactional memory works like transactional databases to provide safe, concurrent access to memory. Agents allow encapsulated access to mutable resources. We'll cover some of these concepts in day 3.

Impatient are you? Start with Clojure, we will.

7.2 Day 1: Training Luke

In *Star Wars*, the apprentice Luke joined with Yoda for advanced training in the ways of the Jedi. He had started his training under another. Like Luke, you have already started your training for functional languages. You used closures in Ruby and graduated to higher-order functions in Scala and Erlang. In this chapter, you're going to learn to apply some of those concepts in Clojure.

Go to the Clojure home site at http://www.assembla.com/wiki/show/clojure/Getting_Started. Follow the instructions to install Clojure on your platform and with your preferred development environment. I'm using a prerelease version of Clojure 1.2, and it should be fully ready by the time this book is in your hands. You may first need to install the Java platform, though today, most operating systems come with Java installed. I'm using the leiningen tool[2] to manage my Clojure projects and Java configuration. That tool lets me build a project and insulates me from the Java details such as classpaths. Once that's installed, I can then create a new project:

```
batate$ lein new seven-languages
Created new project in: seven-languages
batate$ cd seven-languages/
seven-languages batate$
```

Then, I can start the Clojure console, called the repl:

```
seven-languages batate$ lein repl
Copying 2 files to /Users/batate/lein/seven-languages/lib
user=>
```

...and I'm off to the races. Underneath, leiningen is installing some dependencies and calling Java with a few Clojure Java archives (jars) and options. Your installation may require you to start the repl some other way. From here on out, I'll just tell you to start the repl.

After all of that work, you have a primitive console. When I ask you to evaluate code, you can use this repl, or you can use one of any number of IDEs or editors that have Clojure support.

Let's type some code:

```
user=> (println "Give me some Clojure!")
Give me some Clojure!
nil
```

So, the console is working. In Clojure, you'll enclose any function call entirely in parentheses. The first element is the function name, and the rest are the arguments. You can nest them, too. Let's demonstrate the concept with a little math.

Calling Basic Functions

```
user=> (- 1)
-1
user=> (+ 1 1)
2
user=> (* 10 10)
100
```

That's just basic math. Division is a little more interesting:

```
user=> (/ 1 3)
1/3
```

2. http://github.com/technomancy/leiningen

```
user=> (/ 2 4)
1/2
user=> (/ 2.0 4)
0.5
user=> (class (/ 1 3))
clojure.lang.Ratio
```

Clojure has a basic data type called a *ratio*. It's a nice feature that will allow delaying computation to avoid the loss of precision. You can still easily work in floats if you so choose. You can easily calculate remainders:

```
user=> (mod 5 4)
1
```

That's short for modulus operator. This notation is called *prefix notation*. Languages to this point have supported infix notation, with the operator between the operands, like 4 + 1 - 2. Many people prefer infix notation because we're used to it. We're used to seeing math expressed in this way. After warming up, you should be getting into the flow of prefix notation. It's a little awkward doing math in this way, but it works. Prefix notation with parentheses does have advantages, though. Consider this expression:

```
user=> (/ (/ 12 2) (/ 6 2))
2
```

There's no ambiguity. Clojure will evaluate this statement in parenthetical order. And check out this expression:

```
user=> (+ 2 2 2 2)
8
```

You can easily add elements to the calculation, if you so choose. You can even use this style when working with subtraction or division:

```
user=> (- 8 1 2)
5
user=> (/ 8 2 2)
2
```

We've evaluated (8 - 1) - 2 and (8 / 2) / 2 in conventional (infix) notation. Or, if you'd like to see the Clojure equivalent using only two operands at a time, it is (- (- 8 1) 2) and (/ (/ 8 2) 2). You can also get some surprisingly powerful results out of simple operator evaluation:

```
user=> (< 1 2 3)
true
user=> (< 1 3 2 4)
false
```

Nice. We can see whether a list is in order with a single operator and an arbitrary number of arguments.

Aside from the prefix notation and the extra wrinkle of multiple parameter lists, Clojure's syntax is very simple. Let's try to push the typing system a little, probing for strong typing and coerced types:

```
user=> (+ 3.0 5)
8.0
user=> (+ 3 5.0)
8.0
```

Clojure works to coerce types for us. In general, you'll find that Clojure supports strong, dynamic typing. Let's get a little more focused and look at some of Clojure's basic building blocks, called *forms*.

Think of a form as a piece of syntax. When Clojure parses code, it first breaks the program down into pieces called *forms*. Then, Clojure can compile or interpret the code. I'm not going to distinguish between code and data, because in Lisp, they are one and the same. Booleans, characters, strings, sets, maps, and vectors are all examples of forms that you'll see throughout this chapter.

Strings and Chars

You've already been introduced to strings, but we can take it a little deeper. You'll enclose strings in double quotes, and use C-style escaping characters, as in Ruby:

```
user=> (println "master yoda\nluke skywalker\ndarth vader")
master yoda
luke skywalker
darth vader
nil
```

No surprises. As an aside, so far, we've used a single argument with println, but the function also works well with zero or more arguments to print a blank line or several values concatenated together.

In Clojure, you can convert things to a string with the str function:

```
user=> (str 1)
"1"
```

If the target underneath is a Java class, str will call the underlying toString function. This function takes more than one argument, like this:

```
user=> (str "yoda, " "luke,  " "darth")
"yoda, luke,  darth"
```

As a result, Clojure developers use str to concatenate strings together. Conveniently, you can concatenate items that are not strings:

```
user=> (str "one: " 1 " two: " 2)
"one: 1 two: 2"
```

You can even concatenate different types together. To represent a character outside of double quotes, you can precede it with a \ character, like this:

```
user=> \a
\a
```

And as usual, you can concatenate them together with str:

```
user=> (str \f \o \r \c \e)
"force"
```

Let's make some comparisons:

```
user=> (= "a" \a)
false
```

So, characters are not strings of length 1.

```
user=> (= (str \a) "a")
true
```

But you can easily convert characters to strings. That's enough string manipulation for now. Let's move on to some boolean expressions.

Booleans and Expressions

Clojure has strong, dynamic typing. Recall that dynamic typing means types are evaluated at run time. You've already seen a few of the types in action, but let's focus that discussion a little bit. A boolean is the result of an expression:

```
user=> (= 1 1.0)
true
user=> (= 1 2)
false
user=> (< 1 2)
true
```

As with most other languages in this book, true is a symbol. But it is also something else. Clojure's types are unified with the underlying Java type system. You can get the underlying class with the class function. Here's the class of a boolean:

```
user=> (class true)
java.lang.Boolean
user=> (class (= 1 1))
java.lang.Boolean
```

So, you can see the JVM peeking through. This type strategy will make things far more convenient for you as you move along. You can use the result of booleans in many expressions. Here is a simple if:

```
user=> (if true (println "True it is."))
True it is.
nil
user=> (if (> 1 2) (println "True it is."))
nil
```

Like Io, we passed in code as the second argument to the if. Conveniently, Lisp lets us treat the data as code. We can make it prettier by breaking the code across multiple lines:

```
user=> (if (< 1 2)
  (println "False it is not."))
False it is not.
nil
```

We can add an else as the third argument:

```
user=> (if false (println "true") (println "false"))
false
nil
```

Now, let's see what else we can use as booleans. First, what passes for a nil in Clojure?

```
user=> (first ())
nil
```

Ah. That's simple. The symbol called nil.

```
user=> (if 0 (println "true"))
true
nil
user=> (if nil (println "true"))
nil
user=> (if "" (println "true"))
true
nil
```

0 and "" are true, but nil is not. We'll introduce other boolean expressions as we need them. Now, let's look at some more complex data structures.

Lists, Maps, Sets, and Vectors

As with all functional languages, core data structures such as lists and tuples do the heavy lifting. In Clojure, three big ones are lists, maps, and vectors. We'll start things off with the collection you've spent most of your time with so far, the list.

Lists

A list is an ordered collection of elements. These elements can be anything, but in idiomatic Clojure, lists are used for code and vectors for data. I'll walk you through lists with data, though, to prevent confusion. Since lists evaluate as functions, you can't do this:

```
user=> (1 2 3)
java.lang.ClassCastException: java.lang.Integer
    cannot be cast to clojure.lang.IFn (NO_SOURCE_FILE:0)
```

If you really want a list made up of 1, 2, and 3, you need to do one of these things, instead:

```
user=> (list 1 2 3)
(1 2 3)
user=> '(1 2 3)
(1 2 3)
```

Then, you can manipulate the lists as usual. The second form is called *quoting*. The four main operations for a list are first (the head), rest (the list minus the head), last (the last element), and cons (construct a new list given a head and a tail):

```
user=> (first '(:r2d2 :c3po))
:r2d2
user=> (last '(:r2d2 :c3po))
:c3po
user=> (rest '(:r2d2 :c3po))
(:c3po)
user=> (cons :battle-droid '(:r2d2 :c3po))
(:battle-droid :r2d2 :c3po)
```

Of course, you can combine these with higher-order functions, but we'll wait to do so until we encounter sequences. Now, let's move to a close cousin of the list, the vector.

Vectors

Like a list, a vector is an ordered collection of elements. Vectors are optimized for random access. You'll surround vectors with square brackets, like this:

```
user=> [:hutt :wookie :ewok]
[:hutt :wookie :ewok]
```

Use lists for code and vectors for data. You can get various elements like this:

```
user=> (first [:hutt :wookie :ewok])
:hutt
user=> (nth [:hutt :wookie :ewok] 2)
:ewok
```

```
user=> (nth [:hutt :wookie :ewok] 0)
:hutt
user=> (last [:hutt :wookie :ewok])
:ewok
user=> ([:hutt :wookie :ewok] 2)
:ewok
```

Note that vectors are functions, too, taking an index as an argument. You can combine two vectors like this:

```
user=> (concat [:darth-vader] [:darth-maul])
(:darth-vader :darth-maul)
```

You may have noticed that repl printed out a list instead of a vector. Many of the functions that return collections use a Clojure abstraction called *sequences*. We'll learn more about them in day 2. For now, just understand that Clojure is returning a sequence and rendering it as a list in the repl.

Clojure lets you get the typical head and tail of a vector, of course:

```
user=> (first [:hutt :wookie :ewok])
:hutt
user=> (rest [:hutt :wookie :ewok])
(:wookie :ewok)
```

We'll use both of these features as we do pattern matching. Both lists and vectors are ordered. Let's move on to some of the unordered collections, sets and maps.

Sets

A set is an unordered collection of elements. The collection has a stable order, but that order is implementation-dependent, so you shouldn't count on it. You'll wrap a set in #{}, like this:

```
user=> #{:x-wing :y-wing :tie-fighter}
#{:x-wing :y-wing :tie-fighter}
```

We can assign those to a variable called spacecraft and then manipulate them:

```
user=> (def spacecraft #{:x-wing :y-wing :tie-fighter})
#'user/spacecraft
user=> spacecraft
#{:x-wing :y-wing :tie-fighter}
user=> (count spacecraft)
3
user=> (sort spacecraft)
(:tie-fighter :x-wing :y-wing)
```

We can also create a sorted set that takes items in any order and returns them in sorted order:

```
user=> (sorted-set 2 3 1)
#{1 2 3}
```

You can merge two sets, like this:

```
user=> (clojure.set/union #{:skywalker} #{:vader})
#{:skywalker :vader}
```

Or compute the difference:

```
(clojure.set/difference #{1 2 3} #{2})
```

I'll give you one last convenient oddity before I move on. Sets are also functions. The set #{:jar-jar, :chewbacca} is an element but also a function. Sets test membership, like this:

```
user=> (#{:jar-jar :chewbacca} :chewbacca)
:chewbacca
user=> (#{:jar-jar :chewbacca} :luke)
nil
```

When you use a set as a function, the function will return the first argument if that argument is a member of the set. That covers the basics for sets. Let's move on to maps.

Maps

As you know, a map is a key-value pair. Using Clojure, you'll represent a map with curly braces, like this:

```
user=> {:chewie :wookie :lea :human}
{:chewie :wookie, :lea :human}
```

These are examples of maps, key-value pairs, but they are tough to read. It would be hard to see an odd number of keys and values, leading to an error:

```
user=> {:jabba :hut :han}
java.lang.ArrayIndexOutOfBoundsException: 3
```

Clojure solves this problem by allowing commas as whitespace, like this:

```
user=> {:darth-vader "obi wan", :luke "yoda"}
{:darth-vader "obi wan", :luke "yoda"}
```

A word preceded with : is a keyword, like symbols in Ruby or atoms in Prolog or Erlang. Clojure has two kinds of forms that are used to name things in this way, *keywords* and *symbols*. Symbols point to something else, and keywords point to themselves. true and map are symbols. Use keywords to name domain entities such as a property in a map as you would use an atom in Erlang.

Let's define a map called mentors:

```
user=> (def mentors {:darth-vader "obi wan", :luke "yoda"})
#'user/mentors
user=> mentors
{:darth-vader "obi wan", :luke "yoda"}
```

Now, you can retrieve a value by passing a key as the first value:

```
user=> (mentors :luke)
"yoda"
```

Maps are also functions. Keywords are also functions:

```
user=> (:luke mentors)
"yoda"
```

:luke, the function, looks itself up in a map. It's odd but useful. As with Ruby, you can use any data type as a key or value. And you can merge two maps with merge:

```
user=> (merge {:y-wing 2, :x-wing 4} {:tie-fighter 2})
{:tie-fighter 2, :y-wing 2, :x-wing 4}
```

You can also specify an operator to use when a hash exists in both maps:

```
user=> (merge-with + {:y-wing 2, :x-wing 4} {:tie-fighter 2 :x-wing 3})
{:tie-fighter 2, :y-wing 2, :x-wing 7}
```

In this case, we combined the 4 and the 3 values associated with the x-wing keys with +. Given an association, you can create a new association with a new key-value pair, like this:

```
user=>(assoc {:one 1} :two 2)
{:two 2, :one 1}
```

You can create a sorted map that takes items in any order and spits them out sorted, like this:

```
user=> (sorted-map 1 :one, 3 :three, 2 :two)
{1 :one, 2 :two, 3 :three}
```

We're gradually adding more structure to data. Now, we can move on to the form that adds behavior, the function.

Defining Functions

Functions are the centerpiece of all kinds of Lisps. Use *defn* to define a function.

```
user=> (defn force-it [] (str "Use the force," "Luke."))
#'user/force-it
```

The simplest form is (defn [params] body). We defined a function called force-it with no parameters. The function simply concatenated two strings together. Call the function like any other:

```
user=> (force-it)
"Use the force,Luke."
```

If you want, you can specify an extra string describing the function:

```
user=> (defn force-it
             "The first function a young Jedi needs"
             []
             (str "Use the force," "Luke"))
```

Then, you can recall documentation for the function with doc:

```
user=> (doc force-it)
-------------------------
user/force-it
([])
  The first function a young Jedi needs
nil
```

Let's add a parameter:

```
user=> (defn force-it
             "The first function a young Jedi needs"
             [jedi]
             (str "Use the force," jedi))
#'user/force-it
user=> (force-it "Luke")
"Use the force,Luke"
```

By the way, you can use this doc feature on any other function that specifies a documentation line:

```
user=> (doc str)
-------------------------
clojure.core/str
([] [x] [x & ys])
  With no args, returns the empty string. With one arg x, returns
  x.toString().  (str nil) returns the empty string. With more than
  one arg, returns the concatenation of the str values of the args.
nil
```

Now that you can define a basic function, let's move on to the parameter list.

Bindings

As in most of the other languages we've looked at so far, the process of assigning parameters based on the inbound arguments is called *binding*. One of the nice things about Clojure is its ability to access any portion of any argument as a parameter. For example, say you had a line, represented as a vector of points, like this:

```
user=> (def line [[0 0] [10 20]])
#'user/line
user=> line
[[0 0] [10 20]]
```

You could build a function to access the end of the line, like this:

```
user=> (defn line-end [ln] (last  ln))
#'user/line-end
user=> (line-end line)
[10 20]
```

But we don't really need the whole line. It would be nicer to bind our parameter to the second element of the line. With Clojure, it's easy:

```
(defn line-end [[_ second]] second)
#'user/line-end
user=> (line-end line)
[10 20]
```

The concept is called *destructuring*. We're taking a data structure apart and grabbing only the pieces that are important to us. Let's take a closer look at the bindings. We have [[_ second]]. The outer brackets define the parameter vector. The inner brackets say we're going to bind to individual elements of a list or vector. _ and second are individual parameters, but it's idiomatic to use _ for parameters you want to ignore. In English, we're saying "The parameters for this function are _ for the first element of the first argument, and second for the second element of the first argument."

We can also nest these bindings. Let's say we have a tic-tac-toe board, and we want to return the value of the middle square. We'll represent the board as three rows of three, like this:

```
user=> (def board [[:x :o :x] [:o :x :o] [:o :x :o]])
#'user/board
```

Now, we want to pick up the second element of the second row of three, like this:

```
user=> (defn center [[_ [_ c _] _]] c)
#'user/center
```

Beautiful! We're essentially nesting the same concept. Let's break it down. The bindings are [[_ [_ c _] _]]. We'll bind one parameter to the inbound argument, [_ [_ c _] _]. That parameter says we're going to ignore the first and third elements, which are the top and bottom rows in our tic-tac-toe board. We'll focus on the middle row, which is [_ c _]. We're expecting another list and grabbing the center one:

```
user=> (center board)
:x
```

We can simplify that function in a couple of different ways. First, we don't have to list any of the wildcard arguments that come after the target arguments:

```
(defn center [[_ [_ c]]] c)
```

Next, destructuring can happen in the argument list or also in a let statement. In any Lisp, you'll use let to bind a variable to a value. We could use let to hide the destructuring from the clients of the center function:

```
(defn center [board]
 (let [[_ [_ c]] board] c))
```

let takes two arguments. First is a vector with the symbol you want to bind ([[_ [_c]]]) followed by the value (board) that you want bound. Next is some expression that presumably uses that value (we just returned c). Both forms produce equivalent results. It all depends on where you want the destructuring to happen. I'll show you a couple of brief examples using let, but understand that you could also use them within an argument list.

You can destructure a map:

```
user=> (def person {:name "Jabba" :profession "Gangster"})
#'user/person
user=> (let [{name :name} person] (str "The person's name is " name))
"The person's name is Jabba"
```

You can also combine maps and vectors:

```
user=> (def villains [{:name "Godzilla" :size "big"} {:name "Ebola" :size "small"}])
#'user/villains
user=> (let [[_ {name :name}] villains] (str "Name of the second villain: " name))
"Name of the second villain: Ebola"
```

We bound to a vector, skipping the first and picking out the name of the second map. You can see the influence of Lisp on Prolog and, by extension, Erlang. Destructuring is simply a form of pattern matching.

Anonymous Functions

In Lisp, functions are just data. Higher-order functions are built into the language from the ground up because code is just like any other kind of data. Anonymous functions let you create unnamed functions. It's a fundamental capability for every language in this book. In Clojure, you'll define a higher-order function with the fn function. Typically, you'll omit the name, so the form looks like (fn [parameters*] body). Let's take an example.

Let's use a higher-order function to build a list of word counts, given a list of words. Let's say we have a list of people's names:

```
user=> (def people ["Lea", "Han Solo"])
#'user/people
```

We can compute the length of one word like this:

```
user=> (count "Lea")
3
```

We can build a list of the lengths of the names, like this:

```
user=> (map count people)
(3 8)
```

You've seen these concepts before. count in this context is a higher-order function. In Clojure, that concept is easy because a function is a list, just like any other list element. You can use the same building blocks to compute a list having twice the lengths of person names, like this:

```
user=> (defn twice-count [w] (* 2 (count w)))
#'user/twice-count
user=> (twice-count "Lando")
10
user=> (map twice-count people)
(6 16)
```

Since that function is so simple, we can write it as an anonymous function, like this:

```
user=> (map (fn [w] (* 2 (count w))) people)
(6 16)
```

We can also use a shorter form:

```
user=> (map #(* 2 (count %)) people)
(6 16)
```

With the short form, # defines an anonymous function, with % bound to each item of the sequence. # is called a *reader macro*.

Anonymous functions give you convenience and leverage to create a function that doesn't need a name *right now*. You've seen them in other languages. Here are some of the functions on collections that use higher-order functions. For all of these functions, we're going to use a common vector, called v:

```
user=> (def v [3 1 2])
#'user/v
```

We'll use that list with several anonymous functions in the following examples.

apply

apply applies a function to an argument list. (apply f '(x y)) works like (f x y), like this:

```
user=> (apply + v)
6
user=> (apply max v)
3
```

filter

The filter function works like find_all in Ruby. It takes a function that is a test and returns the sequence of elements that pass the test. For example, to get only the odd elements or the elements less than 3, use this:

```
user=> (filter odd? v)
(3 1)
user=> (filter #(< % 3) v)
(1 2)
```

We'll take a deeper look at some of the anonymous functions as we look deeper into Clojure sequences. For now, let's take a break and see what Rich Hickey, creator of Clojure, has to say.

Interview with Rich Hickey, Creator of Clojure

Rich Hickey answered some questions for the readers of this book. He had a special interest in why this Lisp version could be more broadly successful than other Lisps, so this interview is a little more extensive than most. I hope you find his answers as fascinating as I did.

Bruce Tate: *Why did you write Clojure?*

Rich Hickey: *I'm just a practitioner who wanted a predominantly functional, extensible, dynamic language, with a solid concurrency story, for the industry-standard platforms of the JVM and CLR and didn't find one.*

Bruce Tate: *What do you like about it the most?*

Rich Hickey: *I like the emphasis on abstractions in the data structures and library and the simplicity. Maybe that's two things, but they are related.*

Bruce Tate: *What feature would you change if you could start over again?*

Rich Hickey: *I'd explore a different approach to numbers. Boxed numbers are certainly a sore spot on the JVM. This is an area I am actively working on.*

Bruce Tate: *What's the most interesting problem you've seen solved with Clojure?*

Rich Hickey: *I think Flightcaster*[3] *(a service that predicts flight delays in real time) leverages many aspects of Clojure—from using the syntactic abstraction of macros to make a DSL for the machine learning and statistical inference bits to the Java interop for working with infrastructure like Hadoop and Cascading.*

Bruce Tate: *But how can Clojure be more broadly successful when so many other dialects of Lisp have failed?*

Rich Hickey: *This is an important question! I'm not sure I would characterize the major dialects of Lisp (Scheme and Common Lisp) as having failed at their missions. Scheme was an attempt at a very small language that captured the essentials of computation, while Common Lisp strove to standardize the many variant dialects of Lisp being used in research. They have failed to catch on as practical tools for general-purpose production programming by developers in industry, something that neither was designed to be.*

Clojure, on the other hand, is designed to be a practical tool for general-purpose production programming by developers in industry and as such adds these additional objectives to the Lisps of old. We work better in teams, we play well with other languages, and we solve some traditional Lisp problems.

Bruce Tate: *How does Clojure work better in a team setting?*

Rich Hickey: *There is a sense in which some Lisps are all about maximally empowering the individual developer, but Clojure recognizes that*

3. http://www.infoq.com/articles/flightcaster-clojure-rails

development is a team effort. For example, it doesn't support user-defined reader macros, which could lead to code being written in small incompatible micro-dialects.

Bruce Tate: *Why did you choose to run on existing virtual machines?*

Rich Hickey: *The existence of large and valuable code bases written in other languages is a fact of life today and wasn't when the older Lisps were invented. The ability to call and be called by other languages is critical, especially on the JVM and CLR.*[4]

The whole idea of standard multilanguage platforms abstracting away the host OS barely existed when the older Lisps were invented. The industry is orders of magnitude larger now, and de facto standards have arisen. Technically, the stratification that supports the reuse of core technologies like sophisticated garbage collectors and dynamic compilers like HotSpot is a good thing. So, Clojure emphasizes language-on-platform rather than language-is-platform.

Bruce Tate: *Fair enough. But how is this Lisp any more approachable?*

Rich Hickey: *Lots of reasons. For example, we wanted to deal with the parentheses "problem." Lisp programmers know the value of code-is-data, but it is wrong to simply dismiss those who are put off by the parentheses. I don't think moving from* `foo(bar, baz)` *to* `(foo bar baz)` *is difficult for developers. But I did take a hard look at the parentheses use in the older Lisps to see whether the story could be better, and it could. Older Lisps use parentheses for everything. We don't. And in older Lisps, there are simply too many parentheses. Clojure takes the opposite approach, doing away with the grouping parentheses, making it slightly harder for macro writers but easier for users.*

The combination of fewer parentheses and almost no overloading of parentheses renders Clojure much easier to scan, visually parse, and understand than older Lisps. Leading double parentheses are more common in Java code, the horrid `((AType)athing).amethod()`*, than in Clojure code.*

What We Learned in Day 1

Clojure is a functional language on the JVM. Like Scala and Erlang, this Lisp dialect is a functional language but not a pure functional language. It allows limited side effects. Unlike other Lisp dialects, Clojure adds a

4. *Microsoft's common language runtime, a virtual machine for the .NET platform*

little syntax, preferring braces for maps and brackets for vectors. You can use commas for whitespace and omit parentheses in some places.

We learned to use the basic Clojure forms. The simpler forms included booleans, characters, numbers, keywords, and strings. We also broke into the various collections. Lists and vectors were ordered containers with vectors optimized for random access and lists optimized for ordered traversal. We also used sets, or unordered collections, and maps, which were key-value pairs.

We defined some named functions, providing a name, parameter list, and function body with an optional documentation string. Next, we used deconstruction with bindings, allowing us to bind any parameter to any part of an inbound argument. The feature was reminiscent of Prolog or Erlang. Finally, we defined some anonymous functions and used them to iterate over a list with the map function.

On day 2, we'll look at recursion in Clojure, a basic building block in most functional languages. We'll also look at sequences and lazy evaluations, some cornerstones of the Clojure models that help layer a common, powerful abstraction on top of collections.

Now, we'll take a break to put into practice what you've learned so far.

Day 1 Self-Study

Clojure is a new language, but you'll still find a surprisingly active, and growing, community. They were among the best that I found as I researched this book.

Find:

- Examples using Clojure sequences
- The formal definition of a Clojure function
- A script for quickly invoking the repl in your environment

Do:

- Implement a function called `(big st n)` that returns true if a string `st` is longer than `n` characters.
- Write a function called `(collection-type col)` that returns `:list`, `:map`, or `:vector` based on the type of collection `col`.

7.3 Day 2: Yoda and the Force

As a Jedi master, Yoda trained apprentices to use and understand the Force, the unifying presence between all living things. In this section, we get to the concepts fundamental to Clojure. We'll talk about sequences, the abstraction layer that unifies all Clojure collections and ties them to Java collections. We'll also look at lazy evaluation, the just-in-time strategy that computes sequence members only when you need them. And then we'll look at that mystical language feature that is the Force for all Lisps, the macro.

Recursion with loop and recur

As you've learned in other languages in this book, functional languages depend on recursion rather than iteration. Here's a recursive program to evaluate the size of a vector:

```
(defn size [v]
    (if (empty? v)
            0
            (inc (size (rest v)))))

(size [1 2 3])
```

It's not hard to understand. The size of an empty list is zero; the size of another list is one more than the size of the tail. We've seen similar solutions for other languages throughout this book.

You've also learned that stacks can grow, so recursive algorithms will continue to consume memory until all memory is exhausted. Functional languages work around this limitation with tail recursion optimization. Clojure does not support implicit tail recursion optimization because of limitations of the JVM. You must explicitly recur through the use of loop and recur. Think of a loop as a let statement.

```
(loop [x x-initial-value, y y-initial-value] (do-something-with x y))
```

Initially, given a vector, loop binds the variables in the even positions to the values in the odd positions. In fact, if you don't specify a recur, loop works exactly like a let:

```
user=> (loop [x 1] x)
1
```

The function recur will invoke the loop again but this time pass new values.

Let's refactor the size function to use recur:

```
(defn size [v]
        (loop [l v, c 0]
        (if (empty? l)
                c
                (recur (rest l) (inc c)))))
```

In the second version of size, we'll use the tail-recursion-optimized loop and recur. Since we won't actually return a value, we'll maintain the result in a variable called an *accumulator*. In this case, c will maintain a count.

This version works like a tail-optimized call, but we're stuck with more kludgy lines of code. Sometimes, the JVM is a double-edged sword. If you want the community, you need to deal with the problems. But since this function is built into some basic collection APIs, you won't often need to use recur. Also, Clojure gives you some excellent alternatives to recursion, including lazy sequences that we'll get to later in this chapter.

With day 2's bad news out of the way, we're free to shift to more pleasant matters. Sequences will start to take us into some of the features that make Clojure special.

Sequences

A sequence is an implementation-independent abstraction around all the various containers in the Clojure ecosystem. Sequences wrap all Clojure collections (sets, maps, vectors, and the like), strings, and even file system structures (streams, directories). They also provide a common abstraction for Java containers, including Java collections, arrays, and strings. In general, if it supports the functions first, rest, and cons, you can wrap it in a sequence.

Earlier, when you were working with vectors, Clojure sometimes responded with a list in the console like this:

```
user=> [1 2 3]
[1 2 3]
user=> (rest [1 2 3])
(2 3)
```

Notice that we started with a vector. The result is not a list. repl actually responded with a sequence. That means we can treat all collections in a generic way. Let's look at the common sequence library. It's too rich and powerful to cover entirely in one section of a chapter, but I'll try to give you a flavor of what's available. I'm going to cover sequence functions that change, test, and create sequences, but I'm going to touch on them only briefly.

Tests

When you want to test a sequence, you will use a function called a *predicate*. These take a sequence and a test function and return a boolean. every? returns true if the test function is true for all items in the sequence:

```
user=> (every? number? [1 2 3 :four])
false
```

So, one of the items is not a number. some is true if the test is true for any of the items in the sequence:[5]

```
(some nil? [1 2 nil])
true
```

One of the items is nil. not-every? and not-any? are the inverses:

```
user=> (not-every? odd? [1 3 5])
false
user=> (not-any? number? [:one :two :three])
true
```

These behave exactly as you would expect. Let's shift to functions that change sequences.

Changing a Sequence

The sequence library has a number of sequences that transform sequences in various ways. You've already seen filter. To grab only the words with a length greater than four, use this:

```
user=> (def words ["luke" "chewie" "han" "lando"])
#'user/words
user=> (filter  (fn [word] (> (count word) 4)) words)
("chewie" "lando")
```

And you've also seen map, which calls a function on all the items in a collection and returns the results. You can build a sequence of squares of all items in a vector:

```
user=> (map (fn [x] (* x x)) [1 1 2 3 5])
(1 1 4 9 25)
```

5. More precisely, some returns the first value that is not nil or false. For example, (some first [[] [1]]) returns 1.

The list comprehension combines maps and filters, as you saw in Erlang and Scala. Recall that a list comprehension combines multiple lists and filters, taking the possible combinations of the lists and applying the filters. First, let's take a simple case. We have a couple of lists, colors and toys:

```
user=> (def colors ["red" "blue"])
#'user/colors
user=> (def toys ["block" "car"])
#'user/toys
```

We can apply a function to all the colors with a list comprehension, similar to the way a map works:

```
user=> (for [x colors] (str "I like " x))
("I like red" "I like blue")
```

[x colors] binds x to an element from the colors list. (str "I like " x) is an arbitrary function that's applied to every x from colors. It gets more interesting when you bind to more than one list:

```
user=> (for [x colors, y toys] (str "I like " x " " y "s"))
("I like red blocks" "I like red cars"
 "I like blue blocks" "I like blue cars")
```

The comprehension created every possible combination from the two lists. We can also apply a filter with the :when keyword in the bindings:

```
user=> (defn small-word? [w] (< (count w) 4))
#'user/small-word?
user=> (for [x colors, y toys, :when (small-word? y)]
          (str "I like " x " " y "s"))
("I like red cars" "I like blue cars")
```

We wrote a filter called small-word?. Any word that is less than four characters is small. We applied the small-word? filter to y with :when (small-word? y). We got all possibilities of (x, y), where x is a member of colors, y is a member of toys, and the size of y is less than four characters. The code is dense but expressive. That's an ideal combination. Let's move on.

You've seen foldl, foldleft, and inject in Erlang, Scala, and Ruby. In Lisp, the equivalent is reduce. To compute a quick total or factorial, use this:

```
user=> (reduce + [1 2 3 4])
10
user=> (reduce * [1 2 3 4 5])
120
```

You can sort a list:

```
user=> (sort [3 1 2 4])
(1 2 3 4)
```

and sort on the result of a function:

```
user=> (defn abs [x] (if (< x 0) (- x) x))
#'user/abs
user=> (sort-by abs [-1 -4 3 2])
(-1 2 3 -4)
```

We define a function called abs to compute an absolute value and then use that function in our sort. These are some of the most important sequence transformation functions in Clojure. Next, we'll move on to functions that create sequences, but to do that, you're going to have to get a little lazier.

Lazy Evaluation

In mathematics, infinite sequences of numbers are often easier to describe. In functional languages, you'd often like to have the same benefits, but you can't actually compute an infinite sequence. The answer is lazy evaluation. Using this strategy, Clojure's sequence library computes values only when they are actually consumed. In fact, most sequences are lazy. Let's walk through creating some finite sequences and move into lazy sequences.

Finite Sequences with range

Unlike Ruby, Clojure supports ranges as functions. A range creates a sequence:

```
user=> (range 1 10)
(1 2 3 4 5 6 7 8 9)
```

Note that the upper bound is not inclusive. The sequence did not include 10. You can specify any increment:

```
user=> (range 1 10 3)
(1 4 7)
```

You don't have to specify the lower bound if there is no increment:

```
user=> (range 10)
(0 1 2 3 4 5 6 7 8 9)
```

Zero is the default lower bound. The sequences created with range are finite. What if you wanted to create a sequence with no upper bound? That would be an infinite sequence. Let's find out how.

Infinite Sequences and take

Let's start with the most basic of infinite sequences, an infinite sequence of one repeated element. We can specify (repeat 1). If you try it in the repl, you'll get 1s until you kill the process. Clearly, we need some way to grab only a finite subset. That function is take:

```
user=> (take 3 (repeat "Use the Force, Luke"))
("Use the Force, Luke" "Use the Force, Luke" "Use the Force, Luke")
```

So, we created an infinite sequence of the repeated string "Use the Force, Luke", and then we took the first three. You can also repeat the elements in a list with cycle:

```
user=> (take 5 (cycle [:lather :rinse :repeat]))
(:lather :rinse :repeat :lather :rinse)
```

We're taking the first five elements of the cycle from the vector [:lather :rinse :repeat]. Fair enough. We can drop the first few elements of a sequence as well:

```
user=> (take 5 (drop 2 (cycle [:lather :rinse :repeat])))
(:repeat :lather :rinse :repeat :lather)
```

Working from the inside out, we again build a cycle, drop the first two, and take the first five after that. But you don't have to work inside out. You can use the new left-to-right operator (->>) to apply each function to a result:

```
user=> (->> [:lather :rinse :repeat] (cycle) (drop 2) (take 5))
(:repeat :lather :rinse :repeat :lather)
```

So, we take a vector, build a sequence with cycle, drop 2, and then take 5. Sometimes, left-to-right code is easier to read. What if you wanted to add some kind of separator between words? You'd use interpose:

```
user=> (take 5 (interpose :and (cycle [:lather :rinse :repeat])))
(:lather :and :rinse :and :repeat)
```

We're taking the keyword :and and placing it between all the elements of an infinite sequence. Think of this function like a generalized version of Ruby's join. What if you wanted an interpose that took interposing members from a sequence? That's interleave:

```
user=> (take 20 (interleave (cycle (range 2)) (cycle (range 3))))
(0 0 1 1 0 2 1 0 0 1 1 2 0 0 1 1 0 2 1 0)
```

We're interleaving two infinite sequences, (cycle (range 2)) and (cycle (range 3)). Then, we take the first 20. As you read the result, even numbers are (0 1 0 1 0 1 0 1 0 1), and odd numbers are (0 1 2 0 1 2 0 1 2 0). Beautiful.

The iterate function provides another way of creating sequences. Check out these examples:

```
user=> (take 5 (iterate inc 1))
(1 2 3 4 5)
user=> (take 5 (iterate dec 0))
(0 -1 -2 -3 -4)
```

iterate takes a function and a starting value. iterate then applies the function to the starting value repeatedly. In these two examples, we called inc and dec.

Here's an example that calculates consecutive pairs in the Fibonacci sequence. Remember, each number of a sequence is the sum of the last two. Given a pair, [a b], we can generate the next with [b, a + b]. We can generate an anonymous function to generate one pair, given the previous value, like this:

```
user=> (defn fib-pair [[a b]]  [b (+ a b)])
#'user/fib-pair
user=> (fib-pair [3 5])
[5 8]
```

Next, we'll use iterate to build an infinite sequence. Don't execute this yet:

```
(iterate fib-pair [1 1])
```

We'll use map to grab the first element from all of those pairs:

```
(map
first
(iterate fib-pair [1 1]))
```

That's an infinite sequence. Now, we can take the first 5:

```
user=> (take 5
         (map
         first
         (iterate fib-pair [1 1])))
(1 1 2 3 5)
```

Or we can grab the number at index 500, like this:

```
(nth (map first (iterate fib-pair [1 1])) 500)
(225... more numbers ...626)
```

The performance is excellent. Using lazy sequences, you can often describe recursive problems like Fibonacci. Factorial is another example:

```
user=> (defn factorial [n] (apply * (take n (iterate inc 1))))
#'user/factorial
user=> (factorial 5)
120
```

We grab n elements from the infinite sequence (iterate inc 1). Then we take n of them and multiply them together with apply *. The solution is dead simple. Now that we've spent some time with lazy sequences, it's time to explore new Clojure functions called defrecord and protocol.

defrecord and protocols

So far, we've talked about Java integration at a high level, but you haven't seen much of the JVM bleed through to the Clojure language. When all is said and done, the JVM is about types and interfaces. (For you non-Java programmers, think of types as Java classes. Think of interfaces as Java classes without implementations.) To make Clojure integrate well with the JVM, the original implementation has a significant amount of Java in it.

As Clojure picked up more speed and began to prove itself as an effective JVM language, there was a strong thrust to implement more of Clojure in Clojure itself. To do so, Clojure developers needed a way to build platform-fast open extensions by programming to abstractions rather than implementations. The results are defrecord for types and protocol, which groups functions together around a type. From a Clojure perspective, the best parts of OO are types and protocols (such as interfaces), and the worst parts are implementation inheritance. Clojure's defrecord and protocol preserve the good parts of OO and leave the rest.

As this book is being written, these language features are important, but they are evolving. I'm going to lean hard on Stuart Halloway, cofounder of Relevance and author of *Programming Clojure* [Hal09], to help walk through a practical implementation. We're going to go back to another functional language on the JVM, Scala. We'll rewrite the Compass program in Clojure. Let's get started.

First, we'll define a protocol. A Clojure protocol is like a contract. Types of this protocol will support a specific set of functions, fields, and arguments. Here's a protocol describing a Compass:

clojure/compass.clj

```
(defprotocol Compass
  (direction [c])
  (left [c])
  (right [c]))
```

This protocol defines an abstraction called Compass and enumerates the functions that a Compass must support—direction, left, and right with the specified number of arguments. We are now free to implement the protocol with defrecord. Next, we'll need the four directions:

```
(def directions [:north :east :south :west])
```

We'll need a function to handle a turn. Recall that our base direction is an integer, 0, 1, 2, and 3 represent :north, :east, :south, and :west, respectively. Every 1 you add to the base will move the compass ninety degrees to the right. We'll take the remainder of the base/4 (more precisely, base/number-of-directions) so that we'll wrap around correctly from :west to :north, like this:

```
(defn turn
  [base amount]
  (rem (+ base amount) (count directions)))
```

The turn works, just as you'd expect. I'll load the compass file and then use the turn functions:

```
user=> (turn 1 1)
2
user=> (turn 3 1)
0
user=> (turn 2 3)
1
```

Said another way, turning right once from :east gives you :south, turning right once from :west gives you :north, and turning right three times from :south gives you :east.

It's time to implement the protocol. We do that with defrecord. We'll do that in pieces. First, we use defrecord to declare we're implementing the protocol, like this:

```
(defrecord SimpleCompass [bearing]
  Compass
```

We're defining a new record called SimpleCompass. It has one field called bearing. Next, we will implement the Compass protocol, beginning with the direction function:

```
(direction [_] (directions bearing))
```

The direction function looks up the element of directions at the bearing index. For example, (directions 3) returns :west. Each argument list has a reference to the instance (e.g., self in Ruby or this in Java), but we're not using it, so we add _ to our argument list. Next, on to left and right:

```
(left [_] (SimpleCompass. (turn bearing 3)))
(right [_] (SimpleCompass. (turn bearing 1)))
```

Remember, in Clojure, we're using immutable values. That means that turning will return a new, modified compass rather than changing the existing compass in place. Both left and right use syntax that you have not seen before. (SomeType. arg) means fire the constructor for SimpleCompass, binding arg to the first parameter. You can verify that entering (String. "new string") into the repl returns the new string "new string".

So, the left and right functions are easy. Each returns a new compass with the appropriate bearing, configured for the new bearing, using the turn function we defined earlier. right turns right ninety degrees once, and left turns right ninety degrees three times. So far, we have a type SimpleCompass that implements the Compass protocol. We just need a function that returns a string representation, but toString is a method on java.lang.Object. That's easy enough to add to our type.

```
Object
(toString [this] (str "[" (direction this) "]")))
```

We then implement part of the Object protocol with the toString method, returning a string that looks like SimpleCompass [:north].

Now, the type is complete. Create a new compass:

```
user=> (def c (SimpleCompass. 0))
#'user/c
```

Turns return a new compass:

```
user=> (left c) ; returns a new compass
#:SimpleCompass{:bearing 3}

user=> c ; original compass unchanged
#:SimpleCompass{:bearing 0}
```

Notice that the old compass is unchanged. Since we're defining a JVM type, you can access all fields as Java fields. But you can also access the fields in the type as Clojure map keywords:

```
user=> (:bearing c)
0
```

Because these types work like maps, you can easily prototype new types as maps and iteratively convert them to types as your design stabilizes. You can also replace types as maps in your tests as stubs or mocks. There are other benefits as well:

- Types play nice with other Clojure concurrency constructs. In day 3, we'll learn how to create mutable references of Clojure objects in ways that maintain transactional integrity, much like relational databases do.

- We implemented a protocol, but you're not limited to the new way of doing things. Since we're building JVM types, the types can interoperate with Java classes and interfaces.

With defrecord and protocol, Clojure offers the ability to build native code for the JVM, without Java. This code can fully interact with other types on the JVM, including Java classes or interfaces. You can use them to subclass Java types or implement interfaces. Java classes can also build on your Clojure types. Of course, this is not the entire Java interop story, but it's an important part. Now that you've learned to extend Java, let's learn how to extend the Clojure language itself with macros.

Macros

For this section, we're going to refer to the Io chapter. We implemented the Ruby unless in Section 3.3, *Messages*, on page 64. The form is (unless test form1). The function will execute form1 if the test is false. We can't simply design a function, because each parameter will execute:

```
user=> ; Broken unless
user=> (defn unless [test body] (if (not test) body))
#'user/unless
user=> (unless true (println "Danger, danger Will Robinson"))
Danger, danger Will Robinson
nil
```

We discussed this problem in Io. Most languages execute parameters first and then put the results on the call stack. In this case, we don't want to evaluate the block unless the condition is false. In Io, the language circumvented this problem by delaying the execution of the unless message. In Lisp, we can use macros. When we type (unless test body), we want Lisp to translate that to (if (not test) body). Macros to the rescue.

A Clojure program executes in two stages. Macro expansion translates all macros in the language to their expanded form. You can see what's happening with a command called macroexpand. We've already used a couple of macros, called *reader macros*. A semicolon (;) is a comment, a single quote mark (') is a quote, and a number sign (#) is an anonymous function. To prevent premature execution, we'll put a quote in front of the expression we want to expand:

```
user=> (macroexpand ''something-we-do-not-want-interpreted)
(quote something-we-do-not-want-interpreted)
```

```
user=> (macroexpand '#(count %))
(fn* [p1__97] (count p1__97))
```

These are macros. In general, macro expansion will let you treat code like lists. If you don't want a function to execute right away, quote it. Clojure will replace the arguments intact. Our unless will look like this:

```
user=> (defmacro unless [test body]
       (list 'if (list 'not test) body))
#'user/unless
```

Note that Clojure substitutes test and body without evaluating them, but we have to quote if and not. We also have to package them in lists. We're building a list of code in the exact form that Clojure will execute. We can macroexpand it:

```
user=> (macroexpand '(unless condition body))
(if (not condition) body)
```

And we can execute it:

```
user=> (unless true (println "No more danger, Will."))
nil
user=> (unless false (println "Now, THIS is The FORCE."))
Now, THIS is The FORCE.
nil
```

What we've done is change the base definition of the language. We are adding our own control structure, without requiring the language designers to add their own keywords. Macro expansion is perhaps the most powerful feature of Lisp, and few languages can do it. The secret sauce is the expression of data as code, not just a string. The code is already in a higher-order data structure.

Let's wrap up day 2. There's a lot of meat here. We should pause to use what we've learned.

What We Learned in Day 2

It's been another packed day. You've added a tremendous set of abstractions to your expanding bag of tricks. Let's review.

First, we learned to use recursion. Since the JVM doesn't support tail-recursion optimization, we had to use loop and recur. That looping construct allowed us to implement many algorithms you would usually implement with recursive function calls, though the syntax was more invasive.

We also used sequences. With them, Clojure encapsulates access to all of its collections. With a common library, we could apply common strategies for dealing with collections. We used different functions to mutate, transform, and search sequences. Higher-order functions added power and simplicity to the sequence libraries.

With lazy sequences, we were able to add another powerful layer to sequences. Lazy sequences simplified algorithms. They also offered delayed execution, potentially significantly improving performance and loosening coupling.

Next, we spent some time implementing types. With defrecord and protocols, we were able to implement types that were full citizens on the JVM.

Finally, we used macros to add features to the language. We learned that there is a step, called *macro expansion*, that occurs before Clojure implements or interprets code. We implemented unless by using an if function within macro expansion.

There's a lot to digest. Take some time to use what you've learned.

Day 2 Self-Study

This day was packed with some of the most sophisticated and powerful elements of the Clojure language. Take some time to explore and understand those features.

Find:

- The implementation of some of the commonly used macros in the Clojure language
- An example of defining your own lazy sequence
- The current status of the defrecord and protocol features (these features were still under development as this book was being developed)

Do:

- Implement an unless with an else condition using macros.
- Write a type using defrecord that implements a protocol.

7.4 Day 3: An Eye for Evil

In *Star Wars*, Yoda was the first to detect the evil in Darth Vader. With Clojure, Rich Hickey has identified the core problems that plague the development of concurrent object-oriented systems. We've said frequently that mutable state is the evil that lurks in the hearts of object-oriented programs. We've shown several different approaches to handling mutable state. Io and Scala used the actor-based model and provided immutable constructs that gave the programmer the power to solve those problems without mutable state. Erlang provided actors with lightweight processes, and a virtual machine that allowed effective monitoring and communication, allowing unprecedented reliability. The Clojure approach to concurrency is different. It uses *software transactional memory* (STM). In this section, we'll look at STM and also several tools to share state across threaded applications.

References and Transactional Memory

Databases use transactions to ensure data integrity. Modern databases use at least two types of concurrency control. Locks prevent two competing transactions from accessing the same row at the same time. Versioning uses multiple versions to allow each transaction to have a private copy of its data. If any transaction interferes with another, the database engine simply reruns that transaction.

Languages like Java use locking to protect the resources of one thread from competing threads that might corrupt them. Locking basically puts the burden of concurrency control on the programmer. We are rapidly learning that this burden is too much to bear.

Languages like Clojure use *software transactional memory* (STM). This strategy uses multiple versions to maintain consistency and integrity. Unlike Scala, Ruby, or Io, when you want to change the state of a reference in Clojure, you must do so within the scope of a transaction. Let's see how it works.

References

In Clojure, a *ref* (short for reference) is a wrapped piece of data. All access must conform to specified rules. In this case, the rules are to support STM. You cannot change a reference outside of a transaction. To see how it works, let's create a reference:

```
user=> (ref "Attack of the Clones")
#<Ref@ffdadcd: "Attack of the Clones">
```

That's not too interesting. We should assign the reference to a value, like this:

```
user=> (def movie (ref "Star Wars"))
#'user/movie
```

You can get the reference back, like this:

```
user=> movie
#<Ref@579d75ee: "Star Wars">
```

But we're really worried about the value in the reference. Use deref:

```
user=> (deref movie)
"Star Wars"
```

Or, you can use the short form of deref:

```
user=> @movie
"Star Wars"
```

That's better. Now, we can easily access the value within our reference. We haven't tried to change the state of the reference yet. Let's try. With Clojure, we'll send a function that will mutate the value. The dereferenced ref will be passed as the first argument of the function:

```
user=> (alter movie str ": The Empire Strikes Back")
java.lang.IllegalStateException: No transaction running (NO_SOURCE_FILE:0)
```

As you can see, you can mutate state only within a transaction. Do so with the dosync function. The preferred way to modify a reference is to alter it with some transforming function, like this:

```
user=> (dosync (alter movie str ": The Empire Strikes Back"))
"Star Wars: The Empire Strikes Back"
```

We could also set some initial value with ref-set:

```
user=> (dosync (ref-set movie "Star Wars: The Revenge of the Sith"))
"Star Wars: The Revenge of the Sith"
```

You can see that the reference changed:

```
user=> @movie
"Star Wars: The Revenge of the Sith"
```

That's what we expected. The reference is different. It may seem painful to modify mutable variables in this way, but Clojure is enforcing a little policy now to save a lot of pain later. We know that programs that behave in this manner will absolutely execute correctly, with respect to race conditions and deadlock. Most of our code will use functional paradigms, and we'll save STM for the problems that could benefit the most from mutability.

Working with Atoms

If you want thread safety for a single reference, uncoordinated with any other activity, then you can use atoms. These data elements allow change outside the context of a transaction. Like a reference, a Clojure atom is an encapsulated bit of state. Let's try it. Create an atom:

```
user=> (atom "Split at your own risk.")
#<Atom@53f64158: "Split at your own risk.">
```

Now, bind an atom:

```
user=> (def danger (atom "Split at your own risk."))
#'user/danger
user=> danger
#<Atom@3a56860b: "Split at your own risk.">
user=> @danger
"Split at your own risk."
```

You can bind danger to a new value with reset!:

```
user=> (reset! danger "Split with impunity")
"Split with impunity"
user=> danger
#<Atom@455fc40c: "Split with impunity">
user=> @danger
"Split with impunity"
```

reset! replaces the entire atom, but the preferred usage is to provide a function to transform the atom. If you're changing a large vector, you can modify an atom in place with swap! like this:

```
user=> (def top-sellers (atom []))
#'user/top-sellers
user=> (swap! top-sellers conj {:title "Seven Languages", :author "Tate"})
[{:title "Seven Languages in Seven Weeks", :author "Tate"}]
user=> (swap! top-sellers conj {:title "Programming Clojure" :author "Halloway"})
[{:title "Seven Languages in Seven Weeks", :author "Tate"}
 {:title "Programming Clojure", :author "Halloway"}]
```

As with a reference, you'll want to create a value once and then change that value with swap!. Let's look at a practical example.

Building an Atom Cache

Now, you've seen both references and atoms. You'll see the same general philosophy when we work with Haskell. You wrap a bit of state in a package that you can later mutate with functions. While references required transactions, atoms do not. Let's build a simple atom cache. It's a perfect problem for an atom. We'll simply use hashes to associate names with values. This example is provided courtesy of Stuart Halloway of Relevance,[6] a consultancy that provides Clojure training and consulting.

We'll need to create the cache, and then we'll need functions to add elements to the cache and remove elements from the cache. First, we'll create the cache:

clojure/atomcache.clj

```
(defn create
  []
  (atom {}))
```

We're simply creating an atom. We'll let the client of this class bind it. Next, we need to be able to get a cache key:

```
(defn get
  [cache key]
  (@cache key))
```

We take the cache and a key as arguments. The cache is an atom, so we dereference it and return the item associated with the key. Finally, we need to put an item in the cache:

```
(defn put
  ([cache value-map]
     (swap! cache merge value-map))
  ([cache key value]
     (swap! cache assoc key value)))
```

We defined two different functions called put. The first version uses merge to allow us to add all of the associations in a map to our cache. The second version uses assoc to add a key and value. Here's the cache in use. We add an item to the cache and then return it:

```
(def ac (create))
(put ac :quote "I'm your father, Luke.")
(println (str "Cached item: " (get ac :quote)))
```

And the output:

```
Cached item: I'm your father, Luke.
```

Atoms and refs are simple and safe ways to handle mutable state, synchronously. In the next few sections, we'll look at a couple of asynchronous examples.

6. http://www.thinkrelevance.com

Working with Agents

Like an atom, an agent is a wrapped piece of data. Like an Io future, the state of a dereferenced agent will block until a value is available. Users can mutate the data asynchronously using functions, and the updates will occur in another thread. Only one function can mutate the state of an agent at a time.

Give it a try. Let's define a function called twice that doubles the value of whatever you pass in:

```
user=> (defn twice [x] (* 2 x))
#'user/twice
```

Next, we'll define an agent called tribbles that has an initial value of one:

```
user=> (def tribbles (agent 1))
#'user/tribbles
```

Now, we can mutate tribbles by sending the agent a value:

```
user=> (send tribbles twice)
#<Agent@554d7745: 1>
```

This function will run in another thread. Let's get the value of the agent:

```
user=> @tribbles
2
```

Reading a value from a ref, agent, or atom will never lock and never block. Reads should be fast, and with the right abstractions around them, they can be. With this function, you can see the difference in the values that you read from each agent:

```
user=> (defn slow-twice [x]
         (do
             (Thread/sleep 5000)
             (* 2 x)))
#'user/slow-twice
user=> @tribbles
2
user=> (send tribbles slow-twice)
#<Agent@554d7745: 16>
user=> @tribbles
2
user=> ; do this five seconds later
user=> @tribbles
4
```

Don't get hung up in the syntax. (Thread/sleep 5000) simply invokes Java's sleep method on Thread. For now, focus on the value of the agent.

We defined a slower version of twice that took five seconds. That was enough time to see the differences in @tribbles over time in the repl.

So, you will get *a* value of tribbles. You might not get the latest changes from your own thread. If you want to be sure to get the latest value *with respect to your own thread*, you can call (await tribbles) or (await-for timeout tribbles), where timeout is a timeout in milliseconds. Keep in mind that await and await-for block only until actions from your thread are dispatched. This says nothing about what other threads may have asked the thread to do. If you think you want the latest value of something, you have already failed. Clojure's tools involve working with a snapshot whose value is instantaneous and potentially out-of-date immediately. That's exactly how versioning databases work for fast concurrency control.

Futures

In Java, you would start threads directly to solve a specific task. Certainly, you can use Java integration to start a thread in this way, but there's often a better way. Say you wanted to create a thread to handle a complex computation around a bit of encapsulated state. You could use an agent. Or say you wanted to start the computation of a value, but you did not want to await the result. As with Io, you could use a future. Let's take a look.

First, let's create a future. The future returns a reference immediately:

```
user=> (def finer-things (future (Thread/sleep 5000) "take time"))
#'user/finer-things
user=> @finer-things
"take time"
```

Depending on how fast you type, you *may* have had to wait for the result. A future takes a body of one or more expressions, returning the value of the last expression. The future starts in another thread. If you dereference it, the future will block until the value becomes available.

So, a future is a concurrency construct that allows an asynchronous return before computation is complete. We can use futures to allow several long-running functions to run in parallel.

What We've Missed

Clojure is a Lisp, which is an extremely rich language in its own right. It's based on the JVM, which has more than a decade of development. The language also mixes in some new and powerful concepts. It would be impossible to cover Clojure in one chapter of a book. There are some pieces that you should know about.

Metadata

Sometimes, it's nice to associate metadata to a type. Clojure allows you to attach and access metadata on both symbols and collections. `(with-meta value metadata)` gives you a new `value` associated with the `metadata`, usually implemented as a map.

Java Integration

Clojure has excellent Java integration. We touched on Java integration very loosely, and we also built a type on the JVM. We did not use the existing Java libraries at all. We also did not extensively cover the Java compatibility forms. For example, `(.toUpperCase "Fred")` calls the `.toUpperCase` member function on the string `"Fred"`.

Multimethods

Object-oriented languages allow one style of organization for behavior and data. Clojure allows you to build your own code organization with multimethods. You can associate a library of functions with a type. You can also implement polymorphism by using multimethods to do method dispatch based on type, metadata, arguments, and even attributes. The concept is powerful and extremely flexible. You could implement, for example, Java-style inheritance, prototype inheritance, or something entirely different.

Thread State

Clojure offers atoms, refs, and agents for various concurrency models. Sometimes, you need to store data per thread instance. Clojure allows you to do so quite simply with `vars`. For example, `(binding [name "value"] ...)` would bind `name` to `"value"` *only for the current thread.*

What We Learned in Day 3

Today, we walked through the concurrency structures. We encountered several interesting concurrency constructs along the way.

Refs allowed us to implement mutable state while maintaining consistency across threads. We used STM, or software transactional memory. For our part, we placed all mutations to refs within transactions, expressed using a `dosync` function.

Next, we used atoms, lightweight concurrency constructs with less protection but a simpler usage model. We modified an atom outside of a transaction.

Finally, we used agents to implement a pool that could be used to do long-running computations. Agents were different from Io actors, because we could mutate the value of the agent with an arbitrary function. Agents also returned a snapshot in time, a value that may be changed at any time.

Day 3 Self-Study

On day 2, your focus was on advanced programming abstractions. Day 3 brought the concurrency constructs of Clojure. In these exercises, you'll put some of what you've learned to the test.

Find:

- A queue implementation that blocks when the queue is empty and waits for a new item in the queue

Do:

- Use refs to create a vector of accounts in memory. Create debit and credit functions to change the balance of an account.

In this section, I'm going to outline a single problem called *sleeping barber*. It was created by Edsger Dijkstra in 1965. It has these characteristics:

- A barber shop takes customers.
- Customers arrive at random intervals, from ten to thirty milliseconds.
- The barber shop has three chairs in the waiting room.
- The barber shop has one barber and one barber chair.
- When the barber's chair is empty, a customer sits in the chair, wakes up the barber, and gets a haircut.
- If the chairs are occupied, all new customers will turn away.
- Haircuts take twenty milliseconds.
- After a customer receives a haircut, he gets up and leaves.

Write a multithreaded program to determine how many haircuts a barber can give in ten seconds.

7.5 Wrapping Up Clojure

Clojure combines the power of a Lisp dialect with the convenience of the JVM. From the JVM, Clojure benefits from the existing community, deployment platform, and code libraries. As a Lisp dialect, Clojure comes with the corresponding strengths and limitations.

The Lisp Paradox

Clojure is perhaps the most powerful and flexible language in this book. Multimethods allow multiparadigm code, and macros let you redefine the language on the fly. No other language in this book provides this powerful combination. That flexibility has proven to be an incredible strength. In *Hackers and Painters*, Graham chronicles a start-up that leveraged productivity with Lisp to achieve productivity that no other vendors could match. Some emerging consultancies are taking the same approach, betting that Clojure will provide a productivity and quality advantage that other languages simply cannot match.

Lisp's flexibility can also be a weakness. Macro expansion is a powerful feature in the hands of an expert but will lead to unmitigated disaster without the proper thought and care. The same ability to effortlessly apply many powerful abstractions in a few lines of code makes Lisp especially demanding for all but the most skilled programmers.

To successfully evaluate Clojure, you need to look at Lisp but also the other unique aspects of the Java ecosystem and the new unique features. Let's take a deeper look at the fundamental strengths of Clojure.

Core Strengths

Clojure is one of a handful of languages vying for the position as the next great popular language on the Java virtual machine. There are many reasons that it is a powerful candidate.

A Good Lisp

Tim Bray, programming language expert and superblogger, called Clojure a good Lisp in a post called "Eleven Theses on Clojure."[7] In fact, he calls Clojure "the best Lisp ever." I would agree that Clojure is a very good Lisp.

7. http://www.tbray.org/ongoing/When/200x/2009/12/01/Clojure-Theses

In this chapter, you saw Rich Hickey's discussion on what makes Clojure such a good Lisp:

- *Reduced parentheses.* Clojure improves readability by opening up the syntax a little, including brackets for vectors, braces for maps, and a combination of characters for sets.
- *The ecosystem.* Lisp's many dialects water down the support and library set that you can have for any single dialect. Ironically, having one more dialect can help solve that problem. By being on the JVM, Clojure can take advantage of Java programmers who are looking for more and the fabulous set of libraries.
- *Restraint.* By exercising restraint and limiting Clojure's syntax to avoid reader macros, Hickey effectively limited Clojure's power but also decreased the likelihood that harmful splinter dialects might emerge.

You might appreciate Lisp as a programming language in its own right. By that measure, you can look at Clojure purely as a new Lisp. On that level, it succeeds.

Concurrency

Clojure's approach to concurrency has the potential to change the way we design concurrent systems completely. STM does place some additional burden on developers because of its novelty, but for the first time, it protects developers by detecting whether state mutations happen within appropriately protected functions. If you're not within a transaction, you can't mutate state.

Java Integration

Clojure has great integration with Java. It uses some native types such as strings and numbers transparently and offers type hints for performance. But Clojure shines by allowing tight JVM integration, so Clojure types can fully participate in Java applications. You'll soon see much more of Clojure itself implemented within the JVM.

Lazy Evaluation

Clojure adds powerful lazy evaluation features. Lazy evaluation can simplify problems. You have seen only a taste of how lazy sequences can shape the way you attack a problem. Lazy sequences can reduce computation overhead significantly by delaying execution until it is actually needed or by preventing execution altogether. Finally, lazy problem solving offers just one more tool to solve difficult problems. You can often use lazy sequences to replace recursion, iteration, or realized collections.

Data as Code

Programs are lists. As with any Lisp, you can represent data as code. Working with Ruby has helped me see the value of writing programs in programs. I think this is the most important capability of any programming language. Functional programs allow metaprogramming through higher-order functions. Lisp extends this idea through evaluating data as code.

Core Weaknesses

Clojure is a language that's firmly targeted as a general-purpose programming language. Whether it can actually be broadly successful on the JVM is yet to be determined. Clojure has wonderful abstractions but many of them. To truly embrace and use those features effectively and safely, a programmer will need to be highly educated and extremely talented. Here are some of my concerns.

Prefix Notation

Representing code in list form is one of the most powerful features in any Lisp, but there is a cost—prefix notation.[8] Typical object-oriented languages have a wildly different syntax. The adjustment to prefix notation is not easy. It requires a better memory and requires a developer to comprehend code from the inside out, rather than outside in. Sometimes, I find that reading Clojure pushes me toward understanding too much detail too soon. At best, Lisp syntax pushes my short-term memory. With experience, I'm told this improves. I've not yet turned that corner.

Readability

Another cost to data as code is the oppressive number of parentheses. Optimizing for people and computers is not at all the same thing. The location and number of parentheses is still a problem. Lisp developers lean heavily on their editors to provide the feedback for matching parentheses, but tools can never fully mask readability problems. Kudos to Rich for improving this problem, but it will still be a problem.

---

8. Clojure does have left-to-right macros, ->> and ->, which mitigate these problems a little.

Learning Curve

Clojure is rich, and the learning curve is oppressive. You need to have an extremely talented and experienced team to make Lisp work. Lazy sequences, functional programming, macro expansion, transactional memory, and the sophistication of the approaches are all powerful concepts that take time to master.

Limited Lisp

All compromises have some cost. By being on the JVM, Clojure limits tail-recursion optimization. Clojure programmers must use the awkward recur syntax. Try implementing `(size x)` that computes the size of a sequence `x` with recursion and with `loop/recur`.

The elimination of user-defined reader macros is also significant. The benefit is clear. Reader macros, when abused, can lead to the splintering of the language. The cost, too, is clear. You lose one more metaprogramming tool.

Accessibility

One of the most beautiful aspects of Ruby or an early Java is its accessibility as a programming language. Both of those languages were relatively easy to pick up. Clojure places tremendous demands on a developer. It has so many abstraction tools and concepts that the result can be overwhelming.

Final Thoughts

Most of Clojure's strengths and weaknesses are related to the power and flexibility. True, you might work hard to learn Clojure. In fact, if you're a Java developer, you're already working hard. You're just spending your time on Java application-level abstractions. You are looking for looser coupling through Spring or aspect-oriented programming, for example. You're just not getting the full benefits of additional flexibility at the language level. For many, that trade-off has worked. I will humbly suggest that the new demands of concurrency and complexity will continue to make the Java platform less and less viable.

If you need an extreme programming model and are willing to pay the price of learning the language, Clojure is a great fit. I think this is a great language for disciplined, educated teams looking for leverage. You can build better software faster with Clojure.

Logic is little tweeting bird chirping in meadow.
► Spock

Chapter 8
Haskell

Haskell represents purity and freedom for many functional programming purists. It's rich and powerful, but the power comes at a price. You can't eat just a couple of bites. Haskell will force you to eat the whole functional programming burrito. Think Spock from *Star Trek*. The quote above[1] is typical, embracing logic and truth. His character has a single-minded purity that has endeared him to generations. Where Scala, Erlang, and Clojure let you use imperative concepts in small doses, Haskell leaves no such wiggle room. This pure functional language will challenge you when it's time to do I/O or accumulate state.

8.1 Introducing Haskell

As always, to understand why a language embraces a certain set of compromises, you should start with the history. In the early and mid-1980s, pure functional programming splintered across several languages. The key concepts driving new research were lazy processing, as we encountered in Clojure, and pure functional programming. A group from the Functional Programming Languages and Computer Architecture conference in 1987 formed and decided to build an open standard for a pure functional language. Out of that group, Haskell was born in 1990 and revised again in 1998. The current standard, called Haskell 98, has been revised several times, including a revision of Haskell 98 and the definition of a new version of Haskell called Haskell Prime.

1. *Star Trek: The Original Series*, Episodes 41 and 42: "I, Mudd"/"The Trouble with Tribbles." Directed by Marc Daniels. 1967; Burbank, CA: 20th CBS Paramount International Television, 2001.

So, Haskell was built from the ground up to be a pure functional language, combining ideas from the best functional languages, with special emphasis on lazy processing.

Haskell has strong, static typing, like Scala. The type model is mostly inferred and is widely considered to be one of the most effective type systems of any functional language. You'll see that the type system allows for polymorphism and very clean designs.

Haskell also supports other concepts you've seen in this book. Haskell allows Erlang-style pattern matching and guards. You'll also find Clojure-style lazy evaluation and list comprehensions from both Clojure and Erlang.

As a pure functional language, Haskell does not do side effects. Instead, a function can return a side effect, which is later executed. You'll see an example of this in day 3, as well as an example of preserving state using a concept called *monads*.

The first couple of days will get you through typical functional programming concepts, such as expressions, defining functions, higher-order functions, and the like. We'll also get into Haskell's typing model, which will give you some new concepts. Day 3 will stretch you. We'll look at the parameterized type system and monads, which are sometimes difficult concepts to grasp. Let's get started.

8.2 Day 1: Logical

Like Spock, you'll find that Haskell's core concepts are easy to grasp. You'll work strictly with defining functions. Given the same input parameters, you'll get the same output parameters, every time. I'm going to use GHC, or the Glasgow Haskell Compiler, version 6.12.1. It's widely available across many platforms, but you can find other implementations as well. As always, I'm going to start in the console. Type ghci:

```
GHCi, version 6.12.1: http://www.haskell.org/ghc/  :? for help
Loading package ghc-prim ... linking ... done.
Loading package integer-gmp ... linking ... done.
Loading package base ... linking ... done.
Loading package ffi-1.0 ... linking ... done.
```

You'll see Haskell load a few packages, and then you're ready to type commands.

Expressions and Primitive Types

We're going to talk about Haskell's type system a little later. In this section, we'll focus on using primitive types. As with many of the other languages, we'll start with numbers and some simple expressions. We'll move quickly into more advanced types such as functions.

Numbers

By now, you know the drill. Type a few expressions:

```
Prelude> 4
4
Prelude> 4 + 1
5
Prelude> 4 + 1.0
5.0
Prelude> 4 + 2.0 * 5
14.0
```

Order of operations works just about like you'd expect:

```
Prelude> 4 * 5 + 1
21
Prelude> 4 * (5 + 1)
24
```

Notice you can group operations with parentheses. You've seen a couple of types of numbers. Let's look at some character data.

Character Data

Strings are represented with double quotes, like this:

```
Prelude> "hello"
"hello"
Prelude> "hello" + " world"

<interactive>:1:0:
    No instance for (Num [Char])
      arising from a use of `+' at <interactive>:1:0-17
    Possible fix: add an instance declaration for (Num [Char])
    In the expression: "hello" + " world"
    In the definition of `it': it = "hello" + " world"
Prelude> "hello" ++ " world"
"hello world"
```

Notice that you'll concatenate with ++ instead of +. You can represent single characters like this:

```
Prelude> 'a'
'a'
Prelude> ['a', 'b']
"ab"
```

Notice that a string is just a list of characters. Let's briefly look at some boolean values.

Booleans

A boolean is another primitive type that works much as they do in most of the other infix notation languages in this book. These are equal and not-equal expressions, returning booleans:

```
Prelude> (4 + 5) == 9
True
Prelude> (5 + 5) /= 10
False
```

Try an if/then statement:

```
Prelude> if (5 == 5) then "true"

<interactive>:1:23: parse error (possibly incorrect indentation)
```

That's the first major departure from other languages in the book. In Haskell, indentation is significant. Haskell is guessing that there's a follow-up line that is not indented correctly. We'll see some indented structures later. We won't talk about layouts, which control indentation patterns; follow predictable indentation strategies that mimic what you see here, and you will be OK. Let's do a full if/then/else statement:

```
Prelude> if (5 == 5) then "true" else "false"
"true"
```

In Haskell, if is a function, not a control structure, meaning it returns a value just like any other function. Let's try a few true/false values:

```
Prelude> if 1 then "true" else "false"

<interactive>:1:3:
    No instance for (Num Bool)
      arising from the literal `1' at <interactive>:1:3
    ...
```

Haskell is strongly typed. if takes strictly boolean types. Let's try to force another type collision:

```
Prelude> "one" + 1

<interactive>:1:0:
    No instance for (Num [Char])
      arising from a use of `+' at <interactive>:1:0-8
      ...
```

This error message gives us the first glimpse into Haskell's type system. It says "There is no function called + that takes a Num argument followed by [Char], a list of characters." Notice that we haven't told Haskell what types things are. The language is inferring types based on clues. At any point, you can see what Haskell's type inference is doing. You can use :t, or you can turn on the :t option that does something similar, like this:

```
Prelude> :set +t
Prelude> 5
5
it :: Integer
Prelude> 5.0
5.0
it :: Double
Prelude> "hello"
"hello"
it :: [Char]
Prelude> (5 == (2 + 3))
True
it :: Bool
```

Now, after every expression, you can see the type that each expression returns. Let me warn you that using :t with numbers is confusing. That has to do with the interplay between numbers and the console. Try to use the :t function:

```
Prelude> :t 5
5 :: (Num t) => t
```

That is not the same as the type we got before, it :: Integer. The console will try to treat numbers as generically as possible, unless you have done a :set t. Rather than a pure type, you get a class, which is a description of a bunch of similar types. We'll learn more in Section 8.4, *Classes*, on page 286.

Functions

The centerpiece of the whole Haskell programming paradigm is the function. Since Haskell has strong, static typing, you'll specify each function in two parts: an optional type specification and the implementation. We're going to go quickly through concepts you've seen in other languages, so hang on tight.

Defining Basic Functions

A Haskell function traditionally has two parts: the type declaration and the function declaration.

Initially, we're going to be defining functions within the console. We'll use the let function to bind values to implementations. Before defining a function, try let. As with Lisp, in Haskell, let binds a variable to a function in a local scope.

```
Prelude> let x = 10
Prelude> x
10
```

When you're coding a Haskell module, you'll declare functions like this:

```
double x = x * 2
```

In the console, though, we'll use let to assign the function in local scope, so we can use it. Here's an example of a simple double function:

```
Prelude> let double x = x * 2
Prelude> double 2
4
```

At this point, we'll switch to using files with programs. We can then work with multiline definitions. Using GHC, the full double definition would look like this:

haskell/double.hs

```
module Main where

    double x = x + x
```

Notice that we added a *module* called Main. In Haskell, modules collect related code into a similar scope. The Main module is special. It is the top-level module. Focus on the double function for now. Load Main into the console, and use it like this:

```
Prelude> :load double.hs
[1 of 1] Compiling Main             ( double.hs, interpreted )
Ok, modules loaded: Main.
*Main> double 5
10
```

So far, we haven't enforced a type. Haskell is being forgiving by inferring a type for us. There's definitely an underlying type definition for each function. Here's an example of a definition with a type definition:

haskell/double_with_type.hs

```
module Main where

    double :: Integer -> Integer
    double x = x + x
```

And we can load it and use it as before:

```
[1 of 1] Compiling Main             ( double_with_type.hs, interpreted )
Ok, modules loaded: Main.
*Main> double 5
10
```

You can see the associated type of the new function:

```
*Main> :t double
double :: Integer -> Integer
```

This definition means that the function double takes an Integer argument (the first Integer) and returns an Integer.

This type definition is limited. If you went back to the earlier, typeless version of double, you'd see something else entirely:

```
*Main> :t double
double :: (Num a) => a -> a
```

Now, that's different! In this case, a is a type variable. The definition means "The function double takes a single argument of some type a and returns a value of that same type a." With this improved definition, we can use this function with any type that supports the + function. Let's start to crank up the power. Let's look at implementing something slightly more interesting, a factorial.

Recursion

Let's start with a little recursion. Here's a recursive one-liner that implements a factorial within the console:

```
Prelude> let fact x = if x == 0 then 1 else fact (x - 1) * x
Prelude> fact 3
6
```

That's a start. The factorial of x is 1 if x is 0, and it's fact (x - 1) * x otherwise. We can do a little better by introducing pattern matching. Actually, this syntax looks and acts a lot like Erlang's pattern matching:

haskell/factorial.hs

```
module Main where
    factorial :: Integer -> Integer
    factorial 0 = 1
    factorial x = x * factorial (x - 1)
```

The definition has three lines. The first declares the type of the argument and return value. The next two are different functional definitions that depend on the pattern match of the inbound arguments. factorial of 0 is 1, and factorial of n is factorial x = x * factorial (x - 1). That definition looks exactly like the mathematical definition. In this case, the order of the patterns is important. Haskell will take the first match. If you wanted to reverse the order, you'd have to use a guard. In Haskell, guards are conditions that restrict the value of the arguments, like this:

haskell/fact_with_guard.hs

```
module Main where
    factorial :: Integer -> Integer
    factorial x
        | x > 1 = x * factorial (x - 1)
        | otherwise = 1
```

In this case, the guards have boolean values on the left and the function to apply on the right. When a guard is satisfied, Haskell calls the appropriate function. Guards often replace pattern matching, and we're using it to initiate the base condition for our recursion.

Tuples and Lists

As you've seen in other languages, Haskell depends on tail-recursion optimization to efficiently deal with recursion. Let's see several versions of a Fibonacci sequence with Haskell. First, we'll see a simple case:

haskell/fib.hs

```
module Main where
    fib :: Integer -> Integer
    fib 0 = 1
    fib 1 = 1
    fib x = fib (x - 1) + fib (x - 2)
```

That's simple enough. fib 0 or fib 1 is 1, and fib x is fib (x - 1) + fib (x - 2). But that solution is inefficient. Let's build a more efficient solution.

Programming with Tuples

We can use tuples to provide a more efficient implementation. A tuple is a collection of a fixed number of items. Tuples in Haskell are comma-separated items in parentheses. This implementation creates a tuple with consecutive Fibonacci numbers and uses a counter to assist in recursion. Here's the base solution:

```
fibTuple :: (Integer, Integer, Integer) -> (Integer, Integer, Integer)
fibTuple (x, y, 0) = (x, y, 0)
fibTuple (x, y, index) = fibTuple (y, x + y, index - 1)
```

fibTuple takes a three-tuple and returns a three-tuple. Be careful here. A single parameter that is a three-tuple is not the same as taking three parameters. To use the function, we'll start recursion with two numbers, 0 and 1. We will also provide a counter. As the counter counts down, the first two numbers get successively larger numbers in the sequence. Successive calls to fibTuple (0, 1, 4) would look like this:

- fibTuple (0, 1, 4)
- fibTuple (1, 1, 3)
- fibTuple (1, 2, 2)
- fibTuple (2, 3, 1)
- fibTuple (3, 5, 0)

You can run the program, like this:

```
Prelude> :load fib_tuple.hs
[1 of 1] Compiling Main             ( fib_tuple.hs, interpreted )
Ok, modules loaded: Main.
*Main> fibTuple(0, 1, 4)
(3, 5, 0)
```

The answer will be in the first position. We can grab the answer like this:

```
fibResult :: (Integer, Integer, Integer) -> Integer
fibResult (x, y, z) = x
```

We just use pattern matching to grab the first position. We can simplify the usage model like this:

```
fib :: Integer -> Integer
fib x = fibResult (fibTuple (0, 1, x))
```

That function uses the two helper functions to build a quite fast Fibonacci generator. Here is the whole program together:

haskell/fib_tuple.hs

```
module Main where
    fibTuple :: (Integer, Integer, Integer) -> (Integer, Integer, Integer)
    fibTuple (x, y, 0) = (x, y, 0)
    fibTuple (x, y, index) = fibTuple (y, x + y, index - 1)

    fibResult :: (Integer, Integer, Integer) -> Integer
    fibResult (x, y, z) = x

    fib :: Integer -> Integer
    fib x = fibResult (fibTuple (0, 1, x))
```

And here are the results (which appear instantaneously):

```
*Main> fib 100
354224848179261915075
*Main> fib 1000
    43466557686937456435688527675040625802564660517371780
    40248172908953655541794905189040387984007925516929592
    25930803226347752096896232398733224711616429964409065
    33187938298969649928516003704476137795166849228875
```

Let's try another approach with function composition.

Using Tuples and Composition

Sometimes, you need to combine functions by chaining them together by passing the results of one function to another. Here's an example that computes the second item of a list by matching the head of the tail of a list:

```
*Main> let second = head . tail
*Main> second [1, 2]
2
*Main> second [3, 4, 5]
4
```

We're just defining a function in the console. second = head . tail is equivalent to second lst = head (tail lst). We're feeding the result of one function into another. Let's use this feature with yet another Fibonacci sequence. We'll compute a single pair, as before, but without a counter:

```
fibNextPair :: (Integer, Integer) -> (Integer, Integer)
fibNextPair (x, y) = (y, x + y)
```

Given two numbers in the sequence, we can always compute the next one. The next job is to recursively compute the next item in the sequence:

```
fibNthPair :: Integer -> (Integer, Integer)
fibNthPair 1 = (1, 1)
fibNthPair n = fibNextPair (fibNthPair (n - 1))
```

The base case is the value (1, 1) for an n of 1. From there, it is simple. We just compute the next item of the sequence based on the last one. We can get any pair in the sequence:

```
*Main> fibNthPair(8)
(21,34)
*Main> fibNthPair(9)
(34,55)
*Main> fibNthPair(10)
(55,89)
```

Now, all that remains is to match the first item of each pair and combine them into a sequence. We'll use a convenient function composition of fst to grab the first element and fibNthPair to build a pair:

haskell/fib_pair.hs

```
module Main where
    fibNextPair :: (Integer, Integer) -> (Integer, Integer)
    fibNextPair (x, y) = (y, x + y)

    fibNthPair :: Integer -> (Integer, Integer)
    fibNthPair 1 = (1, 1)
    fibNthPair n = fibNextPair (fibNthPair (n - 1))

    fib :: Integer -> Integer
    fib = fst . fibNthPair
```

Said another way, we take the first element of the nth tuple. And we're done. With a little work done for tuples, let's solve a few problems with lists.

Traversing Lists

You've seen lists in many different languages. I'm not going to fully rehash them, but I will go over a basic recursion example and then introduce a few functions you haven't seen yet. Breaking a list into the head and tail can work in any binding, like a let statement or a pattern match:

```
let (h:t) = [1, 2, 3, 4]
*Main> h
1
*Main> t
[2,3,4]
```

We're binding the list [1, 2, 3, 4] to (h:t). Think of this construct as the various head|tail constructs you've seen in Prolog, Erlang, and Scala. With this tool, we can do a few simple recursive definitions. Here are size and prod functions for a list:

haskell/lists.hs

```
module Main where
    size [] = 0
    size (h:t) = 1 + size t

    prod [] = 1
    prod (h:t) = h * prod t
```

I'm going to use Haskell's type inference to handle the types of these functions, but the intention is clear. The size of a list is 1 + the size of a tail.

```
Prelude> :load lists.hs
[1 of 1] Compiling Main
    ( lists.hs, interpreted )
Ok, modules loaded: Main.
*Main> size "Fascinating."
12
```

zip is a powerful way to combine lists. Here's the function in action:

```
*Main> zip "kirk" "spock"
[('kirk','spock')]
```

So, we built a tuple of the two items. You can also zip lists together, like this:

```
Prelude> zip ["kirk", "spock"] ["enterprise", "reliant"]
[("kirk","enterprise"),("spock","reliant")]
```

It's an effective way to combine two lists.

So far, the features you've seen in Haskell have been remarkably similar to those covered in other languages. Now, we'll start working with some more advanced constructs. We'll look at advanced lists including ranges and list comprehensions.

Generating Lists

We've already looked at a few ways to process lists with recursion. In this section, we'll look at a few options for generating new lists. In particular, we'll look at recursion, ranges, and list comprehensions.

Recursion

The most basic building block for list construction is the : operator, which combines a head and tail to make a list. You've seen the operator in reverse used in pattern matching as we call a recursive function. Here's : on the left side of a let:

```
Prelude> let h:t = [1, 2, 3]
Prelude> h
1
Prelude> t
[2,3]
```

We can also use : to do construction, instead of deconstruction.

Here's how that might look:

```
Prelude> 1:[2, 3]
[1,2,3]
```

Remember, lists are homogeneous. You can't add a list to a list of integers, for example:

```
Prelude> [1]:[2, 3]

<interactive>:1:8:
    No instance for (Num [t])
      arising from the literal `3' at <interactive>:1:8
```

You could, however, add a list to a list of lists or even an empty list:

```
Prelude> [1]:[[2], [3, 4]]
[[1],[2],[3,4]]
Prelude> [1]:[]
[[1]]
```

Here's list construction in action. Let's say we wanted to create a function that returns the even numbers from a list. One way to write that function is with list construction:

haskell/all_even.hs

```
module Main where
    allEven :: [Integer] -> [Integer]
    allEven [] = []
    allEven (h:t) = if even h then h:allEven t else allEven t
```

Our function takes a list of integers and returns a list of even integers. allEven for an empty list is an empty list. If there is a list, if the head is even, we add the head to allEven applied to the tail. If the head is odd, we discard it by applying allEven to the tail. No problem. Let's look at some other ways to build lists.

Ranges and Composition

As with Ruby and Scala, Haskell includes first-class ranges and some syntactic sugar to support them. Haskell provides a simple form, consisting of the end points of a range:

```
Prelude> [1..2]
[1,2]
Prelude> [1..4]
[1,2,3,4]
```

You specify the endpoints, and Haskell computes the range. The default increment is 1. What if Haskell can't reach the endpoint with the default increment?

```
Prelude> [10..4]
[]
```

You'll get an empty list. You can specify an increment by specifying the next item in the list:

```
Prelude> [10, 8 .. 4]
[10,8,6,4]
```

You can also work in fractional numbers:

```
Prelude> [10, 9.5 .. 4]
[10.0,9.5,9.0,8.5,8.0,7.5,7.0,6.5,6.0,5.5,5.0,4.5,4.0]
```

Ranges are syntactic sugar for creating sequences. The sequences need not be bound. As with Clojure, you can take some of the elements of a sequence:

```
Prelude> take 5 [ 1 ..]
[1,2,3,4,5]
Prelude> take 5 [0, 2 ..]
[0,2,4,6,8]
```

We'll talk more about lazy sequence in day 2. For now, let's look at another way to automatically generate lists, the list comprehension.

List Comprehensions

We first looked at list comprehensions in the Erlang chapter. In Haskell, a list comprehension works the same way. On the left side, you'll see an expression. On the right side, you'll see generators and filters, just as you did with Erlang. Let's look at a few examples. To double all items in a list, we do this:

```
Prelude> [x * 2 | x <- [1, 2, 3]]
[2,4,6]
```

In English, the list comprehension means "Collect x * 2 where x is taken from the list [1, 2, 3]."

As with Erlang, we can also use pattern matching within our list comprehensions. Say we had a list of points representing a polygon and wanted to flip the polygon diagonally. We could just transpose x and y, like this:

```
Prelude> [ (y, x) | (x, y) <- [(1, 2), (2, 3), (3, 1)]]
[(2,1),(3,2),(1,3)]
```

Or, to flip the polygon horizontally, we could subtract x from 4, like this:

```
Prelude> [ (4 - x, y) | (x, y) <- [(1, 2), (2, 3), (3, 1)]]
[(3,2),(2,3),(1,1)]
```

We can also compute combinations. Let's say we wanted to find all of the possible landing parties of two taken from a crew of Kirk, Spock, or McCoy:

```
Prelude> let crew = ["Kirk", "Spock", "McCoy"]
Prelude> [(a, b) | a <- crew, b <- crew]
[("Kirk","Kirk"),("Kirk","Spock"),("Kirk","McCoy"),
("Spock","Kirk"),("Spock","Spock"),("Spock","McCoy"),
("McCoy","Kirk"),("McCoy","Spock"),("McCoy","McCoy")]
```

That composition almost worked but did not remove duplicates. We can add conditions to filter the list comprehension like this:

```
Prelude> [(a, b) | a <- crew, b <- crew, a /= b]
[("Kirk","Spock"),("Kirk","McCoy"),("Spock","Kirk"),
("Spock","McCoy"),("McCoy","Kirk"),("McCoy","Spock")]
```

That is a little better, but order doesn't matter. We can do a little better by including only the options that appear in sorted order, discarding the rest:

```
Prelude> [(a, b) | a <- crew, b <- crew, a < b]
[("Kirk","Spock"),("Kirk","McCoy"),("McCoy","Spock")]
```

With a short, simple list comprehension, we have the answer. List comprehensions are a great tool for rapidly building and transforming lists.

An Interview with Philip Wadler

Now that you've seen some of the core features of Haskell, let's see what someone from the committee that designed Haskell has to say. A theoretical computer science professor at the University of Edinburgh, Philip Wadler is an active contributor of not only Haskell but also Java and XQuery. Previously, he worked or studied at Avaya Labs, Bell Labs, Glasgow, Chalmers, Oxford, CMU, Xerox Parc, and Stanford.

Bruce Tate: *Why did your team create Haskell?*

Philip Wadler: *In the late 1980s there were a large number of different groups creating designs and implementations of functional languages, and we realized we would be stronger working together than apart. The original goals were not modest: we wanted the language to be a foundation for research, suitable for teaching, and up to industrial uses. The entire history is covered in detail in a paper we wrote for the History of Programming Languages conference, which you can find on the Web.*[2]

2. http://www.haskell.org/haskellwiki/History_of_Haskell

Bruce Tate: *What are the things you like about it the most?*

Philip Wadler: *I really enjoy programming with list comprehensions. It's nice to see that they've finally made their way into other languages, like Python.*

Type classes provide a simple form of generic programming. You define a data type, and just by adding one keyword, derived, *you can get routines to compare values, to convert values to and from strings, and so on. I find that very convenient and miss it when I'm using other languages.*

Any good programming language really becomes a means of extending itself to embed other programming languages specialized to the task at hand. Haskell is particularly good as a tool for embedding other languages. Laziness, lambda expressions, monad and arrow notation, type classes, the expressive type system, and template Haskell all support extending the language in various ways.

Bruce Tate: *What are the things you'd change if you had it to do all over again?*

Philip Wadler: *With distribution becoming so important, we need to focus on programs that run on multiple machines, sending values from one to the other. When you send a value, you probably want it to be the value itself (eager evaluation), rather than a program (and the values of all the free variables of the program) that can be evaluated to yield the value. So, in the distributed world, I think it would be better to be eager by default but make it easy to be lazy when you want.*

Bruce Tate: *What's the most interesting problem you've seen solved with Haskell?*

Philip Wadler: *I'm always blown away by the uses folks find for Haskell. I remember years ago being amazed at uses of Haskell for natural-language processing and years after that when it was used for protein folding with an application to fighting AIDS. I just had a look at the Haskell Community page, and it lists forty industrial applications of Haskell. There are now many users in finance: ABN Amro, Credit Suisse, Deutsche Bank, and Standard Chartered. Facebook uses Haskell for an in-house tool to update code in PHP. One of my favorites is the use of Haskell for garbage collection—not the kind we do in software but real garbage collection...programming engines to be used in garbage trucks!*

What We Learned in Day 1

Haskell is a functional programming language. Its first distinguishing characteristic is that it is a pure functional language. A function with the same arguments will always produce the same result. There are no side effects. We spent most of day 1 covering features you have seen in other languages in this book.

We first covered basic expressions and simple data types. Since there are no mutable variable assignments, we used recursion to define some simple math functions and to deal with lists. We worked with basic Haskell expressions and rolled those up into functions. We saw pattern matching and guards as we found in Erlang and Scala. We used lists and tuples as the basic collections as you found in Erlang.

Finally, we took a look at building lists that took us into list comprehensions, ranges, and even lazy sequences. Let's put some of those ideas into practice.

Day 1 Self-Study

By this time, writing functional programs should be getting easier if you've been working through all of the other functional languages. In this section, I'm going to push you a little harder.

Find:

- The Haskell wiki
- A Haskell online group supporting your compiler of choice

Do:

- How many different ways can you find to write `allEven`?
- Write a function that takes a list and returns the same list in reverse.
- Write a function that builds two-tuples with all possible combinations of two of the colors black, white, blue, yellow, and red. Note that you should include only one of `(black, blue)` and `(blue, black)`.
- Write a list comprehension to build a childhood multiplication table. The table would be a list of three-tuples where the first two are integers from 1–12 and the third is the product of the first two.
- Solve the map-coloring problem (Section 4.2, *Map Coloring*, on page 87) using Haskell.

8.3 Day 2: Spock's Great Strength

With some characters, you might not notice their best qualities for quite some time. With Spock, it's easy to grasp his great strengths. He's brilliant, always logical, and completely predictable. Haskell's great strength is also that predictability and simplicity of logic. Many universities teach Haskell in the context of reasoning about programs. Haskell makes creating proofs for correctness far easier than imperative counterparts. In this section, we'll dig into the practical concepts that lead to better predictability. We will start with higher-order functions. Then, we'll talk about Haskell's strategy for combining them. That will take us into partially applied functions and currying. We'll finally look at lazy computation. It's going to be a full day, so let's get started.

Higher-Order Functions

Every language in this book addresses the idea of higher-order programming. Haskell depends on the concept extensively. We will work quickly through anonymous functions and then apply them with the many prebuilt functions that work on lists. I will move much faster than I have with the other languages, because you've seen the concepts before, and there's so much ground to cover. We'll start things with anonymous functions.

Anonymous Functions

As you might expect, anonymous functions in Haskell have a ridiculously simple syntax. The form is `(\param1 .. paramn -> function_body)`. Try it, like this:

```
Prelude> (\x -> x) "Logical."
"Logical."
Prelude> (\x -> x ++ " captain.") "Logical,"
"Logical, captain."
```

Taken alone, they don't add much. Combined with other functions, they become extremely powerful.

map and where

First, we built an anonymous function that just returns the first parameter. Next, we append a string. As you've seen in other languages, anonymous functions are an important feature for list libraries. Haskell has a map:

```
map (\x -> x * x) [1, 2, 3]
```

We're applying the map function to an anonymous function and a list. map applies the anonymous function to each item in the list and collects the results. There's no surprise here, but that form might be a bit much to digest all at once. We can package it all up as a function and break out the anonymous function as a locally scoped function, like this:

haskell/map.hs

```
module Main where
    squareAll list = map square list
        where square x = x * x
```

We've declared a function called squareAll that takes a parameter called list. Next, we use map to apply a function called square to all the items in list. Then, we use a new feature, called where, to declare a local version of square. You don't have to bind functions with where; you can also bind any variable. We'll see some examples of where throughout the rest of the chapter. Here's the result:

```
*Main> :load map.hs
[1 of 1] Compiling Main             ( map.hs, interpreted )
Ok, modules loaded: Main.
*Main> squareAll [1, 2, 3]
[1,4,9]
```

You can also use map with part of a function, called a *section*, like this:

```
Prelude> map (+ 1) [1, 2, 3]
[2,3,4]
```

(+ 1) is actually a partially applied function. The + function takes two parameters, and we've supplied only one. The result is that we get a function like (x + 1), with a single parameter x.

filter, foldl, foldr

The next common function is filter, which applies a test to items in a list, like this:

```
Prelude> odd 5
True
Prelude> filter odd [1, 2, 3, 4, 5]
[1,3,5]
```

You can also fold left and right, just as you did in Clojure and Scala. The functions you will use are variations of foldl and foldr:

```
Prelude> foldl (\x carryOver -> carryOver + x) 0 [1 .. 10]
55
```

We took an initial carry-over value of 0 and then applied the function to every item in the list, using the result of the function as the carryOver argument and each item of the list as the other. Another form of fold is convenient when you are folding with an operator:

```
Prelude> foldl1 (+) [1 .. 3]
6
```

This is using the + operator as a pure function taking two parameters and returning an integer. The result gives you the same thing as evaluating this:

```
Prelude> 1 + 2 + 3
6
```

You can also fold right to left, with foldr1.

As you might imagine, Haskell offers many other functions in the library of list functions, and many of them use higher-order functions. Rather than spend a whole chapter on dealing with them, I'll let you do your own discovery. Now, I want to move on to the ways Haskell combines functions to work together.

Partially Applied Functions and Currying

We've talked briefly about function composition and partially applied functions. These concepts are important and central enough to Haskell that we should spend a little more time here.

Every function in Haskell has one parameter. You might ask yourself, "If that's true, how could you write a function like + that adds two numbers together?"

In fact, it is true. Every function does have one parameter. To simplify the type syntax, let's create a function called prod:

```
Prelude> let prod x y = x * y
Prelude> prod 3 4
12
```

We created a function, and you can see that it works. Let's get the type of the function:

```
Prelude> :t prod
prod :: (Num a) => a -> a -> a
```

The portion Num a => means "In the following type definition, a is a type of Num." You've seen the rest before, and I lied to you about the meaning to simplify things. Now, it's time to set the record straight. Haskell uses a concept to split one function on multiple arguments into multiple functions, each with one argument. Haskell does this job with partial application.

Don't let the term confuse you. Partial application binds *some* of the arguments, but not all. For example, we can partially apply prod to create some other functions:

```
Prelude> let double = prod 2
Prelude> let triple = prod 3
```

Look at the left side of these functions first. We defined prod with two parameters, but we applied only the first one. So, computing prod 2 is easy, Just take the original function of prod x y = x * y, substitute 2 for x, and you have prod y = 2 * y. The functions work just as you'd expect:

```
Prelude> double 3
6
Prelude> triple 4
12
```

So, the mystery is solved. When Haskell computes prod 2 4, it is really computing (prod 2) 4, like this:

- First, apply prod 2. That returns the function (\y -> 2 * y).
- Next, apply (\y -> 2 * y) 4, or 2 * 4, giving you 8.

That process is called *currying*, and just about every multiple-argument function in Haskell gets curried. That leads to greater flexibility and simpler syntax. Most of the time, you don't really have to think about it, because the value of curried and uncurried functions is equivalent.

Lazy Evaluation

Like Clojure's sequence library, Haskell makes extensive use of lazy evaluation. With it, you can build functions that return infinite lists. Often, you'll use list construction to form an infinite list. Take this example that builds an infinite range, starting at x, in steps of y:

haskell/my_range.hs

```
module Main where
    myRange start step = start:(myRange (start + step) step)
```

The syntax is strange, but the overall effect is beautiful. We're building a function called myRange, taking a starting point and a step for our range. We use list composition to build a list with start as the head and (myRange (start + step) step) as the tail. These are the successive evaluations for myRange 1 1:

- 1:myRange (2 1)
- 1:2:myRange (3 1)
- 1:2:3:myRange (4 1)

...and so on.

This recursion will go on infinitely, so we'll typically use the function with others that will limit the recursion. Make sure you load my_range.hs first:

```
*Main> take 10 (myRange 10 1)
[10,11,12,13,14,15,16,17,18,19]
*Main> take 5 (myRange 0 5)
[0,5,10,15,20]
```

Some recursive functions work more efficiently using list construction. Here's an example of the Fibonacci sequence, using lazy evaluation with composition:

haskell/lazy_fib.hs

```
module Main where
    lazyFib x y = x:(lazyFib y (x + y))

    fib = lazyFib 1 1

    fibNth x = head (drop (x - 1) (take (x) fib))
```

The first function builds a sequence where every number is the sum of the previous two. We effectively have a sequence, but we can improve on the API. To be a proper Fibonacci sequence, we must start the sequence with 1 and 1, so fib seeds lazyFib with the first two numbers. Finally, we have one more helper function that allows the user to grab just one number of the sequence with drop and take. Here are the functions in action:

```
*Main> take 5 (lazyFib 0 1)
[1,1,2,3,5]
*Main> take 5 (fib)
[1,1,2,3,5]
*Main> take 5 (drop 20 (lazyFib 0 1))
[10946,17711,28657,46368,75025]
*Main> fibNth 3
2
*Main> fibNth 6
8
```

The three functions are beautiful and concise. We define an infinite sequence, and Haskell computes only the part necessary to do the job. You can really start to have fun when you start to combine infinite sequences together. First, let's add two Fibonacci sequences together, offset by one:

```
*Main> take 5 (zipWith (+) fib (drop 1 fib))
[2,3,5,8,13]
```

Surprise. We get a Fibonacci sequence. These higher-order functions play well together. We called zipWith, which pairs each item of the infinite list by index. We passed it the + function. Or, we could double a range:

```
*Main> take 5 (map (*2) [1 ..])
[2,4,6,8,10]
```

We're using map to apply the partially applied function * 2 to the infinite range [1 ..], and then we're using the infinite range, beginning with 1.

The nice thing about functional languages is that you can compose them in unexpected ways. For example, we can use function composition in conjunction with partially applied functions and lazy sequences effortlessly:

```
*Main> take 5 (map ((* 2) . (* 5)) fib)
[10,10,20,30,50]
```

That code packs a punch, so let's take it apart. Starting from the inside and working out, we first have (* 5). That's a partially applied function. Whatever we pass into the function will be multiplied by five. We pass that result into another partially applied function, (* 2). We pass that composed function into map and apply the function to every element in the infinite fib sequence. We pass that infinite result to take 5 and generate the first five elements of a Fibonacci sequence, multiplied by five and then again by 2.

You can easily see how you'd compose the solutions to problems. You just pass one function to the next. In Haskell, f . g x is shorthand for f(g x). When you're building functions in this way, you might want to apply them from first to last. You'd do so with the . operator. For example, to invert an image, flip it vertically and then flip it horizontally, an image processor might do something like (flipHorizontally . flipVertically . invert) image.

An Interview with Simon Peyton-Jones

To take a quick break, let's hear from another person on the committee that created Haskell. Simon Peyton Jones spent seven years as a lecturer at University College London and nine years as a professor at Glasgow University, before moving to Microsoft Research (Cambridge) in 1998 where his research focus is the implementation and application of functional programming languages for uniprocessor and parallel machines. He is the lead designer of the compiler used in this book.

Bruce Tate: *Tell me about the creation of Haskell.*

Simon Peyton-Jones: *A very unusual thing about Haskell is that it is a successful committee language. Think of any successful language, and the chances are that it was originally developed by one person or a very small team. Haskell is different: it was originally designed by an international group of twenty-ish researchers. We had enough agreement about the core principles of the language—and Haskell is a very principled language—to keep the design coherent.*

Also, Haskell is enjoying a substantial upsurge in popularity some twenty years after it was designed. Languages usually succeed or (mostly) fail in the first few years of their lives, so what is going on? I believe that it is because Haskell's principled adherence to purity, the absence of side effects, is an unfamiliar discipline that has prevented Haskell from being a mainstream language. Those long-term benefits are gradually becoming apparent. Whether or not the mainstream languages of the future look like Haskell, I believe they will have strong mechanisms for controlling side effects.

Bruce Tate: *What are the things you like about it the most?*

Simon Peyton-Jones: *Apart from purity, probably the most unusual and interesting feature of Haskell is its type system. Static types are by far the most widely used program verification technique available today: millions of programmers write types (which are just partial specifications) every day, and compilers check them every time they compile the program. Types are the UML of functional programming: a design language that forms an intimate and permanent part of the program.*

From day 1 Haskell's type system was unusually expressive, mainly because of type classes and higher-kinded type variables. Since then, Haskell has served as a laboratory in which to explore new type system ideas, something I have enjoyed very much. Multiparameter type classes, higher-rank types, first-class polymorphism, implicit parameters, GADTs, and type families...we are having fun! And, more importantly, we are extending the range of properties that can be statically checked by the type system.

Bruce Tate: *What are the things you'd change if you had it to do all over again?*

Simon Peyton-Jones: *I'd like a better record system. There are reasons that Haskell's record system is so simple, but it's still a weak point.*

I'd like a better module system. Specifically, I want to be able to ship a Haskell package P to someone else, saying "P needs to import interfaces I and J from somewhere: you provide them, and it will offer interface K." Haskell has no formal way to say this.

Bruce Tate: *What's the most interesting problem you've seen solved with Haskell?*

Simon Peyton-Jones: *Haskell is a truly general-purpose programming language, which is a strength but also a weakness because it has no single "killer app." That said, it is quite common to find that Haskell is a medium in which people have been able to dream up particularly elegant and unusual ways to solve problems. Look at Conal Elliot's work on functional reactive animation, for example, which rewired my brain by making me think of a "time-varying value" as a single value that could be manipulated by a functional program. On a more mundane (but very useful) level, there are lots of libraries of parser and pretty-printing combinators, each encapsulating great intellectual cleverness behind simple interfaces. In a third domain, Jean-Marc Eber showed me how to design a combinatory library to describe financial derivatives, something I would never have thought of on my own.*

In each case, the medium (Haskell) has allowed a new level of expressiveness that would be much harder to achieve in a mainstream language.

By now, you have enough knowledge to tackle some hard problems in Haskell, but you can't do some easy stuff, such as dealing with I/O, state, and error handling. These problems will take us into some advanced theory. On day 3, we'll look into monads.

What We Learned in Day 2

In day 2, we looked at higher-order functions. We started with the same kinds of list libraries that you've seen in almost every language in this book. You saw map, several versions of fold, and some additional functions like zip and zipWith. After working with them on fixed lists, we then worked with some lazy techniques such as the ones you used with Clojure.

As we worked through advanced functions, we learned to take a function and apply some of the parameters. This technique was called *partially applied functions*. Then, we used partially applied functions to translate a function that took multiple arguments at once (f (x, y)) to a function that took arguments one at a time (f(x)(y)). We learned that in Haskell, all functions are curried, which explained the type signatures of Haskell functions taking multiple arguments. For example, the type signature of the function f x y = x + y is f :: (Num a) => a -> a -> a.

We also learned function composition, a process that used the return from one function as the input of another. We could effectively string functions together this way.

Finally, we worked with lazy evaluation. We were able to define functions that built infinite lists, which would be processed on demand. We defined a Fibonacci sequence in this way and also used composition with lazy sequences to effortlessly produce new lazy sequences.

Day 2 Self-Study

Find:

- Functions that you can use on lists, strings, or tuples
- A way to sort lists

Do:

- Write a sort that takes a list and returns a sorted list.
- Write a sort that takes a list and a function that compares its two arguments and then returns a sorted list.
- Write a Haskell function to convert a string to a number. The string should be in the form of $2,345,678.99 and can possibly have leading zeros.
- Write a function that takes an argument x and returns a lazy sequence that has every third number, starting with x. Then, write a function that includes every fifth number, beginning with y. Combine these functions through composition to return every eighth number, beginning with x + y.

- Use a partially applied function to define a function that will return half of a number and another that will append `\n` to the end of any string.

Here are some more demanding problems if you're looking for something even more interesting:

- Write a function to determine the greatest common denominator of two integers.
- Create a lazy sequence of prime numbers.
- Break a long string into individual lines at proper word boundaries.
- Add line numbers to the previous exercise.
- To the above exercise, add functions to left, right, and fully justify the text with spaces (making both margins straight).

8.4 Day 3: The Mind Meld

In *Star Trek*, Spock had a special talent of connecting with a character with what he called the *mind meld*. Haskell enthusiasts often claim such a connection to their language. For many of them, the language feature that engenders the most respect is the type system. After spending so much time with the language, I can easily see why this is true. The type system is flexible and rich enough to infer most of my intent, staying out of my way unless I need it. I also get a sanity check as I build my functions, especially the abstract ones that compose functions.

Classes and Types

Haskell's type system is one of its strongest features. It allows type inference, so programmers do not have heavier responsibilities. It is also robust enough to catch even subtle programming errors. It is polymorphic, meaning you can treat different forms of the same type the same. In this section, we'll look at a few examples of types and then build some of our own types.

Basic Types

Let's review what you've learned so far with some basic types. First, we'll turn on the type option in the shell:

```
Prelude> :set +t
```

Now, we'll see the types that each statement returns. Try some characters and strings:

```
Prelude> 'c'
'c'
it :: Char
Prelude> "abc"
"abc"
it :: [Char]
Prelude> ['a', 'b', 'c']
"abc"
it :: [Char]
```

it always gives you the value of the last thing you typed, and you can read :: as *is of type*. To Haskell, a character is a primitive type. A string is an array of characters. It doesn't matter how you represent the array of characters, with an array or with the double quotes. To Haskell, the values are the same:

```
Prelude> "abc" == ['a', 'b', 'c']
True
```

There are a few other primitive types, like this:

```
Prelude> True
True
it :: Bool
Prelude> False
False
it :: Bool
```

As we dig deeper into typing, these ideas will help us see what's really going on. Let's define some of our own types.

User-Defined Types

We can define our own data types with the data keyword. The simplest of type declarations uses a finite list of values. Boolean, for example, would be defined like this:

```
data Boolean = True | False
```

That means that the type Boolean will have a single value, either True or False. We can define our own types in the same way. Consider this simplified deck of cards, with two suits and five ranks:

haskell/cards.hs

```
module Main where
    data Suit = Spades | Hearts
    data Rank = Ten | Jack | Queen | King | Ace
```

In this example, Suit and Rank are *type constructors*. We used data to build a new user-defined type. You can load the module like this:

```
*Main> :load cards.hs
[1 of 1] Compiling Main             ( cards.hs, interpreted )
Ok, modules loaded: Main.
*Main> Hearts

<interactive>:1:0:
    No instance for (Show Suit)
      arising from a use of `print' at <interactive>:1:0-5
```

Argh! What happened? Haskell is basically telling us that the console is trying to show these values but doesn't know how. There's a shorthand way to derive the show function as you declare user-defined data types. It works like this:

haskell/cards-with-show.hs

```
module Main where
    data Suit = Spades | Hearts deriving (Show)
    data Rank = Ten | Jack | Queen | King | Ace deriving (Show)
    type Card = (Rank, Suit)
    type Hand = [Card]
```

Notice we added a few alias types to our system. A Card is a tuple with a rank and a suit, and a Hand is a list of cards. We can use these types to build new functions:

```
value :: Rank -> Integer
value Ten = 1
value Jack = 2
value Queen = 3
value King = 4
value Ace = 5

cardValue :: Card -> Integer
cardValue (rank, suit) = value rank
```

For any card game, we need to be able to assign the ranks of a card. That's easy. The suit really doesn't play a role. We simply define a function that computes the value of a Rank and then another that computes a cardValue. Here's the function in action:

```
*Main> :load cards-with-show.hs
[1 of 1] Compiling Main             ( cards-with-show.hs, interpreted )
Ok, modules loaded: Main.
*Main> cardValue (Ten, Hearts)
1
```

We're working with a complex tuple of user-defined types. The type system keeps our intentions clear, so it's easier to reason about what's happening.

Functions and Polymorphism

Earlier, you saw a few function types. Let's look at a simple function:

```
backwards [] = []
backwards (h:t) = backwards t ++ [h]
```

We could add a type to that function that looks like this:

```
backwards :: Hand -> Hand
...
```

That would restrict the backwards function to working with only one kind of list, a list of cards. What we really want is this:

```
backwards :: [a] -> [a]
backwards [] = []
backwards (h:t) = backwards t ++ [h]
```

Now, the function is polymorphic. [a] means we can use a list of any type. It means that we can define a function that takes a list of some type a and returns a list of that same type a. With [a] -> [a], we've built a template of types that will work with our function. Further, we've told the compiler that if you start with a list of Integers, this function will return a list of Integers. Haskell now has enough information to keep you honest.

Let's build a polymorphic data type. Here's one that builds a three-tuple having three points of the same type:

haskell/triplet.hs

```
module Main where
    data Triplet a = Trio a a a deriving (Show)
```

On the left side we have data Triplet a. In this instance, a is a type variable. So now, any three-tuple with elements of the same type will be of type Triplet a. Take a look:

```
*Main> :load triplet.hs
[1 of 1] Compiling Main             ( triplet.hs, interpreted )
Ok, modules loaded: Main.
*Main> :t Trio 'a' 'b' 'c'
Trio 'a' 'b' 'c' :: Triplet Char
```

I used the *data constructor* Trio to build a three-tuple. We'll talk more about the data constructors in the next section. Based on our type declaration, the result was a Triplet a, or more specifically, a Triplet char and will satisfy any function that requires a Triplet a. We've built a whole template of types, describing any three elements whose type is the same.

Recursive Types

You can also have types that are recursive. For example, think about a tree. You can do this in several ways, but in our tree, the values are on the leaf nodes. A node, then, is either a leaf or a list of trees. We could describe the tree like this:

haskell/tree.hs

```
module Main where
    data Tree a = Children [Tree a] | Leaf a deriving (Show)
```

So, we have one type constructor, Tree. We also have two data constructors, Children and Leaf. We can use all of those together to represent trees, like this:

```
Prelude> :load tree.hs
[1 of 1] Compiling Main             ( tree.hs, interpreted )
Ok, modules loaded: Main.
*Main> let leaf = Leaf 1
*Main> leaf
Leaf 1
```

First, we build a tree having a single leaf. We assign the new leaf to a variable. The only job of the data constructor Leaf is to hold the values together with the type. We can access each piece through pattern matching, like this:

```
*Main> let (Leaf value) = leaf
*Main> value
1
```

Let's build some more complex trees.

```
*Main> Children[Leaf 1, Leaf 2]
Children [Leaf 1,Leaf 2]
*Main> let tree = Children[Leaf 1, Children [Leaf 2, Leaf 3]]
*Main> tree
Children [Leaf 1,Children [Leaf 2,Leaf 3]]
```

We build a tree with two children, each one being a leaf. Next, we build a tree with two nodes, a leaf and a right tree. Once again, we can use pattern matching to pick off each piece. We can get more complex from there. The definition is recursive, so we can go as deep as we need through let and pattern matching.

```
*Main> let (Children ch) = tree
*Main> ch
[Leaf 1,Children [Leaf 2,Leaf 3]]
*Main> let (fst:tail) = ch
*Main> fst
Leaf 1
```

We can clearly see the intent of the designer of the type system, and we can peel off the pieces that we need to do the job. This design strategy obviously comes with an overhead, but as you dive into deeper abstractions, sometimes the extra overhead is worth the hassles. In this case, the type system allows us to attach functions to each specific type constructor. Let's look at a function to determine the depth of a tree:

```
depth (Leaf _) = 1
depth (Children c) = 1 + maximum (map depth c)
```

The first pattern in our function is simple. If it's a leaf, regardless of the content of the leaf, the depth of the tree is one.

The next pattern is a little more complicated. If we call depth on Children, we add one to maximum (map depth c). The function maximum computes the maximum element in an array, and you've seen that map depth c will compute a list of the depths of all the children. In this case, you can see how we use the data constructors to help us match the exact pieces of the data structure that will help us do the job.

Classes

So far, we've been through the type system and how it works in a couple of areas. We've built user-defined type constructors and got templates that would allow us to define data types and declare functions that would work with them. Haskell has one more important concept related to types, and it's a big one. The concept is called the *class*, but be careful. It's not an object-oriented class, because there's no data involved. In Haskell, classes let us carefully control polymorphism and overloading.

For example, you can't add two booleans together, but you can add two numbers together. Haskell allows classes for this purpose. Specifically, *a class defines which operations can work on which inputs*. Think of it like a Clojure protocol.

Here's how it works. A class provides some function signatures. A type is an instance of a class if it supports all those functions. For example, in the Haskell library, there's a class called Eq.

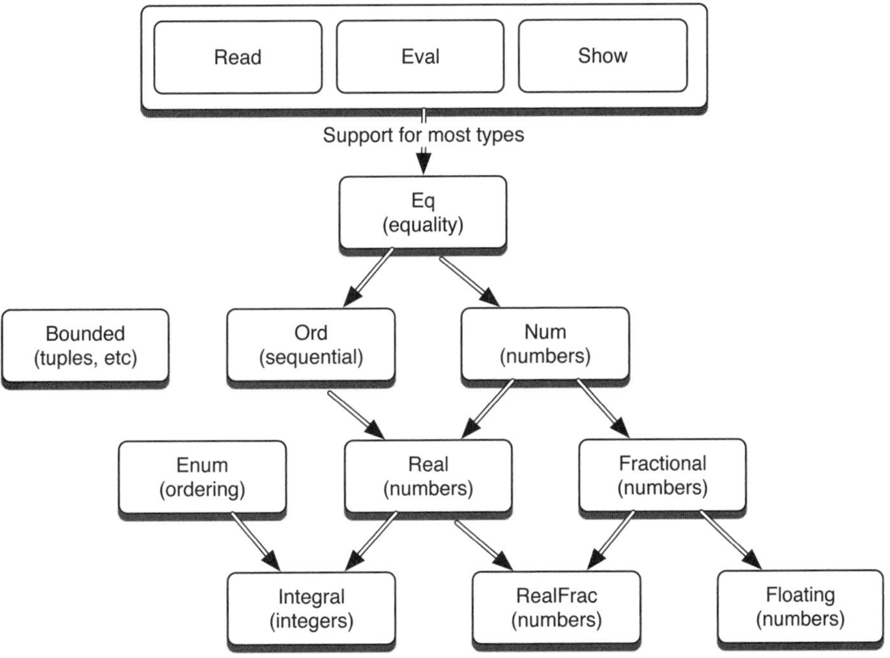

Figure 8.1: IMPORTANT HASKELL CLASSES

Here's what it looks like:

```
class  Eq a  where
   (==), (/=) :: a -> a -> Bool

       -- Minimal complete definition:
       --      (==) or (/=)
   x /= y     =  not (x == y)
   x == y     =  not (x /= y)
```

So, a type is an instance of Eq if it supports both == and /=. You can also specify boilerplate implementations. Also, if an instance defines one of those functions, the other will be provided for free.

Classes do support inheritance, and it behaves like you think it should. For example, the Num class has subclasses Fractional and Real. The hierarchy of the most important Haskell classes in Haskell 98 is shown in Figure 8.1. Remember, instances of these classes are types, not data objects!

Monads

From the time I decided to write this book, I've dreaded writing the section on monads. After some study, I've learned that the concepts are not all that difficult. In this section, I'll walk you through the intuitive description of why we need monads. Then, we'll look at a high-level description of how monads are built. Finally, we'll introduce some syntactic sugar that should really bring home how they work.

I leaned on a couple of tutorials to help shape my understanding. The Haskell wiki[3] has several good examples that I read, and also Understanding Monads[4] has some good practical examples. But you'll probably find that you need to wade through several examples from many different sources to come to an understanding of what monads can do for you.

The Problem: Drunken Pirate

Let's say you have a pirate making a treasure map. He's drunk, so he picks up a known point and a known direction and makes his way to the treasure with a series of staggers and crawls. A stagger moves two steps, and a crawl moves one step. In an imperative language, you will have statements strung together sequentially, where v is the value that holds distance from the original point, like this:

```
def treasure_map(v)
    v = stagger(v)
    v = stagger(v)
    v = crawl(v)
    return( v )
end
```

We have several functions that we call within treasure_map that sequentially transform our state, the distance traveled. The problem is that we have mutable state. We could do the problem in a functional way, like this:

haskell/drunken-pirate.hs

```
module Main where

    stagger :: (Num t) => t -> t
    stagger d = d + 2
    crawl d = d + 1
```

3. http://www.haskell.org/tutorial/monads.html
4. http://en.wikibooks.org/wiki/Haskell/Understanding_monads

```
treasureMap d =
    crawl (
    stagger (
    stagger d))
```

You can see that the functional definition is inconvenient to read. Rather than stagger, stagger, and crawl, we must read crawl, stagger, and stagger, and the arguments are awkwardly placed. Instead, we'd like a strategy that will let us chain several functions together sequentially. We can use a let expression instead:

```
letTreasureMap (v, d) = let d1 = stagger d
                            d2 = stagger d1
                            d3 = crawl d2
                        in d3
```

Haskell allows us to chain let expressions together and express the final form in an in statement. You can see that this version is almost as unsatisfying as the first. The inputs and outputs are the same, so it should be easier to compose these kinds of functions. We want to translate stagger(crawl(x)) into stagger(x) · crawl(x), where · is function composition. That's a monad.

In short, a monad lets us compose functions in ways that have specific properties. In Haskell, we'll use monads for several purposes. First, dealing with things such as I/O is difficult because in a pure functional language, a function should deliver the same results when given the same inputs, but for I/O, you would want your functions to change based on the state of the contents of a file, for example.

Also, code like the drunken pirate earlier works because it preserves state. Monads let you simulate program state. Haskell provides a special syntax, called *do syntax*, to allow programs in the imperative style. Do syntax depends on monads to work.

Finally, something as simple as an error condition is difficult because the type of thing returned is different based on whether the function was successful. Haskell provides the Maybe monad for this purpose. Let's dig a little deeper.

Components of a Monad

At its basic level, a monad has three basic things:

- A type constructor that's based on some type of container. The container could be a simple variable, a list, or anything that can hold a value. We will use the container to hold a function. The container you choose will vary based on what you want your monad to do.

- A function called return that wraps up a function and puts it in the container. The name will make sense later, when we move into do notation. Just remember that return wraps up a function into a monad.

- A bind function called >>= that unwraps a function. We'll use *bind* to chain functions together.

All monads will need to satisfy three rules. I'll mention them briefly here. For some monad m, some function f, and some value x:

- You should be able to use a type constructor to create a monad that will work with some type that can hold a value.

- You should be able to unwrap and wrap values without loss of information. (monad >>= return = monad)

- Nesting bind functions should be the same as calling them sequentially. ((m >>= f) >>= g = m >>= (\x -> f x >>= g))

We won't spend a lot of time on these laws, but the reasons are pretty simple. They allow many useful transformations without losing information. If you really want to dive in, I'll try to leave you plenty of references.

Enough of the theory. Let's build a simple monad. We'll build one from scratch, and then I'll close the chapter with a few useful monads.

Building a Monad from Scratch

The first thing we'll need is a type constructor. Our monad will have a function and a value, like this:

haskell/drunken-monad.hs

```
module Main where
    data Position t = Position t deriving (Show)

    stagger (Position d) = Position (d + 2)
    crawl (Position d) = Position (d + 1)

    rtn x = x
    x >>== f = f x
```

The three main elements of a monad were a type container, a return, and a bind. Our monad is the simplest possible. The type container is a simple type constructor that looks like data Position t = Position t. All it does is define a basic type, based on an arbitrary type template. Next, we need a return that wraps up a function as a value. Since our monad is so simple, we just have to return the value of the monad itself, and it's wrapped up appropriately, with (rtn x = x). Finally, we needed a bind that allows us to compose functions. Ours is called >>==, and we define it to just call the associated function with the value in the monad (x >>== f = f x). We're using >>== and rtn instead of >>= and return to prevent collisions with Haskell's built-in monad functions.

Notice that we also rewrote stagger and crawl to use our homegrown monad instead of naked integers. We can take our monad out for a test-drive. Remember, we were after a syntax that translates from nesting to composition. The revised treasure map looks like this:

```
treasureMap pos = pos >>==
                  stagger >>==
                  stagger >>==
                  crawl >>==
                  rtn
```

And it works as expected:

```
*Main> treasureMap (Position 0)
Position 5
```

Monads and do Notation

That syntax is much better, but you can easily imagine some syntactic sugar to improve it some more. Haskell's do syntax does exactly that. The do syntax comes in handy especially for problems like I/O. In the following code, we read a line from the console and print out the same line in reverse, using do notation:

haskell/io.hs

```
module Main where
    tryIo = do  putStr "Enter your name: " ;
                line <- getLine ;
                let { backwards = reverse line } ;
                return ("Hello. Your name backwards is " ++ backwards)
```

Notice that the beginning of this program is a function declaration. Then, we use the simple do notation to give us the syntactic sugar around monads. That makes our program feel stateful and imperative, but we're actually using monads. You'll want to be aware of a few syntax rules.

Assignment uses <-. In GHCI, you must separate lines with semicolons and include the body of do expressions, and let expressions therein, within braces. If you have multiple lines, you should wrap your code in :{ and }: with each on a separate line. And now, you can finally see why we called our monad's wrapping construct return. It neatly packages a return value in a tidy form that the do syntax can absorb. This code behaves as if it were in a stateful imperative language, but it's using monads to manage the stateful interactions. All I/O is tightly encapsulated and must be captured using one of the I/O monads in a do block.

Different Computational Strategies

Every monad has an associated computational strategy. The identity monad, which we used in the drunken-monad example, just parrots back the thing you put into it. We used it to convert a nested program structure to a sequential program structure. Let's take another example. Strange as it may seem, a list is also a monad, with return and bind (>>=) defined like this:

```
instance Monad [] where
    m >>= f  = concatMap f m
    return x = [x]
```

Recall that a monad needs some container and a type constructor, a return method that wraps up a function, and a bind method that unwraps it. A monad is a class, and [] instantiates it, giving us our type constructor. We next need a function to wrap up a result as return.

For the list, we wrap up the function in the list. To unwrap it, our bind calls the function on every element of the list with map and then concatenates the results together. concat and map are applied in sequence often enough that there's a function that does both for convenience, but we could have easily used concat (map f m).

To give you a feel for the list monad in action, take a look at the following script, in do notation:

```
Main> let cartesian (xs,ys) = do x <- xs; y <- ys; return (x,y)
Main> cartesian ([1..2], [3..4])
[(1,3),(1,4),(2,3),(2,4)]
```

We created a simple function with do notation and monads. We took x from a list of xs, and we took y from a list of xy. Then, we returned each combination of x and y. From that point, our password cracker is easy.

haskell/password.hs

```
module Main where
    crack = do x <- ['a'..'c'] ; y <- ['a'..'c'] ; z <- ['a'..'c'] ;
               let { password = [x, y, z] } ;
               if attempt password
                    then return (password, True)
                    else return (password, False)

    attempt pw = if pw == "cab" then True else False
```

Here, we're using the list monad to compute all possible combinations. Notice that in this context, x <- [lst] means "for each x taken from [lst]." We let Haskell do the heavy lifting. At that point, all you need to do is try each password. Our password is hard-coded into the attempt function. There are many computational strategies that we could have used to solve this problem such as list comprehensions, but this problem showed the computational strategy behind list monads.

Maybe Monad

So far, we've seen the Identity monad and the List monad. With the latter, we learned that monads supported a central computational strategy. In this section, we'll look at the Maybe monad. We'll use this one to handle a common programming problem: some functions might fail. You might think we're talking about the realm of databases and communications, but other far simpler APIs often need to support the idea of failure. Think a string search that returns the index of a string. If the string is present, the return type is an Integer. Otherwise, the type is Nothing.

Stringing together such computations is tedious. Let's say you have a function that is parsing a web page. You want the HTML page, the body within that page, and the first paragraph within that body. You want to code functions that have signatures that look something like this:

```
paragraph XmlDoc -> XmlDoc
...

body XmlDoc -> XmlDoc
...

html XmlDoc -> XmlDoc
...
```

They will support a function that looks something like this:

```
paragraph body (html doc)
```

The problem is that the paragraph, body, and html functions can fail, so you need to allow a type that may be Nothing. Haskell has such a type, called Just. Just x can wrap Nothing, or some type, like this:

```
Prelude> Just "some string"
Just "some string"
Prelude> Just Nothing
Just Nothing
```

You can strip off the Just with pattern matching. So, getting back to our example, the paragraph, body, and html documents can return Just XmlDoc. Then, you could use the Haskell case statement (which works like the Erlang case statement) and pattern matching to give you something like this:

```
case (html doc) of
  Nothing -> Nothing
  Just x  -> case body x of
               Nothing -> Nothing
               Just y  -> paragraph 2 y
```

And that result is deeply unsatisfying, considering we wanted to code paragraph 2 body (html doc). What we really need is the Maybe monad. Here's the definition:

```
data Maybe a = Nothing | Just a

instance Monad Maybe where
    return         = Just
    Nothing  >>= f = Nothing
    (Just x) >>= f = f x

    ...
```

The type we're wrapping is a type constructor that is Maybe a. That type can wrap Nothing or Just a.

return is easy. It just wraps the result in Just. The bind is also easy. For Nothing, it returns a function returning Nothing. For Just x, it returns a function returning x. Either will be wrapped by the return. Now, you can chain together these operations easily:

```
Just someWebPage >>= html >>= body >>= paragraph >>= return
```

So, we can combine the elements flawlessly. It works because the monad takes care of the decision making through the functions that we compose.

What We Learned in Day 3

In this section, we took on three demanding concepts: Haskell types, classes, and monads. We started with types, by looking at the inferred types of existing functions, numbers, booleans, and characters. We then moved on to some user-defined types. As a basic example, we used types to define playing cards made up of suits and ranks for playing cards. We learned how to parameterize types and even use recursive type definitions.

Then, we wrapped up the language with a discussion of monads. Since Haskell is a purely functional language, it can be difficult to express problems in an imperative style or accumulate state as a program executes. Haskell's designers leaned on monads to solve both problems. A monad is a type constructor with a few functions to wrap up functions and chain them together. You can combine monads with different type containers to allow different kinds of computational strategies. We used monads to provide a more natural imperative style for our program and to process multiple possibilities.

Day 3 Self-Study

Find:

- A few monad tutorials
- A list of the monads in Haskell

Do:

- Write a function that looks up a hash table value that uses the `Maybe` monad. Write a hash that stores other hashes, several levels deep. Use the `Maybe` monad to retrieve an element for a hash key several levels deep.
- Represent a maze in Haskell. You'll need a `Maze` type and a `Node` type, as well as a function to return a node given its coordinates. The node should have a list of exits to other nodes.
- Use a List monad to solve the maze.
- Implement a Monad in a nonfunctional language. (See the article series on monads in Ruby.[5])

5. http://moonbase.rydia.net/mental/writings/programming/monads-in-ruby/00introduction.html

8.5 Wrapping Up Haskell

Of all the languages in this book, Haskell was the only one created by committee. After the proliferation of purely functional languages with lazy semantics, a committee was formed to build an open standard that would consolidate existing capabilities and future research. Haskell was born, with version 1.0 defined in 1990. The language and community have grown since then.

Haskell supports a wide variety of functional capabilities including list comprehensions, lazy computing strategies, partially applied functions, and currying. In fact, by default, Haskell functions process one parameter at a time, using currying to support multiple arguments.

The Haskell type system provides an excellent balance of type safety and flexibility. The fully polymorphic template system allows sophisticated support for user-defined types and even type classes that fully support inheritance of interface. Usually, the Haskell programmer is not burdened with type details except in the function declarations, but the type system protects users from all kinds of type errors.

As with any pure functional language, Haskell developers must be creative to deal with imperative-style programs and accumulated state. I/O can also be a challenge. Fortunately, Haskell developers can rely on monads for that purpose. A monad is a type constructor and a container that supports basic functions to wrap and unwrap functions as values. Different container types provide different computational strategies. These functions allow programmers to chain together monads in interesting ways, providing *do syntax*. This syntactic sugar allows imperative-style programs with certain limitations.

Core Strengths

Since Haskell takes the absolute approach of pure functions with no compromise, the advantages and disadvantages can be often extreme. Let's break them down.

Type System

If you like strong typing (and maybe even if you don't), you'll love Haskell's typing system. It is there when you need it but not when you don't. The type system can add a helpful level of protection from common errors, and they can be caught at compile time rather than run time. But the extra safety is only part of the story.

Perhaps the most interesting part of a Haskell type is how easy it is to associate new types with new behaviors. You can build up sophisticated types from the ground up. With type constructors and classes, you can even customize extremely complex types and classes such as Monads effortlessly. With classes, your new custom types can take advantage of existing Haskell libraries.

Expressiveness

The Haskell language has fantastic power. From an abstract sense, it has everything you need to express powerful ideas concisely. Those ideas encompass behavior through a rich functional library and a powerful syntax. The ideas extend to data types where you can create types, even recursive types that bind the right functions to the right data without excessive syntax. In an academic setting, you can find no stronger language for teaching functional programming than Haskell. Everything you will need is in there.

Purity of Programming Model

Pure programming models can radically change the way you approach problems. They force you to leave old programming paradigms behind and embrace different ways of doing things. Pure functional languages give you something you can depend on. Given the same inputs, a function will always return the same values. This property makes it much easier to reason about programs. You can sometimes prove that a program is correct, or not. You can also be free of many of the problems that come from depending on side effects, such as accidental complexity and unstable or slow behavior in concurrent situations.

Lazy Semantics

Once upon a time, dealing with functional languages meant dealing with recursion. Lazy computing strategies offer a whole new set of strategies to deal with data. You can often build programs that perform better and take a fraction of the total lines of code that another strategy might take.

Academic Support

Some of the most important and influential languages such as Pascal grew up in academia, benefitting greatly from research and use in that setting. As the primary teaching language for functional techniques, Haskell continues to improve and grow. Though it is not fully a mainstream language, you'll always be able to find pockets of programmers to do important tasks.

Core Weaknesses

You know by now that no programming language is perfect for every task. Haskell's strengths typically have a flip side as well.

Inflexibility of Programming Model

Being a pure functional language offers some advantages but also a set of headaches. You might have noticed that programming with monads was the last part of the last chapter in a book about programming languages, and rightfully so. The concepts are intellectually demanding. But we used monads to do some things that were trivial in other languages, such as write imperative-style programs, process I/O, and even handle list functions that may or may not find a value. I've said it before about other languages, but I'll say it again here. Though Haskell makes some hard things easy, it also makes some easy things hard.

Certain styles lend themselves to certain programming paradigms. When you're building a step-by-step algorithm, imperative languages work well. Heavy I/O and scripting do not lend themselves to functional languages. Purity in one man's eyes may seem like failure to compromise in another.

Community

Speaking of compromise, you can really see the differences in the approach of Scala and Haskell. Though both are strongly typed, both have radically different philosophies. Scala is all about compromise, and Haskell is all about purity. By making compromises, Scala has initially attracted a much bigger community than Haskell. Though you can't measure success by the size of a programming community, you must have sufficient numbers to succeed, and having more users lends more opportunity and community resources.

Learning Curve

The monad is not the only intellectually demanding concept in Haskell. Currying is used in every function with more than one argument. Most basic functions have parameterized types, and functions on numbers often use a type class. Though the payoff may be well worth it in the end, you must be a strong programmer with firm theoretical footing to have a fighting chance of succeeding with Haskell.

Final Thoughts

Of the functional languages in the book, Haskell was the most difficult to learn. The emphasis on monads and the type system made the learning curve steep. Once I mastered some of the key concepts, things got easier, and it became the most rewarding language I learned. Based on the type system and the elegance of the application of monads, one day we'll look back at this language as one of the most important in this book.

Haskell plays another role, too. The purity of the approach and the academic focus will both improve our understanding of *programming*. The best of the next generation of functional programmers in many places will cut their teeth on Haskell.

Chapter 9

Wrap-Up

Congratulations on making it through seven programming languages. Perhaps you're expecting me to pick winners and losers in this chapter, but this book is not about winners and losers. It's about discovering new ideas. You may have been like me early in my career, buried deeply in commercial projects in large teams with little imagination, the software factories of our generation. In such a world, my exposure to programming languages was extremely limited. I was like a 1970s movie lover in a small town with one theater, getting only the big-money blockbusters.

Since I started building software for myself, I feel like I've just discovered independent films. I've been able to make a living coding Ruby, but I'm not naive enough to think Ruby has all of the answers. Just as independent films are advancing the state of the art in movie making, emerging programming languages are changing the way we think about program organization and construction. Let's review what we've seen throughout the book.

9.1 Programming Models

Programming models change extremely slowly. So far, we've seen new models emerge every twenty years or so. My training started with some procedural languages, Basic and Fortran. In college, I learned a more structured approach with Pascal. At IBM, I started to code C and C++ commercially and was introduced to Java for the first time. I also began writing object-oriented code. My programming experience has spanned more than thirty years, and I've seen only two major programming paradigms. You might be asking yourself why I am so enthusiastic about introducing a few other programming paradigms. It's a fair question.

Though programming paradigms change slowly, they do change. Like a tornado's path, they can leave behind some devastation, taking the form of broken careers and companies that invested poorly. When you find yourself fighting a programming paradigm, you need to start paying attention. Concurrency and reliability are starting to nudge us in the direction of a higher-level programming language. Minimally, I think we're going to start to see more specialized languages to solve specific problems. These are the programming models we encountered.

Object Orientation (Ruby, Scala)

The current "king of the hill" is object orientation, typically in the Java language. This programming paradigm has three major ideas: encapsulation, inheritance, and polymorphism. With Ruby, we experienced dynamic duck typing. Rather than enforcing a contract based on the definition of a class or objects, Ruby enforced typing based on the methods an object could support. We learned that Ruby supported several functional concepts through code blocks.

Scala, too, offered object-oriented programming. Though it supports static typing, it is much less verbose than Java, offering features such as type inference to simplify the syntax. With this feature, Scala automatically deduces the type of variables based on clues in syntax and usage. Scala goes beyond Ruby to introduce functional concepts.

Both of these languages run in widespread production applications today, and both represent significant advances in language design compared to mainstream languages such as Java. There are many variations of object-oriented languages, including the next programming paradigm, prototype languages.

Prototype Programming (Io)

You could actually say that prototype languages are a subset of object-oriented languages, but they are just different enough in practice that I introduced them as a different programming model. Rather than working through a class, all prototypes are object instances. Some specially designated instances serve as prototypes for other object instances. This family of languages includes JavaScript and Io. Simple and expressive, prototype languages are typically dynamically typed and work well for scripting and application development, especially for user interfaces.

As you learned within Io, a simple programming model with a small, consistent syntax can be a powerful combination. We used the Io language in broadly different contexts ranging from scripting concurrent programs together to coding our own DSL. But this prototype programming was not the most specialized paradigm that we encountered.

Constraint-Logic Programming (Prolog)

Prolog comes from a family of programming languages built for constraint-logic programming. The different applications we built with Prolog solved a fairly narrow type of problem, but the results were often spectacular. We defined logical constraints that we knew about our universe and had Prolog find the solution.

When the programming model fit this paradigm, we were able to get results with a fraction of the lines of code that it would take in other languages. This family of language supports many of the most critical applications in the world in domains such as air traffic control and civil engineering. You can also find crude logical rules engines in other languages such as C and Java. Prolog served as the inspiration of Erlang, from another family of languages in this book.

Functional Programming (Scala, Erlang, Clojure, Haskell)

Perhaps the most widely anticipated programming paradigm in this book is functional programming. The degree of purity found in functional programming languages differs, but the concepts are consistent throughout. Functional programs are made up of mathematical functions. Calling the same function more than once will give you the same result each time, and side effects are either frowned on or forbidden. You can compose those functions in a variety of ways.

You've seen that functional programming languages are usually more expressive than object-oriented languages. Your examples were often shorter and simpler than the object-oriented counterparts because you had a broader range of tools for composing programs than you did in the object-oriented paradigm. We introduced higher-order functions and also complex concepts such as currying as two examples that you can't always find in object-oriented languages. As you learned in Haskell, different levels of purity lead to different sets of advantages and disadvantages. One clear win for the functional languages was the absence of side effects, making concurrent programming easier. When mutable state goes away, so do many of the traditional concurrency problems.

Changing Paradigms

If you do decide that you want to do more functional programming, there are several different ways to get there. You can make a clean break from OOP, or you can pick an approach that is slightly more evolutionary.

As we waded through each of the seven languages, you saw languages spanning four decades and at least as many programming paradigms. I hope you can appreciate the evolution of programming languages as well. You saw three distinctly different approaches to evolving paradigms. With Scala, the approach is coexistence. The Scala programmer can construct an object-oriented program using strong functional tendencies. The very nature of the language is that both programming paradigms are first-class. Clojure takes the approach of compatibility. The language is built on the JVM, allowing Clojure applications to use Java objects directly, but the Clojure philosophy is that certain elements of OOP are fundamentally flawed. Unlike Scala, Clojure-Java Interop is provided to leverage frameworks existing on the Java virtual machine, not to broaden the programming language. Haskell and Erlang are basically stand-alone languages. Philosophically, they do not embrace object-oriented programming in any form. So, you can embrace both paradigms, make a clean break, or embrace object-oriented libraries but decide to leave the OOP paradigm behind. Take your pick.

Whether or not you choose to adopt one of the languages in this book, you'll be better for knowing what's out there. As a Java developer, I had to wait a decade for closures, mainly because people like me were uneducated and did not scream loud enough for them. In the meantime, mainstream frameworks like Spring were stuck with anonymous inner classes to solve problems that could have used closures extensively. My fingers bled from the oppressive amount of typing, and my eyes bled because I had to read that stuff. The modern Java developer knows much more, partially because people such as Martin Odersky and Rich Hickey gave us alternatives that are now pushing the state of the art and forcing Java to advance or get left behind.

9.2 Concurrency

A repeated theme in this book is the need for better language constructs and programming models to handle concurrency. Across the languages, the approaches were often strikingly different but extremely effective. Let's walk through some of the approaches we saw.

Controlling Mutable State

By far, the most common theme in the concurrency discussion was the programming model. Object-oriented programming allows side effects and mutable state. Taken together, programs got much more complicated. When you mix in multiple threads and processes, the complexity got too great to manage.

The functional programming language adds structure through an important rule. Multiple invocations of the same function lead to the same result. Variables have a single assignment. When side effects go away, race conditions and all related complexities also go away. Still, we saw tangible techniques that went beyond the basic programming model. Let's take a closer look.

Actors in Io, Erlang, and Scala

Whether using an object or a process, the actor approach is the same. It takes unstructured interprocess communication across any object boundary and transforms it onto structured message passing between first-class constructs, each one supporting a message queue. The Erlang and Scala languages use pattern matching to match inbound messages and conditionally execute them. In Chapter 6, *Erlang*, on page 167, we built an example around Russian roulette to demonstrate a dying process. Recall that we put the bullet in chamber 3:

erlang/roulette.erl

```
-module(roulette).
-export([loop/0]).

% send a number, 1-6
loop() ->
    receive
        3 -> io:format("bang.~n"), exit({roulette,die,at,erlang:time()});
        _ -> io:format("click~n"), loop()
end.
```

We then started a process, assigning the ID to Gun. We could kill the process with Gun ! 3. The Erlang virtual machine and language supported robust monitoring, allowing notification and even restarting processes at the first sign of trouble.

Futures

To the actor model, Io added two additional concurrency constructs: coroutines and futures. Coroutines allowed two objects to multitask cooperatively, with each relinquishing control at the appropriate time. Recall that futures were placeholders for long-running concurrent computations.

We executed the statement futureResult := URL with("http://google.com/") @fetch. Though the result was not immediately available, program control returned immediately, blocking only when we attempted to access the future. An Io future actually morphs into a result when the result becomes available.

Transactional Memory

In Clojure, we saw a number of interesting approaches to concurrency. Software transactional memory (STM) wrapped each distributed access of a shared resource in a transaction. This same approach, but for database objects, maintains database integrity across concurrent invocations. We wrapped each access in a dosync function. With this approach, Clojure developers can break away from strict functional designs where it makes sense and still have integrity across multiple threads and processes.

STM is a relatively new idea that is just creeping into more popular languages. As a Lisp derivative, Clojure is an ideal language for such an approach because Lisp is a multiparadigm language. Users can use different programming paradigms when they make sense with the confidence that the application will maintain integrity and performance, even through highly concurrent accesses.

The next generation of programmers will demand more out of his language. The simple wheel and stick that let you start a thread and wait on a semaphore are no longer good enough. A newer language must have a coherent philosophy supporting concurrency and the tools to match. It may be that the need for concurrency renders whole programming paradigms obsolete, or it may be that older languages will adapt by using stricter controls for mutable variables and smarter concurrency constructs such as actors and futures.

9.3 Programming Constructs

One of the most exciting parts of writing this book was the exposure to the basic building blocks in the various languages of this book. For each new language, I introduced major new concepts. These are some of the programming constructs that you're likely to see in other new languages you might discover. They are among my favorite discoveries.

List Comprehensions

As you saw in Erlang, Clojure, and Haskell,[1] the list comprehension is a compact structure that combines several ideas into a single powerful construct. A list comprehension has a filter, a map, and a Cartesian product.

We first encountered list comprehensions in Erlang. We started with a shopping cart of items such as `Cart = [{pencil, 4, 0.25}, {pen, 1, 1.20}, {paper, 2, 0.20}]`. To add tax to the list, we built a single list comprehension to solve the problem at once, like this:

```
8>    WithTax = [{Product, Quantity, Price, Price * Quantity * 0.08} ||
8>    {Product, Quantity, Price} <- Cart].
[{pencil,4,0.25,0.08},{pen,1,1.2,0.096},{paper,2,0.2,0.032}]
```

Several different language creators mention list comprehensions as one of their favorite features. I agree with this sentiment.

Monads

Perhaps the biggest intellectual growth for me was in the area of monads. With pure functional languages, we could not build programs with mutable state. Instead, we built monads that let us compose functions in a way that helped us structure problems as if they allowed mutable state. Haskell has `do` notation, supported by monads, to solve this problem.

We also found that monads allow us to simplify complex computation. Each of our monads supported a computational strategy. We used the `Maybe` monad to handle failure conditions, such as a `List` search that

1. Scala also supports list comprehensions, but we did not use them.

could potentially return Nothing. We used the List monad to compute a Cartesian product and unlock a combination.

Matching

One of the more common programming features we saw was pattern matching. We first encountered this programming construct in Prolog, but we also saw it in Scala, Erlang, Clojure, and Haskell. Each of these languages leaned on pattern matching to significantly simplify code. The problem domains included parsing, distributed message passing, destructuring, unification, XML processing, and more.

For a typical Erlang pattern match, recall the translate service:

erlang/translate_service.erl

```
-module(translate_service).
-export([loop/0, translate/2]).

loop() ->
    receive
        {From, "casa"} ->
            From ! "house",
            loop();

        {From, "blanca"} ->
            From ! "white",
            loop();

        {From, _} ->
            From ! "I don't understand.",
            loop()

end.

translate(To, Word) ->
    To ! {self(), Word},
    receive
        Translation -> Translation
    end.
```

The loop function matched a process ID (From) followed by a word (casa or blanca) or a wildcard. The pattern match allows the programmer to quickly pick out the important pieces of the message without requiring any parsing from the programmer.

Unification

Prolog uses unification, a close cousin of pattern matching. You learned that Prolog would substitute possible values into a rule to force the left and right sides to match. Prolog would keep trying values until possibilities were exhausted. We looked at a simple Prolog program called concatenate as an example of unification:

prolog/concat.pl

```
concatenate([], List, List).
concatenate([Head|Tail1], List, [Head|Tail2]) :-
  concatenate(Tail1, List, Tail2).
```

We learned that unification makes this program so powerful because it could work in three ways: testing truth, matching the left side, or matching the right side.

9.4 Finding Your Voice

We've talked about movies and characters throughout this book. The joy of movie making means combining your experiences with the actors, sets, and locations that tell the story you want to tell. Everything you do goes into pleasing your audience. The more you know, the better your movies can be.

We need to think about programming in the same way. We, too, have an audience. I'm not talking about the users of our applications, though. I'm talking about the people who read our code. To be a great programmer, you need to write to your audience and find the voice that pleases them. You'll have more room to find that voice and let it evolve if you learn what other languages have to offer. Your voice is your unique way of expressing yourself in code. It will never be any better than the sum of your experience. I hope this book has helped you find your voice. Most of all, I hope you had fun.

Appendix A

Bibliography

[Arm07] Joe Armstrong. *Programming Erlang: Software for a Concurrent World*. The Pragmatic Programmers, LLC, Raleigh, NC, and Dallas, TX, 2007.

[Gra04] Paul Graham. *Hackers and Painters: Big Ideas from the Computer Age*. O'Reilly & Associates, Inc, Sebastopol, CA, 2004.

[Hal09] Stuart Halloway. *Programming Clojure*. The Pragmatic Programmers, LLC, Raleigh, NC, and Dallas, TX, 2009.

[OSV08] Martin Odersky, Lex Spoon, and Bill Venners. *Programming in Scala*. Artima, Inc., Mountain View, CA, 2008.

[TFH08] David Thomas, Chad Fowler, and Andrew Hunt. *Programming Ruby: The Pragmatic Programmers' Guide*. The Pragmatic Programmers, LLC, Raleigh, NC, and Dallas, TX, third edition, 2008.

Index

D

E

F

G

H

The Pragmatic Bookshelf

Available in paperback and DRM-free eBooks, our titles are here to help you stay on top of your game. The following are in print as of August 2010; be sure to check our website at pragprog.com *for newer titles.*

Title	**Year**	**ISBN**	**Pages**
Advanced Rails Recipes: 84 New Ways to Build Stunning Rails Apps	2008	9780978739225	464
Agile Coaching	2009	9781934356432	248
Agile Retrospectives: Making Good Teams Great	2006	9780977616640	200
Agile Web Development with Rails, Third Edition	2009	9781934356166	784
Beginning Mac Programming: Develop with Objective-C and Cocoa	2010	9781934356517	300
Behind Closed Doors: Secrets of Great Management	2005	9780976694021	192
Best of Ruby Quiz	2006	9780976694076	304
Cocoa Programming: A Quick-Start Guide for Developers	2010	9781934356302	450
Core Animation for Mac OS X and the iPhone: Creating Compelling Dynamic User Interfaces	2008	9781934356104	200
Core Data: Apple's API for Persisting Data on Mac OS X	2009	9781934356326	256
Data Crunching: Solve Everyday Problems using Java, Python, and More	2005	9780974514079	208
Debug It! Find, Repair, and Prevent Bugs in Your Code	2009	9781934356289	232
Deploying Rails Applications: A Step-by-Step Guide	2008	9780978739201	280
Design Accessible Web Sites: 36 Keys to Creating Content for All Audiences and Platforms	2007	9781934356029	336
Desktop GIS: Mapping the Planet with Open Source Tools	2008	9781934356067	368
Developing Facebook Platform Applications with Rails	2008	9781934356128	200
Domain-Driven Design Using Naked Objects	2009	9781934356449	375
Enterprise Integration with Ruby	2006	9780976694069	360
Enterprise Recipes with Ruby and Rails	2008	9781934356234	416
Everyday Scripting with Ruby: for Teams, Testers, and You	2007	9780977616619	320
ExpressionEngine 2: A Quick-Start Guide	2010	9781934356524	250
FXRuby: Create Lean and Mean GUIs with Ruby	2008	9781934356074	240
From Java To Ruby: Things Every Manager Should Know	2006	9780976694090	160

Continued on next page

Title	Year	ISBN	Pages
GIS for Web Developers: Adding Where to Your Web Applications	2007	9780974514093	275
Google Maps API, V2: Adding Where to Your Applications	2006	PDF-Only	83
Grails: A Quick-Start Guide	2009	9781934356463	200
Groovy Recipes: Greasing the Wheels of Java	2008	9780978739294	264
Hello, Android: Introducing Google's Mobile Development Platform	2010	9781934356562	320
Interface Oriented Design	2006	9780976694052	240
Land the Tech Job You Love	2009	9781934356265	280
Language Implementation Patterns: Create Your Own Domain-Specific and General Programming Languages	2009	9781934356456	350
Learn to Program, 2nd Edition	2009	9781934356364	240
Manage It! Your Guide to Modern Pragmatic Project Management	2007	9780978739249	360
Manage Your Project Portfolio: Increase Your Capacity and Finish More Projects	2009	9781934356296	200
Mastering Dojo: JavaScript and Ajax Tools for Great Web Experiences	2008	9781934356111	568
Metaprogramming Ruby: Program Like the Ruby Pros	2010	9781934356470	240
Modular Java: Creating Flexible Applications with OSGi and Spring	2009	9781934356401	260
No Fluff Just Stuff 2006 Anthology	2006	9780977616664	240
No Fluff Just Stuff 2007 Anthology	2007	9780978739287	320
Pomodoro Technique Illustrated: The Easy Way to Do More in Less Time	2009	9781934356500	144
Practical Programming: An Introduction to Computer Science Using Python	2009	9781934356272	350
Practices of an Agile Developer	2006	9780974514086	208
Pragmatic Project Automation: How to Build, Deploy, and Monitor Java Applications	2004	9780974514031	176
Pragmatic Thinking and Learning: Refactor Your Wetware	2008	9781934356050	288
Pragmatic Unit Testing in C# with NUnit	2007	9780977616671	176
Pragmatic Unit Testing in Java with JUnit	2003	9780974514017	160
Pragmatic Version Control Using Git	2008	9781934356159	200
Pragmatic Version Control using CVS	2003	9780974514000	176
Pragmatic Version Control using Subversion	2006	9780977616657	248
Programming Clojure	2009	9781934356333	304
Programming Cocoa with Ruby: Create Compelling Mac Apps Using RubyCocoa	2009	9781934356197	300

Continued on next page

Title	Year	ISBN	Pages
Programming Erlang: Software for a Concurrent World	2007	9781934356005	536
Programming Groovy: Dynamic Productivity for the Java Developer	2008	9781934356098	320
Programming Ruby: The Pragmatic Programmers' Guide, Second Edition	2004	9780974514055	864
Programming Ruby 1.9: The Pragmatic Programmers' Guide	2009	9781934356081	960
Programming Scala: Tackle Multi-Core Complexity on the Java Virtual Machine	2009	9781934356319	250
Prototype and script.aculo.us: You Never Knew JavaScript Could Do This!	2007	9781934356012	448
Rails Recipes	2006	9780977616602	350
Rails for .NET Developers	2008	9781934356203	300
Rails for Java Developers	2007	9780977616695	336
Rails for PHP Developers	2008	9781934356043	432
Rapid GUI Development with QtRuby	2005	PDF-Only	83
Release It! Design and Deploy Production-Ready Software	2007	9780978739218	368
SQL Antipatterns: Avoiding the Pitfalls of Database Programming	2010	9781934356555	352
Scripted GUI Testing with Ruby	2008	9781934356180	192
Ship It! A Practical Guide to Successful Software Projects	2005	9780974514048	224
Stripes ...and Java Web Development Is Fun Again	2008	9781934356210	375
Test-Drive ASP.NET MVC	2010	9781934356531	296
TextMate: Power Editing for the Mac	2007	9780978739232	208
The Definitive ANTLR Reference: Building Domain-Specific Languages	2007	9780978739256	384
The Passionate Programmer: Creating a Remarkable Career in Software Development	2009	9781934356340	200
ThoughtWorks Anthology	2008	9781934356142	240
Ubuntu Kung Fu: Tips, Tricks, Hints, and Hacks	2008	9781934356227	400
Web Design for Developers: A Programmer's Guide to Design Tools and Techniques	2009	9781934356135	300
iPhone SDK Development	2009	9781934356258	576

Erlang and Scala

Programming Erlang

Learn how to write truly concurrent programs—programs that run on dozens or even hundreds of local and remote processors. See how to write high-reliability applications—even in the face of network and hardware failure—using the Erlang programming language.

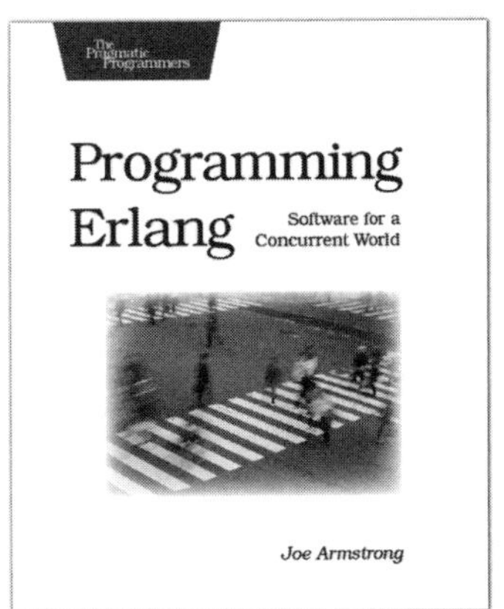

Programming Erlang: Software for a Concurrent World
Joe Armstrong
(536 pages) ISBN: 1-934356-00-X. $36.95
http://pragprog.com/titles/jaerlang

Programming Scala

Scala is an exciting, modern, multi-paradigm language for the JVM. You can use it to write traditional, imperative, object-oriented code. But you can also leverage its higher level of abstraction to take full advantage of modern, multicore systems. *Programming Scala* will show you how to use this powerful functional programming language to create highly scalable, highly concurrent applications on the Java Platform.

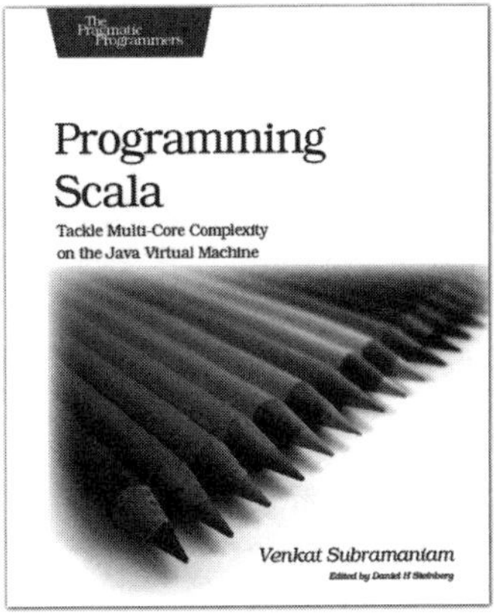

Programming Scala: Tackle Multi-Core Complexity on the Java Virtual Machine
Venkat Subramaniam
(250 pages) ISBN: 9781934356319. $34.95
http://pragprog.com/titles/vsscala

JavaScript and Clojure

Pragmatic Guide to JavaScript

JavaScript is now a powerful, dynamic language with a rich ecosystem of professional-grade development tools, infrastructures, frameworks, and toolkits. You can't afford to ignore it–this book will get you up to speed quickly and painlessly. Presented as two-page tasks, these JavaScript tips will get you started quickly and save you time.

Pragmatic Guide to JavaScript
Christophe Porteneuve
(150 pages) ISBN: 978-1934356-67-8. $25.00
http://pragprog.com/titles/pg_js

Programming Clojure

Clojure is a general-purpose language with direct support for Java, a modern Lisp dialect, and support in both the language and data structures for functional programming. *Programming Clojure* shows you how to write applications that have the beauty and elegance of a good scripting language, the power and reach of the JVM, and a modern, concurrency-safe functional style. Now you can write beautiful code that runs fast and scales well.

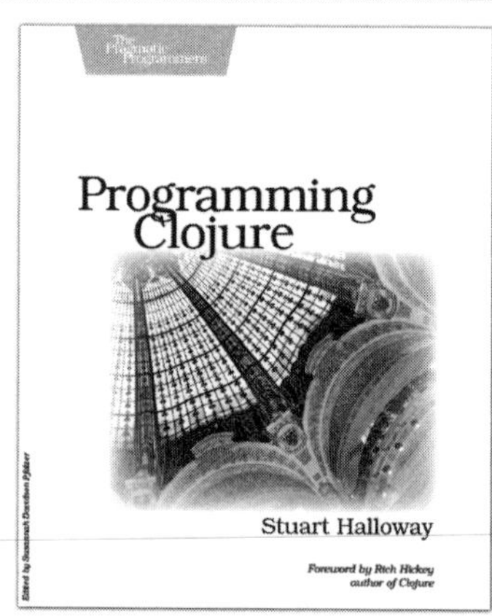

Programming Clojure
Stuart Halloway
(304 pages) ISBN: 9781934356333. $32.95
http://pragprog.com/titles/shcloj

Mac and SQL

Beginning Mac Programming

Aimed at beginning developers without prior programming experience. Takes you through concrete, working examples, giving you the core concepts and principles of development in context so you will be ready to build the applications you've been imagining. It introduces you to Objective-C and the Cocoa framework in clear, easy-to-understand lessons, and demonstrates how you can use them together to write for the Mac, as well as the iPhone and iPod.

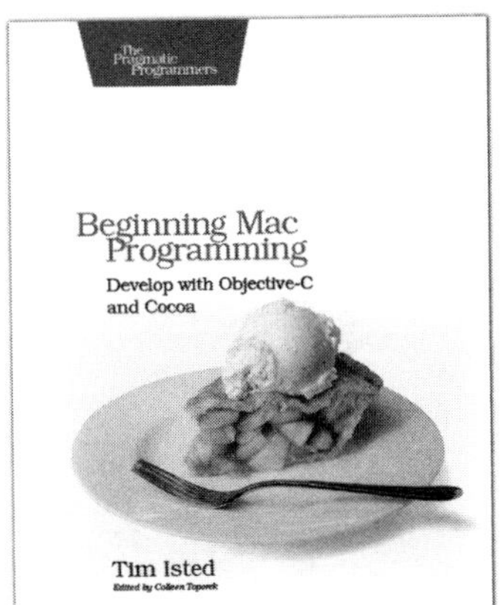

Beginning Mac Programming: Develop with Objective-C and Cocoa
Tim Isted
(300 pages) ISBN: 978-1934356-51-7. $34.95
http://pragprog.com/titles/tibmac

SQL Antipatterns

If you're programming applications that store data, then chances are you're using SQL, either directly or through a mapping layer. But most of the SQL that gets used is inefficient, hard to maintain, and sometimes just plain wrong. This book shows you all the common mistakes, and then leads you through the best fixes. What's more, it shows you what's *behind* these fixes, so you'll learn a lot about relational databases along the way.

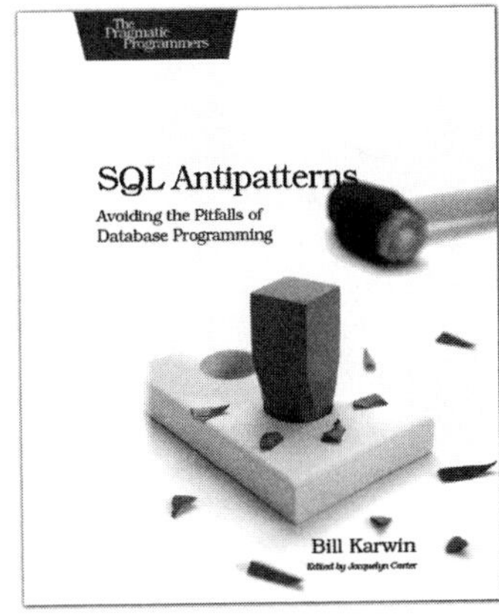

SQL Antipatterns: Avoiding the Pitfalls of Database Programming
Bill Karwin
(300 pages) ISBN: 978-19343565-5-5. $34.95
http://pragprog.com/titles/bksqla

Ruby and Ruby on the Java VM

Programming Ruby 1.9 (The Pickaxe for 1.9)

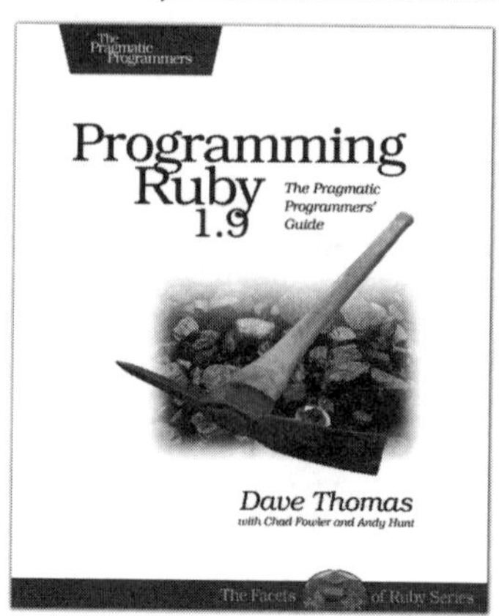

The Pickaxe book, named for the tool on the cover, is the definitive reference to this highly-regarded language.

• Up-to-date and expanded for Ruby version 1.9 • Complete documentation of all the built-in classes, modules, and methods • Complete descriptions of all standard libraries • Learn more about Ruby's web tools, unit testing, and programming philosophy

Programming Ruby 1.9: The Pragmatic Programmers' Guide
Dave Thomas with Chad Fowler and Andy Hunt
(992 pages) ISBN: 978-1-9343560-8-1. $49.95
http://pragprog.com/titles/ruby3

Using JRuby

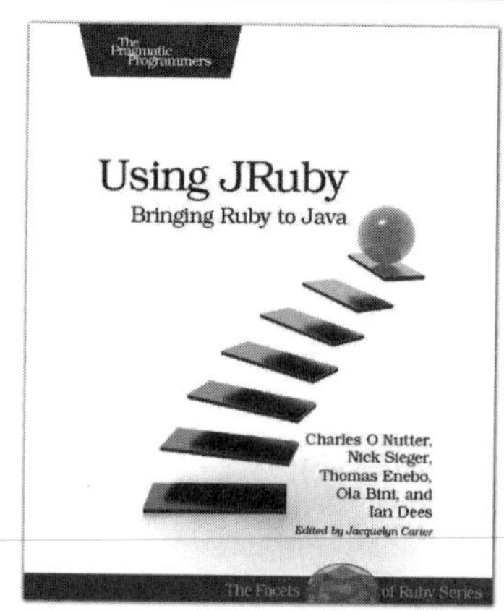

Ruby has the heart, and Java has the reach. With JRuby, you can bring the best of Ruby into the world of Java. Written in 100% Java, JRuby has Ruby's expressiveness and wide array of open-source libraries—it's an even better Ruby. With *Using JRuby*, the entire JRuby core team helps experienced Java developers and Rubyists exploit the interoperability of their respective languages. With JRuby, you'll be surprised at what's now possible.

Using JRuby: Bringing Ruby to Java
Charles O Nutter, Thomas Enebo, Nick Sieger, Ola Bini, and Ian Dees
(300 pages) ISBN: 978-1934356-65-4. $34.95
http://pragprog.com/titles/jruby